Deputy While Immigrant

THE STORY OF A GERMAN WHO BECAME
A DEPUTY SHERIFF IN ARIZONA

TOM PEINE

Seattle, WA 98121

info@indieowlpress.com
IndieOwlPress.com

All rights reserved.
Except as permitted under the U.S. Copyright Act of 1976, no part of this publication may be reproduced, distributed, or transmitted in any form or by any means or stored in a database or retrieval system, without the prior written permission of the author.

This book is written and designed to share the Author's perspectives and knowledge of the subject. The Author and Publisher are not engaged in rendering professional, psychological, or business advice. The Author and Publisher, specifically, disclaim any liability that is incurred from the use or application of the contents of this book.

For permissions and special orders, contact:
info@tompeine.com.

DEPUTY WHILE IMMIGRANT:
THE STORY OF A GERMAN WHO BECAME A DEPUTY SHERIFF IN ARIZONA

Copyright © 2023 Tom Peine

Cover art © Tom Peine
Cover concept by La Rosk
Cover design & Interior layout by Vanessa Anderson
at NightOwlFreelance.com

Paperback ISBN-13: 978-1-949193-26-8
Hardcover ISBN-13: 979-8-8690-0908-1

For Annie, my wonderful wife.

For Tobias, my son, who had to endure the Sonoran Desert after falling in love with the snow of New England.

"To be truly and wholly present even for the briefest moment is to be vulnerable, for we have arrived at the point where the obstacle that fear constructs between ourselves and others dissolves. It is here that the heart is drawn out of hiding and the inherent sympathetic response called compassion arises."
— *Lin Jensen, An Ear to the Ground*

CONTENTS

NOTE TO READERS iii

Chapter 1 - ONE WAY TICKET … 1
Chapter 2 - THAT DAY IN NEW YORK CITY … 7
Chapter 3 - MOVING TO TUCSON … 23
Chapter 4 - THE ACADEMY … 39
Chapter 5 - FIELD TRAINING … 75
Chapter 6 - ROOKIE DAYS … 101
Chapter 7 - ON THE BORDER … 129
Chapter 8 - RINCON … 157
Chapter 9 - RIDE-ALONGS … 219
Chapter 10 - THE "9-9-X" CALLS … 229
Chapter 11 - FROM DEPUTY TO DETECTIVE TO PIO … 247
Chapter 12 - REFLECTION … 267

PIMA COUNTY SHERIFF'S DEPT. 10 CODES … 278 – 279
PIMA COUNTY SHERIFF'S SUPPLEMENTAL CODES … 280

ACKNOWLEDGMENTS … 281
ABOUT THE AUTHOR … 283 - 284

NOTE TO READERS

Dear reader,

While the events described in this book have all taken place, I recalled them to the best of my abilities. Other people present at the time may remember these situations differently or remember details I left out because those weren't a purview of my vantage point. That is the way it goes with memory. There are different versions and perspectives of life's occurrences, and that is a big part of why law enforcement officers collect statements from as many witnesses of an event as possible. My account is just one of many, and I do not intend to offer the one and only valid version. It is simply my reality as I remember it.

There is no intention to provide an underlying theme. This is a collection of personal recollections that were impactful for me, a snapshot of what happened at a specific time and place as seen through my eyes. It is the way life in law enforcement seemed to me, made it special to me, and most importantly, what made it exciting to go to work every day. I never knew what was around the proverbial corner. Every day exposed me to slices of life. Tragedy, happiness, tension, terror, fear, anxiety, relief, and all the other human emotions that could be packed into a work week. It is a big part of what makes the profession of law enforcement officer and other first responders so different. They get intimate glimpses of other people's lives, people they are typically not connected to at all. The only commonality being that they all ended up on the call assignment for a particular person or unit, in this case: mine.

When writing about my experiences, I did so in an attempt to describe them accurately, not to entertain. The entertainment aspect of it may occur at different points in the book for different readers; some may not be entertained in the narrower sense. What I offer is my perspective, my view, my recollection. At the time of its occurrence, some of these situations made me angry or sad, other times it seemed funny or outright hilarious, and some of the experiences stayed with me on a level of intensity I do not always welcome. Recalling these experiences and putting them in a manuscript was a visceral experience, at times difficult.

NOTE TO READERS

I tried to be respectful to those involved. What I experienced as an outsider, who was suddenly thrust into the midst of another person's life, obviously differs significantly from the perception of those directly involved. In my attempts to be mindful of that, I often felt conflicted writing about it at all and never intended for any of it to be invasive. As such, anywhere that seemingly pertinent details have been omitted, that was a purposeful decision to avoid being invasive.

People are often referred to by alternative names, because sensitivity or compassion dictated concealing their identity, or because I do not wish to embarrass anyone.

This book is a reflection of my life experience, of the perpetually changing kaleidoscope of events happening everywhere, all the time, even right now as you read these lines.

Thank you for your interest in my book. I hope you enjoy it.

Sincerely,

Tom Peine

DEPUTY WHILE IMMIGRANT

1

ONE WAY TICKET

It was one of those blazing hot days. The sun was relentless and its rays stung when they hit my skin. My boots left impressions in the dusty soil of the Sonoran Desert, reminding me of Armstrong's footprints left on the moon. The weight of my holstered Glock 22 pistol against my hip felt like a warm reassurance in the remote area that had trails for drug and human smuggling running through it like veins through a body. The sparkling reflection of my polished badge danced on the sandy wall of the dried-out riverbed they call a "wash" down here. This was Southern Arizona, some 40 miles north of the border with Mexico, and I had responded to a 911 call from a hunter, who said he had found human remains.

Two questions we often used to make fun of the perceived oddity of a situation popped into my head. *Where am I? And how did I get here?* The thought made me smile. But seriously, *how did I get here?* If someone would have told me 20 years ago, sitting in a German pub, that I would be a deputy sheriff in Tucson, Arizona one day, I would have immediately asked for whatever drink that person just had. Back then, there was no feasible scenario that would have landed me in the Sonoran Desert.

So how did this German guy from a town in an area known as Eastern Westphalia, Germany, called Gütersloh end up in Tucson? First, since English speakers often have trouble with the pronunciation of the German umlaut, we'll refer to it from here on out as "G-Town." Or you can do as my mother-in-law does and call it "Gootersburg." Either way, I invite you to come along. Slip into my shoes. Walk in my boots. Sit down for a ride-along with this deputy sheriff with the Pima County Sheriff's Department.

Let me start with an introduction. For that purpose, I'll take you back to the month of June 2001:

I walked up to the ticket counter in Frankfurt International Airport and felt my heart beat faster, producing a notable thump in my chest. It was not out of anxiety. As an Enterprise Account Manager working for a U.S. software company, I was used to flying. Based out of Frankfurt, I visited my customers in London and New York, flew for business meetings to Paris, and attended training classes in Mountain View, CA. But this time was different. For the first time in my life, I was flying on a one-way ticket. We were headed for Boston, MA, and a whole lot of anticipation, questions, and uncertainty were traveling with me.

The first time I had visited the United States was three years earlier. A year after, I started dating my current wife, who is a natural born U.S. citizen. One day, she showed up at my apartment near the Bavarian city of Würzburg. She had arrived in Germany only three weeks prior, on orders from the U.S. Department of Defense, and was looking for a permanent place to stay. I was in the process of moving to Cologne, approximately a 3-hour car drive northwest of Würzburg. A year earlier, my then-wife had left, and taken our 3-year-old son, Tobias, with her. Too much in that place reminded me of family life and the disappointment I had experienced. I was ready to move on.

The apartment was a nice, typical, Bavarian-style house on a hillside in a small village called Greussenheim and had been advertised for rent in the local German newspaper. Annie, the woman I should fall in love with and later marry, had brought her commander's secretary with her to take a look at the place. The secretary was German and supposed to act as an interpreter if needed. Outside of my apartment door, I heard Wolfgang, the German landlord, greet the two women at the front door.

Months later, I learned from Annie how they had stood outside waiting for the door to be answered. They looked at the name plate beside the doorbell. Seeing my last name, Peine, Annie said she thought to herself, "How in the hell do you pronounce that?" Little did she know that two years later, she would have to spell out that name virtually every single time she would provide her new last name.

I heard a knock on the apartment's door and said, "Come in! It's open." Not wanting to interfere with Wolfgang showing the place and trying to put the time to good use, I had decided to scrub the ceran-plated stove. The visitors seemed impressed by the layout, size, and location of the apartment. Good! Maybe I could get out of here faster than anticipated. As they continued their walk-through, I heard Wolfgang spilling niceties in broken English all throughout the visit. "Zee apahtment has a prrretty view frrrum ze bellcony." In response, a thick, American-English accent splashed through the apartment and made me feel eerily comfortable. It sounded so interesting; just like in the movies.

Once the tour was completed, the two women said their goodbyes and left, chatting all the way down the driveway. Wolfgang came by to quickly say thank you. He would hear from them hopefully by tomorrow.

The next day, he came downstairs and shared the news that the American seemed interested. She wanted to come back tonight, the commander's secretary in tow, and talk in more detail about a possible rental contract.

The next day, they showed up again. Annie and her German entourage, who I later learned, had grown up in a neighboring village and was yearning to gain another look at Wolfgang, a former police officer and my landlord. Wolfgang left to go upstairs and prepare the paperwork, as it seemed Annie was intent on renting the place. She and her interpreter, who really was not needed nearly as much as anticipated, sat at the dining table and, being a true German gentleman, I offered a beer. Both gladly accepted, and this magic Germanic potion helped to move negotiations along blissfully.

"The curtains over there?"

"Sure."

"How about the lamps in the dining room?"

"Okay."

"Do you want any of the decorations? Oh, and yes, what about the kitchen?"

"The kitchen?"

Annie looked at me with an expression of bewilderment on her face.

"Yes, would you want to buy the kitchen as well? Otherwise, I'd take it with me to my new place."

She looked at the secretary in disbelief, not quite sure if I was trying to be funny or if she was seriously supposed to buy a kitchen in a rental apartment in Germany. After being reassured by the secretary that this was indeed customary, we agreed on a purchase price of 10,000 Deutschmarks, which was the equivalent of approximately $5,000 at the time. A steal, considering that I paid about three times that amount when I had bought it three years earlier. And then it happened. Annie looked at me with a slight smirk and said, "Well, I'm not giving a stranger that kind of money unless he at least takes me out to dinner." And that is how that happened.

Over the course of the coming months, we struggled to make this awkward relationship work. We started a long-distance relationship, separated by a three-hour drive on the autobahn. The fact that I spoke English lulled us into the misconception that there really were not a lot of cultural differences between us. Until the day we almost broke up. "You are always so direct, like a steam train rolling through town," she said. Light-footedness is certainly not a trait Germans are known for, and my attempts at a literal translation of my thoughts were not conducive to a harmonious relationship, either. But with a lot of love, care, and dedication to make it work, we muddled our way through it all. The German and the Alabamian. That's a headline for another book right there.

In 1998, my constant nagging and pushing for us to visit the U.S. finally paid off. Annie suggested we travel to the birthplace of it all—New England. That way I could learn about the history and origins of her country, and the flight time wasn't so bad either. Interesting enough, as a child, my best friend Hans-Peter and I often pretend-played to be U.S. agents. I cannot seem to remember what agency we imagined working for, but it is also entirely possible that we considered such a determination to be unnecessary fluff. Or maybe we just didn't know what "agencies" were or which ones we could have chosen from. My imaginary character was from Boston and his name was Mike Baxter. I forgot what Hans-Peter called himself. It was probably a John or Jim with a last name we considered being distinctly American. And so, we would spend hours on end, idolizing America and feeling mighty powerful when we called each other by our American first names. The names, by the way, were the only English part of our play, as both of us were still in elementary school. At some point, I told Annie about this. How I had never seen images of Boston, at least not knowingly, but I had in my imagination it was a city of red brick buildings with an almost British look to it. Little did I know that I had actually pictured it quite fittingly.

When I got off the airplane at Logan Airport in 1998 for the first time, I had a strange and very confusing experience. I walked into the terminal building and felt as if I had just come home. An eerily unfitting warmth and familiarity took a hold of me. How could I possibly feel this way? What was going on? It puzzles me to this day. From the first day of setting foot on American soil, I felt right at home. I never experienced a day of being homesick. Yes, at times I missed particular aspects of German or European lifestyle. Decent bratwurst comes to mind. But I never felt homesick.

Never before in my life had I met an American before meeting Annie. All I knew was from what I had seen on TV or in one of the many movies coming from across the big pond. The most personal account I had heard of came from my mother. Born in 1932, she had been through World War II as a child with some very vivid memories. She told me of her fear while they were hiding in the basement at the end of the war. U.S. troops were advancing on their small town in southeastern Germany, Thuringia to be exact. Women and children had taken shelter in the basement of the house and were scared to death of what was about to happen. Nazi propaganda had provided the most horrific stories of raping and pillaging "Yankees" having their way with German citizens. But, my mother said, the worst was how they had told the kids that "negro soldiers eat little children." Though my mother was already 13 at the time, she said she was about to pee her pants in fear as they were hunkered down in the cold, musky dark of the cellar. She described how suddenly they heard steps on the floor above them and then heavy steps coming down the stairs. She said the basement door was flung open and an African-American soldier pointed his rifle at the group, obviously in anticipation of possible enemy soldiers. As he noticed there were only women and children inside, he lowered his weapon and walked up straight to my mother. She vividly described how she was about to pass out in sure anticipation of her impending demise when the soldier dug with his hand deep into his pant pocket and pulled out a chocolate bar. My mother was bewildered, yet instantly won over and henceforth declared her love for all things American.

Growing up, Americans were the "good guys" in my book. And in 2001, I was not only visiting again like I had in '98, but going to live there. In the land of the free and the home of the brave.

As I said, I was standing at the counter inside Frankfurt International Airport checking in our luggage—lots of luggage. Everything we would need during the first four to six weeks was in those suitcases. Annie stood behind me at a distance, snapping a picture to preserve the moment. A short while later, we were sitting in our seats on the plane, looking out the window and racing down the runway. Soon, we disappeared into the clouds over Frankfurt. It would be three years before I would return.

2
THAT DAY IN NEW YORK CITY

Though we had chosen a house and started the purchasing process, we were still living in temporary quarters. Don't get me wrong, Marriott is a fine hotel brand. But staying in a Marriott Residence Inn—even with all the comforts it offers—simply isn't home. Both of us were longing to have our own house, our own yard, and more than one room to live in.

My job was going decently well. I had completed my transfer to our Boston office and had officially become a member of the Enterprise Account Team. This was a U.S.-wide group of account managers who looked after large corporate customers, typically with a worldwide reach. My main client was Deutsche Bank, one of the largest financial institutions on the planet at the time, with its employees spread all over the globe. Lots of employees meant lots of potential users for the software solution I sold. Lots of processes meant complexity, and that was something we could help manage with our technology. Efficiency gains were a solid value proposition.

For the past 15 months, I had been working on a large corporate deal, consolidating a variety of licenses previously sold like a patchwork throughout Deutsche Bank entities across the globe. It was an attractive proposition for both sides. Now, we were closing in on a contract that would cover Deutsche Bank's operations worldwide. With my colleagues from within the U.S., in Germany, and in England, we had put together an incredible package for the bank. The only thing missing was the bow on top.

My colleagues in New York City, where Deutsche Bank's headquarters for the Americas were located, had agreed to meet prior to getting together with our customer. We figured that a half hour should suffice to briefly go over some details and see what else might be needed to close the deal with the bank. The deal would be one of the larger deals my company had put on the books.

Deutsche Bank's offices were located right across the street from the World Trade Center, so the Border's Café within the World Trade Center was perfect for our purpose. Deutsche Bank had scheduled our meeting in one of their many locales inside the World Trade Center, on one of the lower floors. The sales team would meet beforehand, briefly go over our strategy, have a cup of coffee, and then stroll over to present everything to the customer.

It was September 10th, and my mind was completely occupied by tomorrow's meeting when I rolled up to the Residence Inn in our rental car. My cellphone pinged, indicating I had received a voicemail. Spotty coverage outside of Boston? I was surprised. When I got into our room, I listened to the message. It was from the airline. My morning flight had been canceled, and they had already re-booked me onto another one a half hour later. Boston to Newark was a popular route. The woman in the message simply advised me of my new departure time.

On the morning of September 11, 2001, Annie drove me to Logan Airport for another day of business in New York City. She dropped me off just outside the check-in area. We kissed goodbye and off I went. It was early and travelers in the terminal were busy reading the newspaper or sifting through business papers. After a slight delay, we were on our way, taking off into the morning sky. The flight seemed longer than usual and a look at my watch confirmed that we were in fact slightly late. I was wondering if I could make up lost time by switching from train to taxi, but quickly dismissed the idea. Holland Tunnel was a mess going toward Manhattan in the morning.

DEPUTY WHILE IMMIGRANT

Once landed, I made my way straight to Newark Penn Station and walked right up to the ticket counter. They were those neat old ticket counters with a surprisingly friendly lady sitting behind the glass. "PATH train return ticket to the World Trade Center, please," I said.

She looked at me and said, "I'm sorry, sir. They had a train wreck in the station there. No trains will be going there for some time."

Fantastic, I thought. I should have taken the taxi after all, but it was too late. Here I was at the train station, so I might as well take a train. "What's the nearest Manhattan train station I can get to, ma'am?"

"That would be Penn Station, New York City," she answered. Going from Penn Station to Penn Station. Fits the way this day was developing so far, I thought. "Yeah, I'll take that."

She issued ticket number 1384624 for $2.50.

On the train, people were talking. I mean, they seemed to talk more animated than usual. As we rumbled over the bridge toward Manhattan Island, I heard the woman next to me tell someone over her cellphone, "I heard it was a sports plane of some kind." And then I saw it for the first time that day. Smoke seemed to be rising from one of the World Trade Center towers visible in a far distance. It was hard to make out any detail, given the distance and the steel struts of the train bridge whizzing by the window. Great, just great, I thought. What is it with this damn day? Then the train submerged in a tunnel for its final approach to New York City Penn Station.

From the platform, I ran up the stairs and briskly made my way toward the exit. The station was packed with people. Everybody seemed to be in a hurry. On a TV screen located in a shop window I passed I caught a glimpse of what looked like smoke billowing out of a skyscraper. *Everything always looks so dramatic when TV cameras zoom in on it.*

I stepped out into the sun and, for a split second, had the wherewithal to appreciate the beautiful sky that pierced the concrete valleys of this pulsating city. And finally, I was lucky. There was a taxi sitting at a red light, just a few steps away. I flagged the driver down and jolted my senses into the unique aroma of the backseat of a New York City cab and told the driver to get me "as close as you can to the Trade Center." He nodded, turned on the meter, and we began to snake our way through traffic toward the financial district in downtown Manhattan.

A few blocks in, we were being passed by fire engines that plowed their way through clogged traffic. Just as soon as one siren seemed to fade away, the next one clawed itself toward us from behind. I tried to call my customer, Daniel Silverman, at Deutsche Bank. There would be rescue personnel everywhere, and they had probably evacuated the floors the plane crashed into. I tried to picture a Cessna or some other small aircraft crashing into the steel structure of the World Trade Center. Not a pretty picture. I could not reach Daniel, and as I tried to reach my coworkers, who I pictured sipping coffee out of paper cups at the Border's Café, my calls kept dropping or went into the annoying standard announcement, "All circuits are busy at this time. Please hang up and try again later."

Fifteen months of work, sleepless nights, endless strategy sessions, and here I was, about to miss an important meeting because some wannabe bush pilot failed to properly circumnavigate one of the tallest buildings in the world. I thought of Alanis Morissette's song "Ironic."

Then, suddenly, my phone rang. It was my wife, Annie. "Where are you?" What an outlandish question, I thought. "In New York City! I'm on my way to the Trade Center to meet with Deutsche Bank." I tried to sound not too annoyed, given all that had happened up to this point, which, of course, my wife couldn't be aware of. I explained, "I know about the crash with the small airplane." Annie's voice suddenly had a commanding ring to it. "Get out! Get out now! That was no small airplane. It was an airliner, and you need to get out while you still can. Do you hear me? They're going to shut the whole place down and then you're trapped." She clearly knew something I didn't, and my instincts told me not to challenge anything she had just said. She was completely aware of what it had taken for me to get to this point and was perfectly at peace with me throwing the Deutsche and the Bank out the window. "Okay," I answered.

"Call me when you're out and in a safe place," she requested.

DEPUTY WHILE IMMIGRANT

I flipped the phone shut, knocked on the Plexiglas window that separated the passenger from the driver's section, and made a whirling motion with my index finger. "Turn around! Back to Penn Station."

My mind was racing and, as if awoken from a dream, I began to notice the hustle all around me. Suddenly, I couldn't get back to the station fast enough. My mind turned into scenario mush and Annie's words and her voice seemed to be on permanent replay in my head. Once again, I tried to call Daniel at Deutsche Bank, but I couldn't get through.

As I entered Penn Station again, a vastly transformed scene greeted me at this major transit hub. It seemed that every one of the little shops had pulled out their televisions into the hallway. People gathered in large groups around them, and those who were not glued to the newscast were all headed for the trains. It was as if I was swimming toward the platform I had emerged from a short while ago. How long ago was that? Time suddenly had become an oxymoronic mix of rush and goo.

I rushed down the stairs and onto the platform where the train was waiting. Was that the same train I came in on? It was packed! It reminded me of those scenes on TV where they showed hopelessly crammed trains in a Tokyo subway station, where folks in uniform were pressing people into the train cars so they could close the doors. Maybe these trains weren't quite as full, but it was clear that people wanted to get out of the city.

And then they came. A small group of maybe three or four Transit Police Officers rushed down the stairs. One or two stayed at the top and blocked people from coming down, seemingly closing down the platform. I squeezed in on the train and ended up jammed in between fellow riders close to the doors. One of the officers could be seen through the scratched-up windows running toward the front of the train, gesturing with his right arm in a downward swipe at the conductor, seemingly telling him to get the train moving out of the station.

The train began to rumble through the dark tunnels right into the belly of this metropolis. It was getting hot quickly. People seemed breathless, though not physically out of breath. The tension was palpable. After a few minutes, daylight broke in through the windows, and as we moved over switches in the tracks, we were all rocking back and forth together. I was looking for something to hold on to when I heard a woman scream nearby. By the time I caught a glimpse of her, she had burst into tears, and everybody was trying to veer through the windows on the left side of the train to see what had caused her reaction. I had to slightly hunch over to see what had made her cry out. It looked way worse than before! Thick smoke was bellowing from the World Trade Center. Both towers were on fire now. The woman who had cried out was being comforted by another passenger next to her. This was bad.

Ahead of me, separated by two or three rows of people, stood a tall man. He was wearing headphones and apparently listening to a radio broadcast. Suddenly, he turned around, looked in my direction, and said, "They just bombed the Pentagon." Passengers behind me asked, "What did he say?" "He said someone bombed the Pentagon," I repeated. Heads started shaking, soft sobbing could be heard. And I thought, so this is how it starts. This is how wars start. And there is nothing I can do. *What's next? Will there be a major military attack?* I thought of Annie, my son Tobias, and my mother, who must have experienced many moments like this.

We arrived at Newark Penn Station. The doors opened, and the train spilled its human cargo onto the platform. We were "greeted" by heavily armed police officers, who directed us toward the stairs and then toward the exit. While we were all going down the stairs, I thought I felt a light tremble underneath my feet, but didn't pay any further attention to it. Maybe a train had passed through on a nearby track. All of this happened in an orderly fashion, and it seemed that not a word was being spoken by any of the evacuees. As I stepped outside the station building, I immediately noticed a large, black armored police vehicle and more cops. Somewhere in between, I learned that all airports were shut down and all air traffic had been suspended.

Fortunately, New York City is within reasonable driving distance from Boston, I thought. So, all I needed was a car. In front of the main exit,

DEPUTY WHILE IMMIGRANT

I noticed two or three car rental shuttles and walked up to the very first one. It was Enterprise Rent-A-Car, and I asked if they might have any cars left. The shuttle driver thought so—at least he hadn't heard otherwise—and off we went. Again, I tried to call Daniel Silverman at Deutsche Bank and again, it was to no avail. I began to worry about him.

I ended up in a neighborhood somewhere in Newark, maybe a five minute or so drive from the train station. As I entered the lobby of the Enterprise Rent-A-Car office, I noticed the TV monitor mounted on the wall behind the customer service agents, facing the customers. Images showed what looked like a full-fledged airliner slicing into one of the towers, causing a massive fireball explosion. Then there were images of giant dust clouds rapidly filling the streets. One of the rental agents was sobbing. Her colleague comforted her and said to me, "Her brother works in the towers. One of the buildings just collapsed. Are you looking for a car?" I had never felt so intrusive before, yet I needed to get back to Boston. "Yes, I need a one-way to Boston, please." A guy walked in from a backroom that seemed connected to a garage. He was the manager and said, "I have one car left, but we don't offer one-way rentals. You would have to return the vehicle back here to this station." How was that possible? Out of options, I agreed, thinking that a car was better than no car. If I had to rent that thing for a month or two, then so be it. He said the car had just been returned and it would take a few moments to have it cleaned, refueled, and ready to go again.

I took a seat in the lobby and noticed two other men in suits sitting on the opposite wall. They were trying to use their phones but looked frustrated. Then I remembered. She said, "Call me when you're in a safe place." I flipped open my phone, dialed the number for our hotel, but it wouldn't go through. All I could hear was the female voice of an automated announcement, "All circuits are busy at this time." I tried again. And what about my customer? I thought about the few facts I felt I knew that might help in estimating possible outcomes. The meeting was supposed to be on a very low floor. Maybe he hadn't even arrived in the conference room yet, but was still in his office across the street when the plane hit. I tried to call him again, and again, then our hotel, then my coworkers, then my manager. "All circuits are busy at this time."

There I was on a faux leather lobby seat, looking at my commiserating peers seated along the other wall, when suddenly a phone ring cut through the voice of the CNN commentator coming from the TV on the wall. There! It rang again. The two other men looked at me. I looked at my phone. My phone was ringing! I flipped it open. "Hello?" It was my wife. "Where are you? Are you okay? Did you get out?" Thank you, thank you! What a relief. Once again, I looked over at the other two men, shrugged my shoulders and felt obliged to mouth the word "Sorry" in their direction. How or why this call got through is beyond me. I gave Annie an update on my situation. She suggested I drive to her brother's house in Marlton, NJ, which was approximately one and a half hours south of Newark. We would decide everything else once I got there. Good plan! She told me she was at the Fleet Bank branch in Concord and how she was using the branch manager's desk phone. She described how the manager there was shaken and tearful. Everybody was in a state of shock. We said our I-love-yous and then hung up.

For the first time, with some of the more immediate plans to get away from all of this seeming to work, my mind slowed down just a little, and I immediately thought of my son again. He was staying with my parents back in G-Town, Germany. What time was it over there right now? They could probably see this on TV. Oh my god, if they learned that I was in New York. I needed to let them know I was okay. I walked up to the counter where the manager was entering information into their booking system. I looked at him and said, "Would you mind if I use your phone to make an international call. My son stays with his…" I couldn't finish the sentence. "Of course, go ahead." He put the phone on top of the counter. "Dial 9 first." Amazing how priorities shift in times of real crisis. In that moment, that man gave me so much comfort with this one gesture of kindness. No questions asked—of course.

I heard the German ringtone on the line and after a few rings, my mother picked up. She wasn't even aware of what was going on yet. It was

DEPUTY WHILE IMMIGRANT

afternoon over there and she had started dinner preparations. Following my instructions, she turned on the TV and immediately saw the images. I assured her I was okay and about to add even more distance between me and the events that were still unfolding. I told her to give my son a kiss, and I would be in touch again as soon as I could, explaining my situation and how I had to keep it short. Then we hung up. "Sir? Your car is ready," the manager said.

We were standing outside, with the car parked at the curb in front of the rental car office, filling out paperwork. A black Crown Victoria pulled up in front of us. Two men in suits got out. One of them carried a shotgun. They entered the rental car office. The manager looked at me and said, "Quick, sign here. Police. They may be looking for additional cars." I scribbled an illegible version of my signature at the bottom of the contract, which may have resembled my name—or not. The manager ripped off my copy, handed it to me, and said, "Good luck."

As I drove away from the rental station, I realized that I had no idea where I was going. About a block down from the rental car office, I scanned the sidewalks for a business or someone on the sidewalk I could ask for directions. (There was no GPS or electronic navigation system.) I noticed that the streets were void of people. Nobody was out, and there were very few cars on the streets, if any. Then I saw a young man walking on the sidewalk. I pulled up to him and rolled down my window. "Hello? Excuse me? Could you tell me how to get to the Interstate?" He answered with a thick German accent, saying, "No. I am sorry. I am only visiting." Really? What were the odds? I couldn't help myself but ask, "Are you German?" He confirmed, and I learned that he had not watched TV and therefore had no idea of what was going on around him. He had stepped out to take a walk and immediately noticed the empty streets. I gave him the Reader's Digest version of what I knew up to this point and asked if he needed any help. He said he was okay and briskly walked back in the direction he had come from.

Somehow, I figured out how to get to the Interstate. Relieved to see the sign toward the on-ramp, my mind played the "You'll be safe soon" movie. The simple notion of soon to be with family members gave me an instant boost of motivation. As I traveled up the ramp, the Manhattan skyline became visible on the driver's side. I looked across the water to the north and saw what was now a giant smoking gap. They were gone! The iconic sight of the Twin Towers was no more. It was so surreal that I wished someone would wake me up from the nightmare.

Driving southbound was just as surreal an experience. Usually, these freeways are buzzing with traffic. Thousands of people constantly coming and going, often filling these roadways to capacity. Not today. There were a few other cars going southbound with me, but there was virtually no traffic going toward the city. Upon reaching the first toll-both, I immediately noticed the lights of a police cruiser up ahead. The barriers at the booth were open and police officers were waving cars through. Almost like an encouragement. "Come on! Leave! Get out of here!"

Another 15 or so minutes into my drive, the next eerie scene developed on the opposite, New York-bound side. Ambulances—lots of them. They were driving toward the site of horror to help with all the injured; I was sure. With their emergency lights activated, but no sirens, it looked like a silent procession toward the carnage. Throughout my drive, I made several more attempts to reach Daniel at Deutsche Bank. Once I regained network coverage and got through, his phone went straight to voicemail.

It was around that time, due to the regained coverage, my phone indicated that I had received a few voice messages. The first one was from Nathaniel, my coworker who was supposed to be at the Border's Café. It sounded like he had the phone on speaker and had walked away from it, maybe toward a window. I heard him talk about a possible bomb at the Trade Center, his description of one of the towers on fire and how he had had me on redial for a while, but said he was "freaking out" as I didn't answer. Clearly, he had never made it to the Trade Center and made this call fairly early as the events unfolded when it was still unclear as to what exactly had happened.

Another call was from our HR department in San Diego. It was the HR Director, who asked me to please call them or Nathaniel or my boss.

DEPUTY WHILE IMMIGRANT

She said, "We are worried to death about you!" Later on, I found out that I was the last person in the whole company they were able to account for that day. In a phone call with my boss, I relayed what had transpired and learned that my coworkers were all okay. I told him about my concerns as I was not able to reach Daniel at Deutsche Bank, despite attempts to call him since I had regained cell phone service. My boss said he'd take care of headquarter notification and for me to get some rest. We'd figure the rest out as we moved into the coming days.

I arrived in Marlton and parked in front of my in-law's house. Annie's brother and his wife were the first family members of hers I had met back in 1998. We had added a side trip to New Jersey during our visit and therefore knew each other. It felt fantastic and so comforting to be with people I was familiar with. We exchanged long hugs and their loving welcome felt like a fluffy blanket on a cold winter night. My sister-in-law cried and her husband asked if I wanted a beer. We went over to the den where they had a large back-projection TV running. It showed the footage of the planes crashing into the towers, then the towers collapsing, people covered in dust, running for their lives, all on a constant loop of visual terror. My stomach began to turn, and I thankfully declined all offers of food.

After an hour or so in the den with family members, I stepped outside to be alone for a few minutes. Up to this point, everything had been such a rush of madness that was now subsiding. My full senses and emotions slowly returned. I was no longer in fight-or-flight mode. I paced back and forth on the lawn beside the house. That is when it hit me—all of it at once. I cried, sobbed with tears running down my cheeks. It was no particular thought or memory that brought this on. It just completely overcame me. Being out there, looking at the evening sky, watching the birds in the trees, crying, I lost myself in the moment and couldn't really tell how long I spent out there by myself. When my sister-in-law came out to invite me to dinner at her parents' house next door, I pulled myself together somewhat and walked back with her, entering her parent's house through the backdoor, rejoining the family, who had migrated over for dinner. We all sat at the dining table. Grace was said and in doing so, the family expressed their thankfulness for my safety, paired with wishes for those who might still need to be rescued.

Another call to my mother and son in Germany reassured them that I was okay. On the radio and TV, there were constant calls for blood donations in anticipation of the need for all the injured. The family here decided to go to one of the quickly established donation centers.

Needless to say, I didn't eat or sleep much that night. All I could think of was how I wanted to be with Annie.

The next morning, I decided to go back to Newark and return the vehicle to Enterprise Rent-A-Car in order to switch to a vehicle from another company that would allow me a one-way rental. I gave my in-laws each a hug goodbye and headed back toward the Interstate.

The knot in my stomach became prominent again and more so the closer I came to Newark. When I passed Newark International Airport, which abuts the freeway, they had parked airplanes all the way up to the fence line. This was where you would typically look across a wide-open grass area and the runway toward the terminal buildings in a distance. Now, that same area was filled with aircraft from all over the world. They had been ordered to land to clear the airspace over the United States. Obviously, the airport ran out of space where they'd typically park these giants. They had improvised. The off-ramps toward the airport were blocked by giant snow plows they had parked in the middle of the road, manned by armed personnel, presumably police officers. I know people on the trucks were armed because as I drove past one of them, I noticed the barrel of a rifle or shotgun sticking out of the driver's side window, angled toward the sky.

The return of the car at the Enterprise Rent-A-Car station was quick. They called me a cab, and I asked the driver if we could get to any of the airport car rental offices. He said he wasn't sure, but we could try. We were lucky the first time and drove up to an Avis station next to Newark International Airport. I asked the cabbie to standby while I checked to see if they had any cars left. Their lot didn't look promising. I figured that some of the cars parked there belonged to employees, leaving a very limited supply available for rent.

I walked into the lobby and saw only a couple of other customers inside. I approached the counter and asked if they had any cars left. The agent explained they had only two vans left. Before asking any other questions or having any other conversation, I simply said, "I'll take one of them" and handed her my credit card. While the service agent prepared the paperwork, I walked back outside, paid the cab, and gave him a good tip. When I returned to the service agent, I explained that I needed a one-way rental. She said of course that would be no problem and that they would waive the otherwise customary fee for this special request. People arrived after me and were told there were no more vehicles available. Before I left, I thought there might be others who needed to go in the same direction but didn't get a car. So, I asked two of the new arrivals where they needed to go and told them I was headed for Boston. They had other, incompatible destinations. Once the paperwork was completed, I boarded my Chrysler family van and headed toward Massachusetts.

Half of the day had already passed by the time I was finally on my way home. My stomach demanded I stop for some food, but I wasn't in the mood for a big meal and decided to stop somewhere along the way. On the Garden State Parkway, I came upon a rest stop located between the two directional lanes. The place was busy and only offered the typical burger-type fast food. As I did not want to lose any significant amount of time, I ordered one of their junk meals and decided to eat in the van. I grabbed the bag of food and on my way out I noticed the local New York City daily newspapers displaying the now infamous images on their front pages.

Memories of another historical moment I had experienced came back to me. The morning after the reunification of East and West Germany, newspapers were available for free on the streets of my hometown back in Germany, glowing with the celebratory headlines that appropriately framed the momentous occasion. The headlines and pictures on the front pages at this rest stop were very similar in their historic vibe, just not in a celebratory way. They seemed more like an outcry, a scream. Just like I did in 1989 and again in 1990, I bought two of each of the papers. I thought of them as a memento, something tangible to bring back and preserve as if I needed some kind of proof that I was there that day.

Back in the van, I once again tried to reach Daniel Silverman. I did not count how many times I had tried to call him the previous day but was never able to connect with him. The phone rang, and then I heard Daniel's voice on the other end. "Tom?" He sounded tired. The first thing out of my mouth was, "Oh thank God! Are you okay?" Then he went on to explain how he was, in fact, in the Deutsche Bank building across the street from the World Trade Center when the first plane hit. This was the old Bankers Trust building. They had been told to stay put and not evacuate the building. But once the second plane hit, Daniel said it was every man for himself and he just took off. He said he ran for city block after city block and finally made it out of Manhattan and home. He went on to say that he was on a train on his way to the bank's disaster recovery site and would contact me from there. We disconnected, and I felt a huge sense of relief.

After I finished my first substantial meal since breakfast the previous day, I took the van back onto the Interstate and continued my way north. I turned on the radio. The airwaves had seemingly transformed into one gigantic news and talk radio show. The hosts on every station provided even the most minute update on investigative findings or rescue efforts. The frustrating part was that none of it sounded like it would offer much comfort to those who were waiting for word on or from missing loved ones. Between repetitive reports, a seemingly endless stream of listeners shared their stories. Then came a fast-growing number of call-ins from people all over the Northeast and elsewhere. They briefly introduced themselves and explained how they were construction workers, plumbers, electricians, even a guy with a crane truck. They called to say they were about to leave from their businesses or hometowns. Some were already on the road. All of them were headed to the same destination: the place that would, from here on, be known as "Ground Zero." They asked who they should report to or where exactly to go. People called to say that their businesses were preparing meals for all the first responders and other folks involved in the rescue efforts. Private people called in to ask what they could do or where they could send money. It was an amazing, breathtaking, and beautiful outpouring of support. I drove across the Tappan Zee Bridge with tears rolling down my face.

A few hours later, I rolled into the parking lot of the Marriott Residence Inn in Weston. I grabbed my luggage, went inside and upstairs to the second floor, where I started running toward our room. I knocked on the door. Annie opened, and without saying another word, we hugged. We held each other tightly and cried.

3

MOVING TO TUCSON

After pulling over onto the dirt shoulder, I opened the driver's side door and put one foot out. It felt like stepping into an oven. Having fully emerged from the car, I looked over at Annie, who rose from the passenger side. She squinted and said, "Man, that's like your face getting hit by a blast furnace." It was well beyond 100 degrees Fahrenheit, paired with a humidity level in the single digit percentages.

We were just outside of Tucson, Arizona, in a small community of houses scattered in the desert. The place was called Vail and was located in unincorporated Pima County. It was only a few days prior to my birthday in April 2005. Annie and I had come out to visit with her brother, who was a Chief Master Sergeant with the U.S. Air Force stationed at Davis Monthan Air Force Base, and his family.

It wasn't all about family, but also about business and finances. The years following 9/11 were challenging for us. Though we had bought a beautiful house in Maynard, MA and had made friends with the best neighbors one can possibly imagine, finances had begun to spiral downward. On the positive side, in 2002, my German-born son Tobias (Tobi) decided to come to the United States and live with us. He was the child from my first marriage, and up to that point, had lived in G-Town. At the tender age of nine, he opted to move across the Atlantic and stay with us. His mother had made the gut-wrenching decision to support his choice, and in October of that year, he joined us, and we turned into a small family of three.

The deal with Deutsche Bank ultimately closed and was a glowing success for both client and vendor. But the company I worked for at the time, Remedy Inc., had been sold to a competitor. A development that didn't go well. Management of the new parent company, Peregrine Inc., had "cooked the books" and ended up in prison. A new buyer purchased the—still intact—former Remedy entity and became part of the new owner, BMC Software. By 2004, I began to suffer serious burn-out. I lost my drive and motivation, the two most critical ingredients to being a successful salesperson. Software sales were sluggish across the economy and the cost of living in Massachusetts was sky high.

To take matters into my own hands, I decided to quit my corporate job and become an independent consultant. Working for myself instead of lining other people's pockets sounded like a good idea. The only problem was that I miscalculated the time it would take to generate enough cash flow to sustain the business. A partnership with a friend ended up derailing the whole concept, as it turned out that our ideas about how to grow the business were just too different.

Ultimately, my partner and I made the decision to dissolve the business and go our separate ways. Annie started looking into ways we could "reset" and give it another go elsewhere. It also seemed a good opportunity to look for a new home in a warmer climate. Being from Germany, I had some serious catching up to do with respect to my exposure to sunlight. Though Tobias, a true snow lover, was hesitant about the idea, Annie began to apply for federal government jobs in places like Texas, Arizona, and Colorado. (Though the snow in Colorado ended up getting it removed from the list of desirable locations.)

The job that came through for Annie was with the U.S. Department of the Interior, and her office would be located on Ft. Huachuca in Arizona. A brief visit to the base's host town of Sierra Vista, AZ, southeast of Tucson assured us that we wanted to live much closer to or even in Tucson. As a home in Tucson would have made for an excruciatingly long commute every morning for Annie, we opted for Vail with its location almost halfway in between the two towns. It meant she would have to cope with "only" about an hour-and-a-half round-trip every day. Vail's school district also had stellar reviews, which weighed heavily on our decision to make it our new homebase.

So, there we were. The homes we were looking at were still under construction. It turned out that all the houses had already been sold, except for two models. The on-site sales agent gave us 24 hours to think it over or he would sell to one of the other interested parties. A brief check with our realtor to see if this could be true or if it was simply a clever sales strategy returned only a nauseatingly simple nod from the realtor and the words "red hot market."

After four years of living in the United States, I found myself on a dust lot in the Sonoran Desert, looking at a home that was still only partially finished. Latino construction workers were buzzing throughout the house and mariachi music was blasting from a radio on the bare concrete floor of the living room. We stepped into the main room. The southern exterior wall was all windows, with a pristine and unobstructed view of the Santa Rita Mountain range in a distance. It was like one of those pictures in a travel catalog showing a faraway place people dream of. It was breathtaking, and I was mesmerized. Though the surroundings looked a bit rough, (i.e., undeveloped), and a dirt road abutted the property, I looked at Annie and quietly said, "This is it." We had looked at several other places, but this was, well, it.

Let me tell you, for a guy from Eastern Westphalia, Germany, who grew up in what was considered a "spacious" townhome of 1,300 square feet, this place was a palatial 2,810 square feet of house on an acre lot. We even talked about putting a swimming pool in the backyard. The realtor recommended a contractor who would deliver great craftsmanship at a fair price for a wall around the perimeter. Wait what? We just got rid of a big old wall in my country about ten years ago. The one in Berlin, you know. Why would I want to build one in my backyard? The response was a reality check for both of us. We learned about the local wildlife and how we would most likely be interested in some sort of barrier between them and us, especially out here.

The list of beasts our realtor riddled down included mountain lions, bears, coyotes, larger snakes, and so on. Did he just nonchalantly say "larger" snakes? What about the small ones? And what type of snakes were we talking about? Answer: No, the little guys would still make their way through the irrigation guard in the wall. They're harder to keep out. But the big, fat, adult rattle snakes would not fit through the small holes in those bricks at the foot of the wall. I felt cold sweat beads building on my forehead as I pictured myself sucking snake venom out of my son's leg while my wife frantically rode on a horse to reach the next phone booth to call for a rescue helicopter. The realtor said with a slightly annoyed undertone in his voice, "Well, y'all will get used to all the critters out here."

The next morning, we returned to the sales guy's single-wide trailer office to sign the purchasing contract. It was my 40th birthday.

When I called my mother a few days later to tell her about our upcoming move and the beautiful surroundings, she reacted with disbelief. "In the desert? Thomas, will they even have work for you? What are you going to do out there?" I guess the term desert naturally set off a kaleidoscope in her mind mixing pictures of sand dunes, Bedouins, camels, and the odd, palm-circled oasis in the distance. My description of Tucson included that of an international airport, the Raytheon Missile Systems factory, a military air base, and the picture of a city of roughly 700,000. To this day, I'm not sure I was able to alleviate her concerns for our economic survival. But over time, she came around to love the place.

We moved into our new home over the 4th of July holiday. The house was a Santa-Fe-style bungalow located in a gated community. Well, let me frame that properly. The main entrance road into the neighborhood had a gate installed, which constituted the controlled access. However, those gates remained open for the first two years or so, and there was no surrounding fence or other barrier.

Part of the sales pitch was also the prospect of a shopping center and mixed-use development across the Interstate, maybe a third of a mile down the road from our new home. The "Passages of Tucson," as it was called, certainly created a bit of a hype among the salespeople and made the prospect of living out in the desert seem more feasible.

What was unbeatable was the view from our back patio. Looking straight at a desert mountain range and no other noteworthy development nearby, except for a few homes on 1-acre-plus lots sprinkled into the landscape. It was an enchanting view. Many a night we found ourselves sitting out there in the warm desert air marveling at a vista others had to travel far to experience. For us, it was home now.

One of those balmy desert nights on the patio came with some nosy (and at times noisy), unexpected visitors. A group of coyotes strolled along the dirt road behind our house and curiously stopped to see who was seated there, illuminated only by candlelight. It was an eerie feeling, and we decided to expedite the construction of the property wall to enclose our backyard. As for the other critters, our realtor was right. We did get used to them and actually named some of them. First and most prominent was a large, hairy tarantula we called Agatha. Now you may shiver when thinking of a big, hairy spider walking on your patio as you leisurely lounge in your garden furniture. But I had to seriously reverse my opinion of these marvelous creatures. First of all, they're slow and—more importantly—not aggressive if left alone. Some of the local school kids, including kids in Tobias's class, would let them crawl on their hands and, much to the dismay of the teachers, bring them to class. The tarantulas, however, were not the kind of insects I was concerned about. It was more the tiny, beige Arizona bark scorpions, which are considered to be North America's most poisonous representatives of their species and made the top ten list for most poisonous scorpions in the world. Centipedes are also on the definitely-avoid list. They're ugly, fast, and deliver a painful sting. It is a lively and poisonous universe out there in the Sonoran Desert. We identified tarantula wasps, Gila monsters, wolf spiders, black widows, termites that will eat your house—you get the picture.

We pulled together all our money from the sale of our house in Massachusetts and besides constructing the backyard wall, we hired a landscape and pool designer to build us a custom swimming pool, deep enough to accommodate a diving board. The latter design requirement was added by Tobias, who had begun to attend classes at Old Vail Middle School. The plans for the pool looked fabulous and certainly gave the whole property a more luxurious touch.

As my parents came for a first visit, the work on the excavation for the pool began. The contractor pulled the excavator to the site of our future little oasis in the desert. The bucket at the end of the excavator's arm swung down to take a big bite out of the dusty soil, but nearly jolted the operator out of his seat as it hit the ground with a resounding bang. They tried several more times in different spots, but the soil seemed near impenetrable. The tough material took a toll on the contractor's nerves and on the bucket's teeth. The next morning, the crew exchanged the bucket for a giant jack hammer and kept switching back and forth between the two tools. What was scheduled to be a day's worth of excavation work stretched into a week of tremor-inducing hammer-and-scoop action.

As we took possession of our new home and wrestled our property out of the tight grip of the Sonoran Desert, Annie began her work in Ft. Huachuca, and I took on the task of exploring the local job market. For several weeks, I kept going through the job ads in the Arizona Daily Star, the local newspaper, but mostly came up empty-handed. All I knew was that I did not want to go back to sales. Maybe I would find a new calling, something where I could help others. I'm a people person, so I really wanted to work in an environment that would provide for that. Then one day, destiny seemed to be on my side. The local Wells Fargo branch had advertised positions in their customer service department. Not really a new calling or even a step away from sales, but as we drove through what could be considered the town center of Vail, we noticed a sign advertising the site of a future Wells Fargo branch to be built right about two miles from our house. Being a banker by trade, I gathered my papers and put together an application.

About two weeks later, while perusing the job section again, there was another advertisement that jumped out at me. In glorious, bold, black and white letters, it spelled out that the Pima County Sheriff's Department was looking for Deputy Sheriff recruits.

Some may wonder why I would even read such an ad. The short answer is the humanitarian and the boy in me jumped to attention. The long answer requires a bit of personal history. At around the age of 12 or 13, the police in my home state of North-Rhine Westphalia had an exhibition inside the main local department store called "Hertie" in downtown G-Town. Walking through the exhibit, seeing all the gear they showcased, I was enthralled. I even got to sit on a BMW police motorcycle, where a police officer took a Polaroid picture of me. I had always looked up to police officers as the epitome of righteousness and readily bought into the advertised notion of cops being your friend and helper. They definitely were the good guys, and a seed had been planted. Over the years, the desire to join the police force grew in me.

The law enforcement profession in Germany is structured differently from that in the USA. There are only state police forces, plus the Federal Police, who were in charge of airports and border protection when I was a child. You could join the police force anytime between the age of 16 and 32. Serving as a police officer would automatically relieve you from the then compulsory service in the German armed forces or Bundeswehr and was considered employment for life. Meaning you would go through a 3-year-long training while living in police barracks and then embark on your law enforcement career until you retired at age 60. Just like the military, the German police service has their own healthcare system, paid for by the government and at no cost to the officer.

While in the 10th grade of a type of high school called "Realschule," which mostly prepared youth for a vocational education, I visited with the local recruiting officer for the state police. This particular type of grade school lasted only 10 years. Following graduation, you would either move on to join the last three years of the 13-year-long string to prepare for college or sign up for a three-year education in a trade or business setting. And it was a crowded field. Typically, hundreds of teenagers would apply for an apprenticeship with a particular local business. It was difficult to get the type of placement one would desire.

Walking into the local police headquarters and speaking with the recruiter was a very exciting experience. I was serious about this! Armed with several glossy brochures that highlighted the training and professional life of young officers, I came home with a head full of glorious fantasies. But would I even pass the test? All these people seemed to be very athletic and an athlete I was not. Sport was not my forte or, more accurately, not something my parents had particularly encouraged. I had been a pretty decent marksman and member of a local sports shooting club. An attempt at judo had not panned out too well, as the local coach was obsessed with training his students to fall properly for such an extended period that over the course of several months, I never made it into the first grappling group. All I took away from judo practice was a serious infestation of head lice.

My parents were, well, apprehensive regarding my career choice. My father kept pointing out the toughness of the duty, especially the fact that you'd have to work on weekends and during off hours. Dad served as a non-commissioned officer in the German Luftwaffe and was a technician for the American-made F-104 Starfighter jet. But except for a few stories here and there, he frequently talked about how his service had not been a real challenge for him. I recall him saying, "It's not a place to build a career. All you do is take orders and do as you're told." It seemed to be his mission to keep me out of any kind of uniformed services. He talked about all the demonstrations going on at the time. There were massive rallies of people opposed to nuclear power or additional runways at Frankfurt International Airport. Thousands of protesters would face thousands of riot police officers in sometimes violent standoffs. We kept discussing the fact that before reaching patrol duties, there was a period of several years where you had to serve in the riot police, who lived in barracks. My parents argued that the earning prospects weren't as favorable, and how they had heard of many officers who became disillusioned after years of service on the street.

At the same time, my parents had a personal friend for years who worked as a homicide detective. Interesting enough, they always spoke very highly of him and his profession. But then again, he was portrayed as some sort of intellectual genius and only the super-smart would ever make it into one of the coveted slots in the detective division. My school grades were certainly nothing to be proud of and, therefore, I tried to picture a life inside a patrol car. Maybe I could become a helicopter pilot?

Their attempts to persuade me to choose an economically more profitable career path failed. In early 1982, I made my way to the riot police barracks in Münster, Germany, and participated in one of the selection processes, which lasted two days. Having received the invitation letter with detailed instructions on what to bring with me and what to expect, I showed up with a duffel bag at the barrack's front gate and reported to one of the police officer guards there. I was impressed with the officer's appearance. While he was friendly, he had this aura of authority about him. Would I be one of them someday?

An escort picked me up and brought me to one of the large, elongated brick buildings which served as housing units. It was a large compound that housed not only the selection service but also a large contingent of riot police. Once in my dorm room, I met with three other candidates who had taken possession of their bunks already. We went over to the small cafeteria on base. There we met other candidates and shared our expectations and anxieties for the testing days ahead of us.

Over the course of the next two days, the field of police officer candidates was whittled down dramatically from a field of sixty to four. It was a constant process of stressful anticipation. We were brought into a classroom, received brief instructions on the upcoming test, which was subsequently handed out. A large, oversized stopwatch on the desk of the observing officer in the room would show how much time we had left. If you were caught cheating or glancing at your neighbor's test sheet, you were eliminated from the process immediately. No questions asked, no recourse.

It was a battery of several written and multiple-choice tests throughout the day, covering a wide variety of topics and subjects. After the completion of each individual test, we were brought into a waiting room. The tests were graded right away, somewhere in a different room. The waiting time seemed endless. Each time it was concluded by an officer briskly opening the door to the waiting room and reading out loud a list of names. Those called up were then escorted out of the room and we never saw them again. The remaining candidates were brought back into the classroom for the next test. It was a stressful process.

At the conclusion of Day 1, the field had been reduced significantly. I seem to remember that only a few candidates were left. The lead officer came into the classroom and congratulated us. He said we had done well and affirmed what we already knew; that this was a hell of a test battery. He explained that tomorrow would be different. We'd have a psychological test, a personal interview, a physical fitness test, and a medical exam—if we made it that far. He urged us to pay special attention to the news tonight and to make sure to read the newspaper in the morning, as it was customary to quiz the candidates on recent events during the personal interview. That night, we sat together in the cafeteria again, reminiscing about the day and congratulating each other for making it this far. We didn't last very long, though, and ended up going to bed early.

The next morning, May 14, 1981, we went for breakfast in the "chow hall" and filed through a set of newspapers we had bought. And there it was in large headlines on the front page: There had been an assassination attempt on the pope in Rome. Who would do such a thing? We pored over the article and tried to remember as many of the details as possible. Other news of the day would certainly take a back seat in comparison.

My psychological evaluation apparently did not reveal any reason for exclusion from further participation in the selection process and my interview also went well. Next, we were asked to change into our sports gear and brought to a space under the roof of one of the buildings. It was freezing cold up there and the lead officer apologized to us, a measly group of four remaining candidates, for the low temperature. The room offered some seriously dated gym equipment, including some medicine balls of worn, brown leather. I briefly wondered if they were pre-or post-

DEPUTY WHILE IMMIGRANT

World War II inventory.

A circuit had been set up with an officer assigned to each of us to record our individual score. We did pull-ups, sit-ups, push-ups, sit-ups while thrusting a medicine ball, and others. Afterward, still in our gym clothes, we went straight down to the medical wing for our exam.

At the end of the day, the four of us received a warm handshake and were congratulated as we had passed. A brief verbal instruction as to what would happen next in the process was provided as well. I received yellow carbon copies of several documents I had to sign and was then sent on my way back home. Passing through the main gate on my way back to the train station, I began to wrap my head around the fact that I was now a member of a very small group of candidates who had passed a stringent, arduous selection process so many others had failed. I felt glorious and smiled the entire train ride home, looking through the windows at the passing fields of Westphalia.

That year, though several others had tried, I was the only one of my entire class to be accepted into the police service. My start date was documented as October 1, 1982, in a letter of appointment from the Selection Service of the State Police of North-Rhine Westphalia.

It would have been all good had it not been for those pesky grades. In the short amount of time left in the school year, I was unable to overcome the effects of my excessive absences during the preceding months. With less than passing grades in three subjects, I failed to graduate. Crushed and devastated, I watched all of my classmates graduate and leave school to begin their professional careers, while I stayed behind to do it all over again. In Germany, it was and is not uncommon to repeat a grade. If you fail two subjects in any particular year, you'll be held back automatically. However, most of those who shared my destiny of being a repeater had done so in earlier years. Instead, I had to watch them all leave and then do what we called my "honorary lap."

So, what did that mean for me becoming a police officer? Upon inquiry with the Selection Service by my father, they told him over the phone that all I had to do was graduate next year and come in again for a follow up on my medical exam, as obviously things might have changed due to injury or other unpredictable events. The rest of the test battery, however, need not be repeated and would remain valid. Phew! No big deal, I thought, and poured my heart into studying.

To nobody's surprise, the results were vastly improved grades. As spring of 1983 came around, my father once again called the Selection Service. He explained that he was trying to gauge what the likelihood of me failing the medical exam was, given the fact that it was to take place in late spring. No, there were no major medical events. But if there was a possibility that I could fail the exam, he'd have me start applying for other apprenticeships. So, in case I'd be rejected, I would not run out of time to secure a job education in this rather crowded field of applicants streaming into the marketplace. The officer on the other end told my father, "Mr. Peine, short of your son showing up in a wheelchair, there is nothing to worry about." Relying on that rather upbeat statement, I rested on my laurels and simply waited for the day of the exam.

Upon arrival at the police barracks in Münster in May of 1983, I was allowed to head straight for the medical unit and was seen in short order. After the same general exam that I went through a year earlier: stress EKG, measuring blood pressure, height and weight, vision test, hearing test, providing a urine sample, et cetera, I sat on the edge of the exam table and waited. Though having no particular reason to doubt that I would be fine, I was a nervous wreck with goose bumps all over my body. The doctor came back into the exam room after having left for several minutes. He asked me some additional questions and went back into the next room. The door remained cracked open, and though I could not hear exactly what was being said, I could see three people in white lab coats, presumably all doctors, discussing what I figured were the results of my tests. Their voices sounded concerned, and they kept going over paper files. After a while, the doctor who had examined me came back in and said he was very sorry to be the bearer of bad news, but they had "discovered" that I might have high blood pressure.

I could not believe what I had just heard. In between feelings of being shattered and pissed off at the same time, I helplessly asked if there was something I could do. Maybe I could exercise more or change my diet, do something. "No, I am sorry. I'm afraid this is final, Mr. Peine." The train ride home this time was the exact opposite of the delighted journey back a year earlier. The fields outside the train car window seemed gray and bleak. My ego was in shambles, and I felt betrayed, beat, and clueless as to what I would do next.

Once home again, my parents were furious, and my father launched another futile attempt to turn matters around, to no avail. It was not going to happen. No spiffy police uniform in October, no becoming a protector of the weak, and no career in what I thought would be my dream job. My father of course went on a lengthy diatribe about how he had warned me about "those government people." Good for nothing else but sucking up our tax money and in return bothering us with speeding tickets. Yes, I received the whole "I-told-you-so" treatment—the whole enchilada.

In a race to the finish line and out of pure desperation, I landed an apprenticeship to become a grocer. Telling my parents, "Not a thousand horses will get me back into school," I started work in a local delicatessen and fine foods store on August 1, 1983. Once on the job, I had a rather rude awakening. The store owner would quiz me on the total price for a random collection of individually sold rolls from the baked goods section. "Two sesame rolls, one regular, a cheese-crust roll, and three of the poppy-seed rolls. How much?" With teaching topics such as mopping the shop floor, properly irrigating salted herring (which almost made me puke), and trying to study up on the difference between German summer sausage, salami, and other red-meat sausages with lard sprinkles, I quickly reached the end of my rope. Three weeks later, I quit and enrolled in the local business high school for a 2-year course to prepare for college or enter a business apprenticeship with a reduced term.

Following my graduation from business high school, I secured one of the coveted apprentice slots at our local savings and loans bank, turning myself into a banker. Law enforcement as a profession disappeared from my consciousness. Uniformed service, however, still entered my life, albeit involuntarily. By the end of my apprenticeship, the German military had already been lurking in the background, waiting for their moment. In 1987, the year I graduated as a banker, the country still had compulsory military service for all men between the ages of 18 and 32. Within weeks of my graduation, I found the dreaded blue envelope in the mail. I was instructed to report to the Osnabrück central train station to board a train for bootcamp. 15 months of mandatory military duty as a conscript soldier in a signal battalion followed.

The advertisement in the Arizona Daily Star had rekindled the spark, bringing it back to the forefront of my mind. It spelled out the requirements, and though I looked for an age limit, I could not find one. I was 40 years old, after all. My process of naturalization had just concluded and on September 16, 2005, I had been sworn in as a U.S. citizen, which would cover one of the many requirements in order to qualify as an applicant. In a moment filled with blissful memories and limited critical thinking, I decided to go for it. Maybe the third time would be the charm. The initial fitness and multiple-choice tests were advertised for September 24, 2005. All I had to do was call in and provide my information to secure a slot in the process. That old wish of mine, that dream of a career in law enforcement, had been reignited in an instant. I had to tell Annie.

When she came home from work that night, I broke the news. She had been very supportive of my application with Wells Fargo. While it was certainly not the kind of high-paying, impactful job I had while I worked in the world of enterprise sales, it was a job with a reputable organization, which would provide some much-needed stability and income.

When I brought up the Sheriff's Department announcement, she gave me the same kind of look she did back in the months following 9/11, when I felt urged to do something, to somehow contribute. During those days, I had spoken to a Navy recruiter. I had gone through the ASVAB in preparation for my consultation with the recruiter and learned that I had attained the high score of the day. The recruiter was obviously excited, and I just barely fit into the upper end of their age requirements. However, based on my then status of a permanent resident, opposed to the citizenship I had now, all prospective assignments were measly jobs, where I saw little chance of doing something meaningful and living up to my true potential. So I walked away from the effort. But the look on her face back then was awkwardly identical.

"Okay, so now you want to be a cop? I mean, you're 40. Please! Honey! Buy a Harley or something. I'd really like for you to look into that bank job." The situation did not improve when I explained that the Deputy Sheriff position would pay less than the Wells Fargo job. But it would increase year after year, and it would be an awesome opportunity to finally pursue that dream job of mine, albeit with a slight delay of more than 20 years. You have to know that my wife is a strong-minded person. I fell in love with her because she knew what she wanted, was not afraid of anything life might throw at her, and she was always up for an adventure. Though her career was a textbook example of increasing responsibility in a specific field of federal government work, she had accomplished as much as she had through her can-do attitude. Prior to coming to Germany, she had been employed in California, North Carolina, preceded by an 18-month-stint in South Korea. Yes, shy to take a risk, she was not. And now she appeared staunchly opposed to the fulfillment of my childhood dream.

I reluctantly agreed to continue with the bank application. However, at the same time, we agreed that, just in case Wells Fargo wouldn't work out, I would continue with the selection process for the Deputy Sheriff position. For days I walked around the house moping, complaining, discussing, challenging. Things didn't get any easier when Wells Fargo made me a job offer. But given the fact that my approach began to resemble Chinese water torture, Annie finally gave in. "Okay then, go ahead. Let's see how far you'll get in that process," she said. And yes, I noticed the undertone of her wishing I'd fail.

4

THE ACADEMY

The selection process for Deputy Sheriff with the Pima County Sheriff's Department was in part very similar to the one I had gone through 24 years earlier in Germany. First came the physical fitness test for which I had begun to exercise in preparation. An effort that I expected to pay off. If you received a passing score on your fitness, you would continue to the tests for English comprehension, writing, math, memory, psychology, ability to observe, and others.

Next up was an oral board interview scheduled for September 27, 2005. This was the strangest interview I had ever experienced. They called it a "structured interview." In the interview room, you had a panel of interviewers seated behind a row of tables. The panel consisted of a Sergeant and three Deputy Sheriffs. Centered in front of them stood a single table with a chair: my chair. My interview, like all interviews during this process, would last all but 15 minutes. Each applicant was asked the same four questions, which you also received on a set of note cards turned upside down. I was instructed to leave them turned over until told otherwise. The sergeant then introduced the panel and gave additional instructions. Next, I was asked to turn over the first notecard and one of the panel members read the question aloud. After indicating that I had understood the question, the clock started running. I answered as best as I could, trying to keep track of time in my head. Once I finished my response, I turned over the note card, which indicated to the panel that

I was done. There was a hard stop after 15 minutes. Being too brief and not using enough of the 15 minutes was considered a malus. Running longer than 15 minutes got you cut off without being able to finish your statement. The panel members would not ask any questions or for clarifications from the applicants. You walk in, they read the questions out loud, you answer. Thank you very much. Good luck. Next!

In the first week of October 2005, I received a letter from the Sheriff's Department telling me I had passed all tests up to that point. The selection process continued with a polygraph interview. Up to that day, I had only known these machines and interviews from spy movies, some of which involved the subsequent torturing of the interviewee. I was determined not to end up in a dungeon facing a hooded interrogator. My polygraph examiner was actually a woman who worked for a private contractor. An interview preceding the actual test was meant to eliminate any potential false positives due to a misunderstood question or context that may require explanation before simply answering yes or no.

I sat down in the interview room and was hooked up to the polygraph. That meant the examiner applied a blood pressure sleeve, chest strap and a sensor on my fingertip. She looked at my hands and said, "Ooh, sweaty palms. That's good. Makes for a clear read." It was a miserable experience. All my childhood sins rush back into my mind. I told the examiner about the time when I was six years old and slipped a pack of Wrigley's gum into my pant pocket, for reasons I cannot remember (we could afford chewing gum), while my mother checked out at our local grocer. Back home, my mother discovered my misdeed, made me go back to the grocery store to return the gum to the store owner and apologize. The shame of having committed such a senseless offense stuck with me to this day, or at least until I was 18.

"Have you ever had contact with law enforcement other than during a traffic stop?" "Yes," I answered. In the interview preceding the test, I had to admit to a teenage stupidity. It was December 30th, the day before New Year's Eve the year I turned 18. Being of legal age, my friends and I had gone out to buy firecrackers and properly welcome the new year.

DEPUTY WHILE IMMIGRANT

It was the first time we could legally do so ourselves. Bursting with anticipation of how and where we would discharge all these explosives, we allowed ourselves a little preview. Of course, this was illegal, as the use of firework was allowed only on New Year's Eve and New Year's Day. But it all didn't seem quite thrilling enough yet. Walking through one of G-Town's finest neighborhoods—right around the perimeter of the city's main park, we laid eyes on a set of decorative lanterns on top of a front yard fence. Wedging two large firecrackers in between the cast iron décor and the yellow tinted glass of the light fixture, I lit the fuse, and we took off running. With a loud boom, the explosion of the firecracker turned the glass into shrapnel that flew all over the front yard and the sidewalk. You could hear the shards of glass hit the ground. The explosion echoed from nearby houses and trees, which made it sound even more menacing. We were amazed, impressed, and thoroughly entertained by our moronic tour de force. We continued to walk through this neighborhood, leisurely dropping smaller firecrackers here and there when suddenly the headlights of a car shone through our legs from behind. The car did not pass us, and we turned around to see what was going on. As we looked head-on into the glaring headlights of a car, a blue emergency light on top of the roof was turned on.

"Cops!" my friend yelled.

As the officers got out of their patrol car, I attempted to "stealthily" dispose of the remaining firecrackers by throwing them into the brush off the sidewalk next to me. Officer Eagle-Eye, however, pointed his flashlight right at my face and said, "What did you just toss into the brush there?" I gave the only reasonable response, "Nothing." German Polizei is not necessarily known for its great sense of humor. We ended up with our hands against the roof of the patrol car and were patted down. The second officer, who had briefly descended into the brush, reemerged and announced he had found the firecrackers I had tossed. Then we learned about the reason why they had stopped us. At the house of a local attorney, "someone" had blown a nice, expensive outdoor light fixture to shreds, and the word "idiot" may have been used. The attorney had called the police to press charges for vandalism. *Who would do such a thing?* We fell on our proverbial sword and admitted that we were indeed those idiots, albeit remorseful idiots. Officers took our information and released us with the advisory that we would be contacted within the next few days regarding possible charges. The blissful ignorance of teenage stupidity had come to an abrupt end.

When I returned home that night and had to tell my parents of our explosive-laden exploits, my dad simply looked at me with an expression of disappointment and disbelief.

"Well, now what are you going to do?"

"I don't know. I thought you might be able to…"

"Oh no, my friend! Don't even try to go there. This one you'll have to figure out all by yourself."

"But I will have to go to the police!"

"You told me just this morning how proud you were of being 18 and you'd go buy some fireworks. Here's the thing with adulthood. You can do things like that now, but you also have to bear the consequences of your actions all by yourself."

"I don't know what to do, though."

"Maybe you should consider the humble route and go see the homeowner to offer paying for the damage."

The next morning, me and my friends found ourselves at the front door of said attorney's residence to plead for mercy, leniency, and forgiveness. Our teenage brains had simply short-circuited in the presence of the legally available explosive ordinance. Much to our disbelief, we learned about the exorbitant price tag for one of these lanterns and were indeed offered the opportunity to pay for it. In exchange, the attorney would drop the charges. We repentantly accepted the offer and for the next four weeks I found myself taking odd jobs all over G-Town in order to keep my conscience—and my criminal record—clean and my future job prospects intact. That would remain my only brush with the law until it was brought back up unexpectedly 22 years later in the offices of Southwest Polygraph in Tucson, AZ.

DEPUTY WHILE IMMIGRANT

In the following days, the Sheriff's Department testing continued with a psychological evaluation, a medical examination, and drug screen. The medical exam had been scheduled for November 21, 2005, and it was there in the waiting room that I met William "Will" Novak for the first time. We struck up a conversation and quickly determined that we were both in the process for Deputy Sheriff. We also figured out that there was more we had in common. Will also came out of the corporate world and was the son of Czech immigrants. He was a lot of fun and a very smart fellow. We instantly liked each other and ended up driving together to and from class every day for the duration of the entire academy.

The intensive background investigation conducted by the Sheriff's Department also gave a green light, and finally I was notified that I should report for duty at the Pima County Sheriff's Department Law Enforcement Academy on the morning of January 23, 2006.

It was a dark and freezing morning. All the recruits showed up early, wearing the required uniform of the day, which was a white shirt, black tie, black pants, and tennis shoes. We had learned from our experience during the academy orientation a few days prior that it was best to follow instructions to the letter. And the instruction was to make sure we'd show up on time. Whereas, "on time" had been defined as "If you're five minutes early, you're on time. If you're on time, you're late." The phrase was strangely similar to the one I was given during my military service in the German Bundeswehr. There, the motto was "Fünf Minuten vor der Zeit ist des Soldaten Pünktlichkeit" which means, "Five minutes ahead of time is the soldier's punctuality."

We filed into our classroom that was part of a small complex behind the Pima County jail. It was an older building and actually too small a space for this undertaking. There was one classroom and two sets of locker rooms, one for male and one for female recruits. Our class had a strength of 42 recruits in the beginning, which would soon be reduced through attrition. This academy was basically the final step of the selection process and, in the end, only 33 of us would make it all the way to graduation. Even less would make it all the way through field training and to patrolling the streets of Pima County. There was no gym. Instead, there was a patio in the back with a metal roof, sans any workout equipment. Alternatively, there was the nearby parking lot we referred to as "the open-air gym." There was also an obstacle course behind the academy building containing a six-foot wall, a set of monkey bars, and a brick wall with an opening resembling a window. Finally, to the eastside of the building, there was a sandbox, also known as "the pit." More about that later.

We formed a single file line ending at a desk where one of the class counselors would fill out some initial paperwork and register attendance. Once class attendance was confirmed and we had taken our seats, the classroom turned quiet. The room bristled with anticipation. We sat there wide-eyed, ready to go. An interior door with one-way-mirrored glass, transparent only to the other side, opened and a deputy in a dress uniform (AKA class A) stepped into the room. He wore a black campaign hat, also known as a Mounty, with a large silver badge in the front. His eyes were covered by dark sunglasses, making his appearance distinctly formidable, which was clearly the point because sunglasses were hardly necessary at this early hour, given that it was still dark outside and there were only neon lights inside the classroom. This man had a crisp appearance. His uniform was perfectly pressed, brass shined, shoes polished to a spit shine. This was the drill instructor or class officer. From there on out, I referred to him as "The Hat." He greeted us with a stern, but otherwise friendly, "Good Morning." The class responded in unison with a loud, resounding, "Good Morning, sir!" And then snap! The Hat suddenly began to yell at us. "Stand up! On your feet! That was pathetic!" And so it went.

The Hat then properly introduced himself. His verbal delivery had changed to a loud, forceful, unapologetic, assertive tone. "I am your assigned class officer for the next twenty weeks!" He emphasized every word in *"next 20 weeks,"* making it sound all the more daunting. This vocal onslaught seamlessly transitioned into a continuous flow of verbal harassment. I don't remember a word being spoken by him in a regular volume suitable for indoor conversation for the next half hour or so. Everything that came out of that man's mouth was constantly at maximum volume. Within a few minutes, The Hat had found so many things wrong with us, our behavior, our attitude, our "uniforms," the world as a whole, that we ended up in the pit for the first time.

Now, the combination of The Hat and the pit was a bad development during an academy day by any stretch of the imagination. The pit is a large sandbox filled with deep, grainy sand, which manages to creep into every part of your clothes, your shoes, it sticks to your skin, and would frequently show up in the shower tub at night when I tried to rinse off the stress of the academy at home. The pit is roughly 20 x 20 feet in size. We ran over there and stood in several lines, filling the entire area of the pit. Next, we were made to drop on all fours, followed by a series of exercises such as push-ups, another one we called "dead bug" because you would lie on your back with your extremities straight up into the air, jumping jacks, et cetera. This would go on for 15–20 minutes, or longer if it was deemed appropriate by The Hat. Upon returning from the pit, we were full of sand, which left a noticeable trail toward the classroom. Sand was in my mouth, my hair, my ears, my shoes. We regularly ended up looking quite disheveled due to the strenuous exercises. The sand on the floor and the subpar appearance of our uniforms would, in turn, lead to a return visit to the pit. It was a lose-lose situation.

On this first day, we learned several very important things necessary to survive the academy:

1. Wherever you go on the academy grounds, you move in double-time. (Referring to a specific way of quick-stepping everywhere you went.)
2. When you move from point A to point B on the academy grounds, you move at right angles only. Yup, you got that right. No curving, no crazy 16-degree variation in your walking direction. Ninety degrees and ninety degrees only. It was annoying, but strangely entertaining at the same time.
3. Whenever you encountered someone else on the academy grounds other than your classmates, you stopped, got into a pose of

"Attention" and reported to the individual you encountered by stating your name, what you're up to, and finished with a request for permission to proceed.
4. Any statement you made had to begin and end with the term "Sir" or "Ma' am."

So, you would end up in a situation where you're double-timing in right-angles toward the bathroom and suddenly encounter someone in civilian clothes. You would immediately freeze in place, hug the closest wall with your back, and then proceed with the loud statement of "Sir/Ma'am! Recruit Peine, on the way to the bathroom. Requesting permission to proceed, Sir/Ma'am!" If you did well, the person you encountered would release you by mumbling, "Carry on." If you screwed up, you might find yourself dropping to the floor, performing a set of 10 or 20 push-ups to remediate your failure to perform as instructed. It may sound funny, but it was not. Here I am, 40 years old, running around an academy compound like a directionally challenged chicken, constantly preparing in my head to explain why I was roaming freely through these sacred halls. Actually, the example of having to use the bathroom facilities is a poor choice on my part. If you in fact had to relieve yourself during class or at any other time outside the assigned bathroom breaks, you definitely would have received a public dressing down for your lack of self-control and failure to use the break times appropriated for such activities. In a worst-case scenario, your behavior might trigger a visit to the pit by the entire class. In particularly egregious cases, that visit may have been paired with an appearance of The Hat. And you already know how that goes. By the end of day one, I was positively exhausted. During our drive home, Will and I reminisced how strange an experience this was for us, coming straight out of the corporate world and thrown into this authoritative environment. With that said, we decided that—most likely—they knew what they were doing and had our success in mind.

On the morning of day two, things went pretty much the same way:

"Good Morning!"

"That was pathetic!"

DEPUTY WHILE IMMIGRANT

Running to the pit, joined by The Hat.

Stream of consciousness yelling at the class.

Performing strenuous exercises in the sand.

Then back to class, failing a uniform inspection by The Hat and back to the pit we went.

We actually did have a class or two in between as well. Classes in which I learned that the term "sheriff" came from England. Yes, there was the well-known Sheriff of Nottingham, who struggled with Robin Hood and his antics. It was interesting to see that the job had its roots in the Anglo-Saxon shires. "The Shire Reeve," which later morphed into the term Sheriff, was the senior official with local responsibilities under the crown. (Wikipedia)

We also enjoyed a visit by a senior ranking member of the department, a Bureau Chief, who talked about integrity and what it meant to do the right thing even if no one was looking. We learned about the meaning of the badge and how it was not only a symbol of power given to the bearer under state law, but that it also stood as a representation of the trust citizens would place in us and our commitment to honorably discharge the duties of our office. There was a lot of meaning in small things and often significant history behind all of it. It made a deep impression on me and certainly instilled a sense of belonging to a special order.

In the afternoon, the intellectual input found an abrupt end as we were called to zig-zag onto the patio behind the academy. Once there, we were instructed that we would go through what was known as a survival drill. We were shown a parkour set up in the parking lot. We were to perform a set of "suicide runs" for one minute at full strength, followed by as many push-ups as we could muster for one minute. The goal was to exhaust ourselves and weaken our strength before we would go into the final stage of the drill. We had been paired up with another classmate and were instructed that after the push-ups, we would put on boxing gloves and then punch each other. Only punches to the head were allowed, no body shots. We were supposed to hit with 50% force. The goal was to expose the recruits to physical violence and see how they would react. It was meant to be an experience where you realize that even though you were taking a hit, you were still able to function, think, and fight back. For some, it was no big deal. Maybe they had engaged in their share of physical fights before.

For me, this was a difficult challenge. Back in my childhood days, I had been bullied for years. On my way to school, there was a particular stretch I was scared to pass. One of the main bullies lived in a housing project right off the bike path, and he had given me a bloody nose more than once. Becoming a victim, however, was rooted even earlier in my childhood. For several years, I had been cared for by my maternal grandmother. She was a proponent of the "finer" things in life. Her mantra was that one should strive for a proper education, have impeccable manners, dress and eat well to be recognized as a viable and credible member of society. Violence, especially the street kind, had no place in her worldview. She had witnessed atrocities during the Jewish pogrom in November 1938 and probably other evil acts committed by her fellow citizens wearing brown shirts and swastikas. It was clear that those and other experiences had left her with a sense of disgust toward any kind of physical violence. That mindset was instilled in me, and I was told to "stay away from those bad kids who hit each other." When facing aggression, she instructed me to cry for help and run the other way. Both experiences caught up with me during this very drill.

I was paired with another male recruit about my size (6' 4"), though he was heavier built than me. We went through the runs and push-ups, which left me gasping for air. Classmates assisted in slipping the boxing gloves, (which I had never worn before in my life), over my hands and then dropped to our knees underneath the awning in the back of the academy encircled by the rest of the class. The whole scene perfectly resembled school yard fights, where the kids would chant, "Fight, fight, fight!"

This time it was not the call for a fight, but people were still yelling, cheering us on, and clapping their hands. I looked at the other guy and thought, I have no reason whatsoever to hit this person. He actually seems to be a nice guy. Wham! No time to think this through any further. Under loud cheers from our classmates, he had delivered his first blow to my head, and it wrung my bell. Wham! Another one from the other side. The third blow I was able to block, but it felt weaker. He was bigger than me. So why did he not continue to hit as hard? Was he scared, too? My proverbial red curtain dropped, and I began to pummel my opponent. Blow after blow and he did not hit back. He actually bent over slightly, and the person I had just looked at so favorably suddenly turned into prey. Fueled by my cheering classmates, I kept hitting him and felt how my punches got harder. We were stopped briefly to reset, and my opponent was asked if he was okay. When he nodded, we kept going. Immediately, I began to strike him again and again. He had to go down. I wanted him down. Nobody had instructed us to deliver a knock-out. My uncoordinated punches, however, had an impact. Suddenly, I heard a whistle blow from a distance, and someone pulled me backward, separating me from my opponent. It was over. I felt a rush go through my body. Other recruits patted me on the shoulders. I had beaten the bigger guy and I could have kept going. Okay, okay. Gloves off, we shook hands. It was time for the next pair to hit the matt.

What happened? Was this the kind of transformation they were seeking? I immediately felt emboldened and more capable than ever to face the dangers lurking out on the streets of Pima County. The physical aspect was always one I had struggled with, but in the end decided to trust the time-tested methods of a law enforcement academy to prepare me appropriately. For a first experience with those methods, I had learned about the power of positive reinforcement and the power of a winner's mindset. As soon as I felt I could actually hold my own, I felt the adrenaline rushing toward my fists and felt the confidence needed to succeed in a physical struggle.

We started losing classmates on a regular basis. The first dropout was a man close to my age. He looked at me right before heading toward the counselor's office to turn in his resignation and said, "I'm a grown man. I don't need to be here, getting yelled at, getting belittled by these people. I have better things to do." That was on the morning of day two. So, I thought, you go through this entire selection process, all the interviews and tests, only to throw in the towel after a day? I shook my inner head and wished him the best of luck.

The classroom portion was tough. Every week, on Fridays, there was a test covering the materials taught during the previous four days. We had to score at least 80% on the test in order to pass. Miss it once and you're placed on academic probation. Miss it twice and you're out. Study groups were established and once a week my group would meet at our house after a long day at the academy. We would go through all the materials and some study hints we received during the previous days of instruction. There was obviously a lot of legal language we had to learn as part of the Arizona Revised Statutes, case law, legal opinions, and other police-related materials. But I was fascinated by all of it. Maybe, I thought, being a German in this environment wasn't all that bad after all. See, the country I grew up in cherishes obedience to rules. Rules give Germans a sense of safety, security, and predictability. You will see a person stand on the sidewalk facing a pedestrian signal in the middle of the night. There are no cars on the road. The person on the sidewalk will activate the push button to request a walk signal, then stand at the light and wait. There are still no cars. The traffic light turns red and the pedestrian signal illuminates the word "Walk" (in Germany, it is actually a small green figure in a posture that indicates a walking person). Now they'll cross, because that's the rule. Seriously, can you picture that anywhere in the U.S.? Try crossing the street on a pedestrian "Stop" signal anywhere in Germany. Other people will yell at you, mention little kids, who may or may not be around at the time, and chastise you for being a poor example to them. Other people at the light will give you the stink eye for such an egregious and blatant rule infraction. Yes, as a German, I felt at home in the world of rules and laws.

We were actually the first class to go through the Sheriff's Department's own academy. We learned that years back there had been another Sheriff's Department academy, but once the Southern Arizona Law Enforcement Training Center (SALETC) had been established, it seemed to be the more prudent approach to participate in a regional setting. The regional academy with participants from a variety of agencies in the area promoted a sense of comradery among recruits and sure was helpful if you'd run into each other in the field later on. Mind you, there's a variety of agencies in a place like Pima County. Not as straight forward as in Germany: state police, federal police, end of story. No, no, no. Here there was the Sheriff's Department, city police departments (plural), university/college police, airport police, railroad police, federal agents, Border Patrol, tribal police, park rangers, state police, and I'm probably forgetting a few here. Everybody and their uncle seemed to have their own police force. Not only could that potentially impede enforcement action or investigations but also emergency responses. There were workarounds, and most of the time it worked surprisingly well, given the logistical and legal constraints of such a model. But when it didn't work, it was pretty messy. However, the Sheriff had decided that the drawbacks of a mixed academy outweighed the advantages, and brought back the department's own academy. And there we were, the first class out of our own academy. The class size certainly justified the notion.

Part of the academy process was that the class would be tasked with picking a motto under which they would operate moving forward. It was their motto that would be yelled out loudly each time the class reported for duty in its entirety and should represent the spirit of those attending. After some discussion one afternoon, we voted on a set of suggestions and chose "First class lead the way." From there on out, we'd yell across academy grounds when standing in formation to report for duty, "Class 06-1. First class lead the way." This motto was later embroidered on a guidon, which accompanied the class wherever we went and was carried by a dedicated recruit selected for this duty. The guidon still hangs in the gym of the now much expanded academy today.

The class also elected a class president, a deputy, and a treasurer. The class president was the main contact for academy personnel, including The Hat, to address class matters where the class as a whole was affected. The class president was also expected to ensure cohesion of the class, to look out for those who struggled and to represent the class during ceremonial events. He or she was considered a primus inter pares: first among equals. The treasurer was responsible for the funds raised during a social project the class had to choose and for the funds raised to pay for the graduation dinner.

The election and motto selection came upon us during week two. The Hat came in and advised that this was what we would be doing during the next 30 minutes or so and then left the room as abruptly as he had appeared. We looked at each other and began a rather disorderly discussion. A recruit named Ethan stepped forward and volunteered to take charge of the process. A wild back and forth about suggestions for a motto ensued and after a short while, the process had escalated to a degree where one of the counselors had come back into the room and urged us to do this orderly and efficiently. None of this was Ethan's fault. We were just a very lively, bone-headed group of people aged 21 to 43. After the "warning shot" by the counselor, I stood up, went to the front of the class, and tried to help Ethan get a vote going. I explained how it would be unfavorable to wait for The Hat to return to the room and have us choose a motto while we were all eating sand in the pit. The argument had some undeniable logic to it and so we voted. Next came the vote for the class president. We were out of time, and I had been the only one to present a logical argument and describe the threat we all faced if we didn't handle the situation appropriately. Needless to say, someone threw my name out as a candidate. Ethan said he'd run for the job as well. Following the vote count, I had a job I neither really wanted, nor knew how to do, and Ethan, who was from Boston, became my sidekick as deputy. And with that, we were in charge.

Curiously, the class vote was overridden by The Hat only two weeks later, as we apparently still had not made enough progress in becoming a cohesive unit. During a break, I was called into The Hat's office and told that he had made the decision to take a drastic step in order "to shake things up." He explained that I would be removed from my post as class president and my deputy would take charge instead. He added that this was in no way a reflection on my performance as class president, but that something more extreme had to happen to awaken that spirit of cohesion and for these independent-minded individuals to learn they had to fall in line. A forced removal of the president due to a "lack of performance" would be a very unusual, albeit crystal-clear indicator that ignoring a well-meaning fellow recruit would lead to consequences for that recruit and the entire class. Given the horror of the past two weeks, being called out by The Hat several times for issues with the class that were entirely out of my control or where I was lacking the power to "enforce" anything, I was delighted. I told him that I would be perfectly fine with my deputy taking over.

The daily ritual always involved a wide variety of ways to gather material against us. On the morning of day one, there was the motorcycle deputy who had run radar on the road leading from the Interstate toward the academy. All those who had run over the posted speed limit of 35 mph were put on the naughty list, aka "the shit list." You did not want to be on the shit list, as it was the only possible way to be included in a "special session" in the pit. (The Hat and the pit combined with a mention on the shit list were the ultimate in negative outcomes for the day.) Other ways to end up on the shit list were illegal or missing equipment on or in your vehicle, doors left unlocked—or in police lingo: unsecured. Expired tags, being late, forgetting a piece of equipment (recruits were required to bring every piece of equipment they had been issued to class every day), having unintended contact with law enforcement, et cetera. The you-are-on-the-shit-list playbook was that we were all in the pit, together with The Hat, sweating, hurting, and eating sand all while being yelled at and then… The Hat would reach in his pant pocket and unveil a yellow piece of notepaper. He would call a recruit's name followed by the unmistakable order of "Front and center!" The class, who remained in some sort of physically strenuous position in the often baking-hot sand, would learn about some egregious infraction the recruit standing front and center had committed. We learned about such terrible mistakes such as driving 37 mph in a 35-mph-zone, leaving a piece of uniform visible in the interior of the car, window tint that was too dark, and other "horrendous" things. While the recruit, or sometimes it was several recruits, stood front and center, the rest of the class was made to burn some extra calories in the pit. I remember well how I'd look out of the corner of my eye and watch with horror how The Hat would retrieve a whole bundle of yellow shit lists from his pocket. Needless to say, we spent some valuable time in the pit.

One day during the first or second week of our training, it was once again time to visit the pit. Following the usual invitation by The Hat, we ran in right angles and obediently landed in the pit. To our surprise, we were joined by representatives of the local media. Folks with photo and video cameras, and notepads not unlike the shit list, carefully observed us being tortured. The head of the academy, a Sergeant would seemingly explain things to the attending reporters and answered questions. The reporters busily took lots of notes and the photographers got their action shots of us sweating in the pit and The Hat performing at his best. Nonetheless, we were all proud seeing ourselves on the local TV news that night and in the paper the next morning.

From an article in the Arizona Daily Star published on January 24, 2006:

> *"'Sir, yes sir' echoed off "A" Mountain and the walls of the Pima County jail on Monday as the Sheriff's Department brought its recruit training in-house for the first time in eight years.*
>
> *Forty-two deputy recruits spent much of their first day of class in "the pit," an oversized sandbox behind the jail used for physical training and endurance drills.*
>
> *'If you can perform under arduous physical training, you can perform on the street,' barked the drill instructor as the recruits sweated it out, doing push-ups in dress clothes."*

DEPUTY WHILE IMMIGRANT

Another tool we had to learn to use was the radio, our lifeline. From the very first days of the academy, we were issued a handheld radio to listen to live radio traffic from deputies in the field and develop what was known as the "radio ear." Having a radio ear referred to the fact that you could pay attention to ongoing radio traffic while doing something else. This was especially important as you would rely on the fact that fellow deputies would listen and be aware of what you were doing while you're on a call or traffic stop. In case things go bad, other deputies had at least a basic grasp of where you were and what type of call you were involved in. Especially if you needed help from others to respond to your location or help establish a perimeter, or be on the lookout for a fleeing vehicle, it was extremely important everyone would listen and maintain a general awareness of what else was going on in the district.

In order to understand radio chatter, we had to learn a special kind of language called the Ten Codes and the Supplemental Codes. These codes were established to keep radio traffic brief, render it almost useless for the uninitiated and provide a sense of safety if something confidential needed to be said over the airwaves. This is where the radio mainstay of "10-4" or a simple acknowledgement comes into play. Ten Codes[1] would become such an integral part of our lives that most of our family members would become versed in them as well. Not only from the time where they helped us memorize all the codes by quizzing us, but also because they slowly but surely snuck into our private conversations. I cannot count the instances where I acknowledged something my wife told me over the phone by saying "10-4," or by telling her that she could meet me at "103," which stood for Supplemental Code 103 (pronounced "one-o-three")[2] or the Sheriff's Department's administration building.

Among these codes were several that would certainly get your attention. Someone who would advise another deputy to "10-0" or use caution, or when deputies announced they were responding to a scene "Code 3," which stood for expedited response using lights and siren.

---

1 10-CODES KEY, PAGES 278 - 279
2 SUPPLEMENTAL-CODES KEY, PAGE 280

And then there were those codes that would make your blood freeze. Code 9-9-9 (Officer needs help urgently) and Code 9-9-8 (Officer involved shooting), both of which were announced across all frequencies simultaneously, accompanied by a warble tone that was our S-O-S of sorts. If you heard the warble tones announcing a 9-9-8 or 9-9-9 and were not on a call, you would start toward that location and continue to listen to the radio in order to receive further instructions from your shift supervisor. Depending on how far away the troubled deputy was or how dire the situation was, the response was coordinated by the sergeant, who would advise how many units or deputies would go. Obviously, you couldn't just send every single deputy because you have to maintain the ability to respond to emergencies still happening in your own district. Even detectives in their offices who had their radios turned on would momentarily stop what they were doing to listen to the information and to hear the location of the emergency. To this day, hearing that tone in recordings makes my heart skip a beat. The idea that one of us was in deep trouble, urgently needed help, or was in a potential life and death scenario caused a physical reaction and sent the proverbial chill down my spine—and I wasn't the only one. It was so serious that we would add breaks into the radio transmission of license plate numbers that resembled these codes. If a deputy would call out a license plate reading "ABC 999" over the radio, they would say, "Arizona, Alpha Bravo Charlie Nine Break Nine Break Nine." This was to ensure it was not misinterpreted as a potential emergency call in case the transmission was garbled or fractured.

We were constantly quizzed on radio codes. The Hat would walk around while we stood in formation and riddle down an imaginary radio call consisting mainly of a string of codes. The recruit facing The Hat would have to translate The Hat's mock-transmission into plain English. If you failed to properly interpret what had been said, the entire class was punished by having to drop and perform push-ups.

We settled into a routine and the weeks went by. Coming home was often not as pleasant as you might imagine. Typically, I went straight to the bedroom, stripped myself of the dirty, sweaty clothes and then jumped under the shower to turn myself into a human being again. After especially hard days with grueling workouts, I sank into the hot bathtub to soak my aching body in a solution of Epsom salt. I could feel every single one of those 40 years, most of which I had spent sitting behind a desk. When I joined Tobias and Annie for dinner, I often had a cup of coffee; otherwise, I would have simply collapsed right at the table. Narcolepsy is as close a description of my then daily bedtime routine as I can give. There were nights where I remembered how I had sat down on the mattress and that was the end. I did not remember how I laid down, tucked myself underneath the blanket, seeing my wife come to bed… nothing. Over the course of the first half of the academy, I lost 12 pounds. Mind you, I was not overweight to begin with. In order to stop the weight loss, Annie prepared a high-calorie diet and meals were supplemented by protein shakes. My metabolism certainly was in good working order. How I managed to sit down and study each night, I don't recall.

Over time, I slowly changed into a cop, and the metamorphosis became tangible. Small but important, potentially life-saving changes took place. Constant vigilance was engrained into our behavior. Learning all these police basics was akin to a complete reprogramming of how we would go about our day. We learned about the different states of alertness we should be in at all times (green at your home or friend's house, yellow outside of your house but still on your own property, and red everywhere else). This kind of vigilance was new to most of us. Only our fellow recruits who were combat veterans readily slipped into this behavioral pattern, just that it wasn't Fallujah but Tucson. I was a yelled at once for carrying a notebook in my right or "strong hand." Strong hand is the hand you used to pull the trigger on your weapon. Always keep your strong hand free and unoccupied so you can react and draw down on a threat at any given moment. The department did not require deputies and detectives to carry a gun while off duty, but it was recommended and most of us did, once we were out on the streets. We might be the only individual present in a given scenario who had the training and equipment to stop someone from harming other people.

We learned and drilled to be aware of our surroundings, being observant. When in a restaurant, I started sitting in the corner, with my back to the wall, "unexposed" as we called it, and facing the main entrance if possible. I'd scan the room to get an idea of the people inside and possible threats. While out shopping with the family, I began to scan my surroundings, checking out people in my vicinity, looking for odd behavior or the give-away bulge in their clothing. At first it was stressful, but over time it became second nature. I would immediately hone in on the person who seemed to be constantly checking his surroundings and fidgeting with merchandise in front of them. The guy in the long coat on a warm summer day would become a magnet to my eyes. Roughly how many people were in this restaurant and where were the emergency exits? My family learned that we would have a code word. In case we were somewhere in a public place, and I would notice something dangerous going on, I'd simply mention our code word. In return, my wife knew, should it ever come to that, to immediately take our son and leave, call 911 tell them where we were, that I was an off-duty Deputy Sheriff, and provide a description of me so responding law enforcement would know what the good guy looked like.

Instructors also told us about the "life in a fishbowl." Once your neighbors, friends, other school parents, or your spouse's coworkers learned about your profession, your own obedience to rules and laws became the focus of their attention.

"Were you speeding when I was behind you on Broadway the other day?"

"Did you see the deputy who lives next door to us cross the street this morning? That's called jay walking!"

"The deputy's husband always double parks at the grocery store."

And boy were the instructors right! They were also right about the fact that everyone, yes everyone, wants to tell you their cop story as soon as they learn that you are a peace officer. "Oh, you're a Deputy. You know, last year on our trip to Hawaii, we were pulled over by a cop. My whole family was in the car, and he was rude!" It was as if you're working as a Firefighter and I'd say, "You know, when I visited my parents in Phoenix the other day, there was a house fire on the way there and the fire department had blocked the road. The firefighter who stopped us and told us to find a different route was so rude." Who does that? Suddenly, the actions of another person reflected on me, no matter how geographically or otherwise distant from me they were, only because we shared a profession. In the shortest amount of time, I heard a litany of "bad cop" stories, and all I could do was to say, "I would never do such a thing." I quickly learned the lesson of one "bad apple" spoiling the whole basket. Not that this doesn't happen in other industries I had previously worked in, but it was never conveyed as viscerally as in reference to negative encounters with police officers.

Later on in my career, I came to compare it with the job of a referee. They are needed as enforcer of the rules of the game to maintain an orderly flow of play. Rules of the game alone will not automatically make everyone adhere to them. Most people don't particularly like the referee. Often, they are blamed for a team's loss or demise and not so much the actions of the team on the field. It was the way the referee interpreted the rules, didn't see what really happened, had a grudge against your team, et cetera. Cops are the referees of society. We have given ourselves a set of rules called the law. People break the law all the time. Cops break the law. And the same pattern of shift in responsibility takes place. Suddenly, it is not about the fact that the driver was speeding. No, it's the cop who obviously had nothing better to do than harass innocent citizens. It is the cop who injected himself into someone's private life following a 911 call about a woman screaming from the apartment. Rarely is it the citizen's fault. It's the cop who caught them in the act of violating a rule. Many people refuse to take responsibility for their actions.

Other kinds of indoctrination happened as well. There was the instructor who felt it necessary to make sure we had what he considered "the right mindset." He presented the story of the sheep dog, the sheep, and the wolves, an excerpt from a book called "On Killing: The Psychological Cost of Learning to Kill in War" by Dave Grossman. Why this should relate to the role of police in patrolling their own citizens, serving their own community, I was not sure. Then again, it's an academy setting, and you do not have much of a choice or room for debate either.

Remember the us-and-them mentality? This is where it manifested for some in the class—and apparently some of the academy staff. In short, it is a story about how there are only three kinds of people in the world. To hell with diversity, we'll go with just three. There are those who are ignorant, non-observant, blasé, unaware, and naïve when it comes to what the author considers the "true" nature of human existence. On the other hand, are there those who are the opposite, who get it. They are vigilant, observant, prepared, sharp, and ready to defend whatever needs defending. The first kind are from here on out referred to as the sheep and the others, the defender-types, are the sheep dog. Now the sheep dogs are protecting the sheep. The sheep need protection because their oblivious ways will inevitably lead to their quickly perishing and falling victim to the wolves, who are constantly roaming around the perimeter (of our communities). The sheep don't like the sheep dog but need them for their survival. The sheep dog needs to herd or in the human realm constantly "tell" the sheep what to do, where to go, and sometimes needs to use force to make the sheep do what they need to do in order to survive and not fall prey to the wolves. The deputy giving the class pointed out the story was not part of the official curriculum; however, he introduced it as a way of helpful and "realistic" self-perception for cops. He stressed it was not the official policy of the department and just one way of looking at things, but then he added how we would soon discover the truth of the story for ourselves.

This compartmentalization, the categorizing of people we would encounter: worthy and less worthy, strong and weak, superior and inferior, good versus evil, rang all alarm bells for me. I grew up in a culture with a specific sensitivity based on its history toward pitting one group against another. Appealing to one's primitive sense of wanting to belong to the winning side, the superior one, to be part of something special, can have disastrous consequences. Leading people down a path of self-perception that somehow separates them qualitatively from others means to enter a very slippery slope. Peace officers who identify as separate from or superior to the community they are policing will ultimately not be part of a solution, but create a problem, an obstacle, a barrier.

When driving home that night, Will and I talked about it in the car and how we were uncomfortable with looking at the world that way. Yes, there were bad guys or "wolves" out there. But people didn't automatically fall victim because they were always ignorant, naïve, and react only out of fear. Cops weren't always the superheroes coming to the rescue. The generalization of the idea is what kept me thinking about it. Or was it simply a picture that reflects reality? A reality I had not experienced yet, because of my sheltered upbringing in a society where violence was generally frowned upon and where firearms were, for the most part, illegal to own or possess. Was it an inconvenient truth or a telltale sign of a bitter and depressingly negatively skewed look at the world? Who or what determined which category (sheep, sheep dog, wolf) a person would end up in? Could they transition from one into the other? Personally, I thought—and still think—it is ludicrous to compartmentalize people that way. Characters and behaviors are fluid, ever-evolving, dependent on circumstances and environmental factors. We all live in this world, in this country, state, county, city, neighborhood together. And the police are part of it, not separate—if they so choose or not.

Another aspect of the idea of a life under constant threat was the often-quoted phrase "Be polite, be professional, have a plan to kill everyone you meet." A quote by General "Mad Dog" Mattis. Yes, you had to be ready to defend your own or the life of others at a moment's notice. When confronted with a lethal threat, you may not have the time to think it all through at length. You simply have to act in order to survive. But couldn't this particular kind of conditioning potentially lead to overreaction? Why should I consider killing the person in front of me in the checkout line, or the Uber driver, or my neighbor? To have that kind of mindset on the battlefield or in a theater of war might be helpful, but to use it in a generalized sense, in an everyday setting seemed ill conceived to me. It was a change in thinking patterns from evaluating a possible situation as an "if"-scenario to a "when"-scenario. To think of a situation as "*When* someone attacks me…" rather than "*If* someone attacks me…" leaves less room for the option of it not happening. It made it almost certain that it was going to happen someday. Was that the development of a high degree of vigilance or the creation of lethal sheep dogs?

Over time, I found a sense of relief in the fact that many of our leaders took these broad-brush strokes and rather simplistic approaches and prescribed thought patterns either with an extra grain of salt or openly opposed them. It was often the field supervisors, the Sergeants and Lieutenants, who would point out the particular situation the victim may have been in at the time the crime was committed. They would stress the hopelessness of the situation a perpetrator may have found himself or herself in. Suspect and arrestees were, for the overwhelming majority of incidents, talked to respectfully, despite the fact that they were suspected of having committed a crime. Don't get me wrong here. There are evil people out there, and they have to be dealt with decisively. We just had to make sure we would not sink to their level and misconstrue that because of their evil acts or nature, we reciprocate in the same. That was exactly what set us apart.

I am happy to say that during my tenure with the department, I encountered fine leadership with a very differentiated look at society and the work we did. The instructors also continued to stress how it was important to find the right balance between the letter of the law and spirit of the law when taking enforcement action. But it also taught me to maintain awareness toward my own mindset and that of my coworkers.

As the 20 weeks went by, there were other noteworthy moments. Such as the time where poor Will, my buddy from the corporate world, had significant trouble with staying awake during class. At times, he would nod off and was caught by instructors. As you may imagine, this didn't sit well with The Hat. At that particular time, we had passed the period of communal punishment and had moved to the phase where people were held accountable for their misdeeds individually. His sleepiness resulted in the requirement of carrying a pillow with him wherever he went. A truly embarrassing task to perform. Unfortunately, the pillow on his person at all times did not solve his sleep deprivation and so he was caught again. For another week we saw Will walk around with a pillow *and* a blanket. The poor guy reminded me of the Peanuts cartoon character Linus. Will remedied the situation by consuming copious amounts of Coke every day, which just about carried him through to the end of class. Years later, he found out that he had suffered from sleep apnea, leading to his constant fatigue.

As our academy progressed, we reached yet another milestone. One day, at the end of class, a counselor addressed us and stated that the next morning we were expected to show up in class C deputy uniforms. Finally! No more white shirt, black tie, black pants, and tennis shoes, lovingly referred to as the "Forest Gump suit." It meant progressing from the silly attire and stepping into the role of a Deputy Sheriff in the making. We were all very excited and discussed what type of shirt to wear. We agreed to short sleeves vs. long sleeves and reminded each other of all the items that belonged on the uniform. On the duty belt, there needed to be the holster for the OC spray, the baton holster, radio holster, handcuff case, gun holster, and magazine pockets. All the belts had to look identical in their setup. Most of the holsters were still empty, as we had not qualified with the tools to be contained therein. In the gun holster, we carried a blue plastic replica of our duty gun to be issued, a Glock 22, which was a .40 caliber handgun.

Upon arrival in the parking lot the next morning, recruits were way more frantic than usual. Not every individual has the same sense of accuracy, shoe shine, or a proper understanding of how to neatly tuck in a shirt. We had made the mistake of not running a mock inspection the previous night to ensure we'd all look the same the next morning. Needless to say, it was a mess, and when I arrived, we had all but 15 minutes left before morning formation. Every morning, we would line up outside, in front of the academy building for the hoisting of the flag. A ceremony during which a three-man team, called the flag parade, with one of us carrying the folded U.S. flag, would hoist the flag. Meanwhile, the rest of the class would stand at attention and observe the ceremony. It was an inspiring start to our day, yet riddled with obstacles for the non-initiated. Precise military turns and movements had to be performed while paying close attention to not violate flag handling protocol. Once the flag was atop the mast, the class president would report to The Hat the strength of the class that morning, including known reasons for anyone's absence or lack thereof.

And that is how it went on this particular morning. As soon as the flag flew above our heads and the morning report had been delivered, The Hat began a uniform inspection. I seem to remember that he made it approximately three or four recruits deep, finding something wrong with their attire or equipment on each and every one. At about the third or fourth unsightly recruit, The Hat had an all-out meltdown. In an unprecedented barrage of verbal onslaught, we were sent to the locker rooms to change back into the Forest Gump suit. Time: 3 minutes.

After proudly wearing our disheveled uniforms for all but 20 minutes, including the time of adjustment in the parking lot, we zig-zagged toward the lockers. The small locker room was laid out for approximately 10 to 15 people. It was now filled with a group of 30 nervous recruits, trying to change uniform in 360 seconds. It was a scene of socks flying, shoes being ripped off, folks in Forest Gump Suit on the top half of their body and Deputy uniform on the bottom half. Some of us were sitting, some standing, and it felt as if you constantly had someone's butt sticking in your face. The atmosphere was ripe with the smell of sweat. If you showed up a moment too late, you may have had to wait, as there was simply not enough room for all of us to change at the same time. Then someone yelled out, "30 seconds" and the scene turned into a madhouse.

We came running back out to the front of the academy building where The Hat was waiting, still fuming from what he had found during the uniform inspection. Unfortunately, everybody was back wearing Forest Gump suits after approximately 3 minutes 20 seconds. Meaning we had failed to obey the order of being back within 3 minutes. Needless to say, that some of the "uniforms" did not look as stellar as expected. The Hat had us drop on all fours, and we began a rigorous routine of push-ups, dead bugs, and so on. My memory becomes blurry at this point.

Then there was the day, further along in our process of becoming deputies, where we were out at the shooting range again, this time for scenario training. The shooting range was a complex on the outskirts of Tucson, about a 10-minute drive from my house, out in the desert. Picture several sets of shooting ranges and a small compound of buildings designed for scenario-based training, aptly named "Survival City." It was scheduled from 2:00 p.m. to 10:00 p.m. to include nighttime scenarios. Around 6:00 p.m., we were given the opportunity to have dinner. During a previous day at the range, counselors allowed us to order pizza for the whole class. I concluded it would be a good idea to repeat that this time around. As my classmates sat down to eat the food they had brought along, I found two other recruits who wanted to join me in a pizza feast. I called the nearest pizza delivery and placed an order, which they said would be on its way shortly. My taste buds and salivary glands reacted to the pure thought of high caloric pizza and what a treat it would be during this long day. In between, we were called out to participate in scenarios and mine involved a traffic stop. The observing instructor and I boarded the patrol car and went out onto the nearby road, which, while public, barely ever had any traffic, except before and after the shift change at a small power station nearby. We encountered a sedan, and I was instructed to conduct a traffic stop on the vehicle. I don't recall any particulars about the mock traffic stop, but I am sure something went awry, as that was part of the learning experience. After it was all over, I received my debriefing from the instructor and the other role players and then returned to the shooting range. I got out of the patrol car and the next recruit jumped into the driver's seat for her turn.

Across the parking lot, I noticed an unsettling scene. There was a small civilian hatchback with an illuminated pizza delivery sign atop its roof. Next to the delivery car stood The Hat facing what was likely the delivery driver, who was holding a set of pizza boxes. Not good! Not good at all!

Quickly running all sorts of scenarios through my head, the combination of people and things in this picture did not offer any positive outcomes. Bear in mind that I ran possible outcome scenarios in my head all the time during these days. And there it was. "Peine!" The Hat's commanding voice reverberated throughout the parking lot and may have been noticed by the workers at the power plant about a quarter of a mile away. "Sir, yes, sir!" I responded while running toward the awkward scene. Once I reached the two men, I posted myself at a respectful distance, awaiting my destiny at attention. Only moving my eyes, I glanced at the delivery driver, who was on the shorter side, and made The Hat seem even more intimidating. The driver appeared absolutely terrified and stared at The Hat, not knowing if his death was near or if he would be hauled off to the nearby state prison within the next few minutes.

"Peine. Did you order pizza?" The Hat asked.

"Sir, yes, Sir!" I replied.

"Well, then go ahead and pay the man," The Hat rightfully demanded of me.

Under his watchful eyes, I pulled out my wallet and quickly mumbled, "How much?" at the driver. He told me the amount due and with my hands shaking, I handed over the money. I noticed a slight tremor in the delivery driver's hands as well as he took the cash and then handed me the pizza boxes. He looked up at The Hat and asked, "Can I leave now?"

The Hat responded in his normal voice, "Of course you can."

The young man then bolted toward the driver's side of his car, backed out of the parking space, and left the grounds, driving back toward civilization.

I was left alone with The Hat and the pizza boxes. "What the hell were you thinking, Peine? Did anyone allow you or tell you to order pizza for delivery?"

I tried to gather my thoughts and phrase a response that would have the least negative consequences. "Sir, I was not thinking, and nobody allowed me to order pizza, sir." *Ah, that didn't come out right.*

DEPUTY WHILE IMMIGRANT

The Hat's response was, "Never *at this point in the academy* have I ever experienced anyone doing something so ridiculous! I would have expected better from you, Peine!" Inadvertently referring to his time as a class counselor in the previous, regional academy as well gave his scolding more emphasis.

In complete submission and unable to think clearly, I only responded, "Sir, yes, sir!"

"You will submit a 500-word memo about common sense the day after tomorrow!" was The Hat's verdict.

"Sir, yes, sir!"

I took my pizza boxes and right-angled my way to the classroom. There, my classmates—those who were not involved in the order process—had listened to what had transpired outside. They chuckled and looked at me with surprise. "What did you do?" After giving my description of events, some of my fellow recruits felt the need to share their feedback and "advice" of how I had apparently lost my awareness for the type of setting I was in. They were right. Momentarily, I had functioned much like an independently thinking, hungry 41-year-old. It should not happen again, or at least not be quite so obvious. I wrote the 500-word memo the next day and delivered it to The Hat's office without further incident.

Early the next week, we were ordered out in formation in front of the academy for a scheduled uniform inspection. The Hat would walk past each recruit, accompanied by a counselor who acted as a scribe. With a stoic expression on his face, he would mumble whatever was found at fault with a recruit's appearance and the scribe would make a note for the recruit's file. As it was my turn, he walked up in front of me, made a right-face turn, and took a step toward me. He looked me up and down and mumbled toward the scribe, "Okay." Then he leaned forward with the brim of his campaign hat almost touching my forehead. "How was the pizza, Peine?" he asked quietly. "Sir, it was delicious, sir." I responded truthfully. "Well, at least it was worth it," The Hat responded. His comment planted a smile on my face. And just for a split second, I thought I noticed a sliver of a smile on his face as well.

TOM PEINE

    Finally, only a few things were left to be done to obtain all the necessary certifications before we could graduate. I will focus on the two most anxiously anticipated. First was the exposure to oleoresin capsicum or OC spray, commonly referred to as "pepper spray." Secondly, there was the Taser, which we'll cover later. On what was referred to as our "OC exposure day," we spent the better part of the morning learning about OC spray itself. Oleoresin capsicum is an extract from the fruit of the chili plant, and it is weaponized by putting it into a small, pressurized can that would reside on our duty belts. We learned of the effects this substance has on those who are exposed to it, including but not limited to redness of the skin, swelling of the eyes, redness of the eyes, temporary loss of clear vision, extreme secretion from the nasal glands, and the sensation of breathing difficulty. Following the theoretical instruction of the morning, we went outside toward the obstacle course in the afternoon, where a patrol car was parked with an unmarked car in front of it. We were told that this was a traffic stop scenario, and all we had to do was make contact with the driver. We all knew what was about to come and suddenly, despite the temperature being in the 90s, I felt ice cold. The order in which we would go was voluntary. I watched a few scenarios in agony. The driver of the civilian car got out and faced the deputy who had stopped him. After a very brief exchange, he suddenly pulled a can of OC spray and hosed the deputy's face with an orange liquid that was dispensed from the nozzle of the can. The following reactions were individual versions of outcries, bending over, instinctively drawing the weapon, moaning, wincing, and other equally dreadful displays of human agony. After building up enough courage, I raised my hand to be next and took my seat in the patrol car.

    The instructor asked, "Are you ready?" Was I ready? No! "Sir, yes, sir," I said with fake confidence. As instructed, I called out the traffic stop over the radio, which had been switched to a training frequency. Replaying all the other scenarios I had watched over the past 10 minutes or so, I got out of the police car, built myself up tall and approached the hatchback in front of me. As I approached, the driver got out of his car and gestured wildly while making statements along the lines of why he was being harassed by police. Though I knew it would be in vain, I conducted myself with as much professional courtesy as I could, when the driver suddenly produced something with his right hand. It felt as if someone had poured thousands of electrically charged needles into my eyes and all over my face, accompanied by an incredibly hot, burning sensation. My eyes instinctively closed, and I was not able to open them again. The instructor, seemingly far away, kept telling me what to do. "Fight! Fight! Fight!" Through the tiny slits that my eyes had become, I vaguely made out what I knew to be two other recruits holding punching pads. I began to punch away in the direction of the pads and broke into a pepper-laden sweat. I drew my plastic weapon. I was practically blind, yet tried to see something. Holy jeepers, my face was burning up. In truly sophisticated fashion, I used the index finger and thumb of my left hand to pry open my left eye. The sunlight was near unbearable, and all I could see was an orange blur. My nose had also begun to run profusely. Thick, clear snot ran down my face and at the chin joined the tears coming down my cheeks. I distinctly remember that because together, they had created a flow of hot, burning goo, which was trying to find a way down my neck and into my shirt. "Take cover behind your car! Get on the radio! Call for help!" the instructor said from somewhere nearby. "Fox 4-6, Code 9-9-9!" I managed to bark into the mic of my handheld radio. "I have been exposed to OC." That's all I could muster. The instructor began to yell, "The driver is still there. What kind of weapon does he have? What's the weapon?" I again pried open my left eye and couldn't see a thing. I simply riddled down a bunch of weapons I could come up with. "Knife, gun, grenade," I yelled out, all while threateningly waving my blue plastic gun in the general direction of a large, dark orange shape somewhere ahead of me in the distance. "Okay, okay. Scenario over!" came the instruction.

Two classmates came, one on each side, took me by the arms and lead me over to where the sergeant of the academy stood by a plastic tub on the ground. He was holding a large shower head fixed to the tip of a garden hose and said, "We'll rinse it off right here. It'll help." As soon as the cold water hit my face, it felt as if my airways instantaneously swelled shut. I had a lot of trouble breathing and began to gasp for air. Long, clear strings of nasal secretion hung from my nostrils, and I felt absolutely terrible. Splash! Here came some more water. I managed to yowl "Stop! Stop!" and walked off to the side. The other two recruits came back and escorted me to an area under the roof over the patio, where a giant, airplane-propeller-sized fan had been placed. It was running at full throttle and a group of pathetic looking recruits stood right in front of the airflow, like a bunch of oxygen junkies in a wind tunnel. We stood together like red-faced invalids, with orange spots on our t-shirts, eyes mostly swollen shut, looking like Rocky Balboa after a 12-round fight yelling out for "Adrianne!" We were simply trying to breathe. It took me about 15 minutes to come around and another 30 minutes after that to recover fully.

The instructors for the remaining two afternoon classes took it noticeably easy on us. Before being sent home, we were each issued a spray can of this hellfire juice and proudly placed it into the canister holster on our duty belts. That night, I was very careful when taking a shower (we were forewarned by academy staff) so as not to create a burning run-off from the remaining residue on my face, which could potentially cause some serious genital discomfort on its way toward the drain. I was able to avoid any penile damage but did experience trouble breathing again. That was some powerful stuff.

The next day, one of the recruits had left his OC spray canister inside his private car. Outside temperatures cranked up well into the low 100s, with temperatures inside our cars being well above that. Evidently, the interior temperature of the car was beyond what the spray can was designed to withstand. When the recruit came back to his car, it was filled with a fine mist of, you guessed it, oleoresin capsicum. For several days he arrived at the academy teary-eyed.

The final certification we needed before finishing up the academy was the Taser. It was probably the most anxiety-laden anticipation I experienced during the academy. We had been told about that requirement on day one. And I was not looking forward to it. The setup leading up to the exposure was identical to the one we had gone through with the OC spray. Class in the morning with plenty of information about the fantastic effectiveness of the tool and how to use it properly. We learned that—unlike the movies often portrayed—it was only a temporary incapacitation of the person on the receiving end of the wires. The immobility only lasts while the Taser is emitting current into the wires to the probes embedded in the subject's skin: 50,000 volts that are distinctly different from one of those stun guns you could buy online. Those would simply deliver a shock to anyone who momentarily came into contact with the two electrodes. The Taser, we learned, affects the person it is directed against in two different ways. One was the incapacitation, which was accomplished by the particular frequency with which the electrical current was delivered. It leads to the override of the central nervous system and the affected muscles contract. That means, if the right muscle groups are affected, the individual subjected to a Taser will fall (if standing) and be unable to move, experiencing a seizure-like condition. The second was the pain component. As the subject is fully conscious while the Taser is deployed, they also feel strong pain, which is intended to bring them into compliance.

We were told the Taser would only be deployed for five seconds. *So, how bad could it be?* We were lined up in three rows on the patio. Each line had a Taser instructor standing at the front, Taser at the ready. Each recruit who was about to be exposed would step into the middle of the grappling mat laid out under the roof. Two fellow recruits would hold their classmate by their upper arm and safely guide them to the ground when their legs gave out after the Taser prongs made contact. Our fear of possibly urinating or defecating on ourselves while "taking the ride" had been thoroughly addressed and alleviated. The key information being that the electric current streaming through our body would trigger our muscles to contract, not relax.

And then it was my turn. I stepped onto the center of the mat, and everything around me seemed to fade away. The voices were muffled. All I listened for was the warning from the instructor. The hands of my fellow classmates touched my upper arms, and I heard the instructor's warning call, "Taser! Taser! Taser!" I don't even remember the typical pop coming from the explosion that tears apart the plastic blast door of the Taser cartridge, sending its two harpoon shaped probes on their flight path toward my back. They embedded themselves thoroughly into my tissue, none of which I felt. All I felt was an overwhelming pain sensation and, fully aware of what was happening around me, how my classmates laid me onto the mat as my knees had simply given in and my legs had turned to Jell-O. If you have ever touched a live wire while doing some electrical work at home, you know how uncomfortable the brief jolt can be. Try to imagine this about 500 times worse, encompassing not just one finger or the hand, but your entire body. A constant shock that seemed to be delivered in waves through every bone, organ, and cell in my body. Now look at your watch or use your phone to time five seconds. I cried out in pain. Then it stopped just as abruptly as it started. I felt as if had just run a 5K.

One of my classmates had to remove the two metal Taser prongs stuck about a foot and a half apart near my left shoulder and further down to the right of my spine. We had to pull out our classmate's probes as part of the certification process, so we knew how to properly do it. We learned that we would be allowed to remove the probes following this instruction, whereas a paramedic would have to leave the prongs embedded, cut the copper wire, and take the injured person to the hospital to have the probes removed by a doctor. The instructor told one of my classmates what to do. Then I felt two quick yanks. It didn't hurt. As a matter of fact, I barely felt it. The two punctures were wiped down with a sterile wipe and covered with a Band-Aid. I got up and got back on the mat to help the next recruit. (I still have the T-shirt with the two holes in the back.)

Twenty weeks came to an end, and we had passed our final exam in writing and passed the final evaluation scenarios out at the shooting range and Survival City. The remaining few days were filled with preparation for the graduation ceremony and the formal dinner on the night prior to the public celebration.

DEPUTY WHILE IMMIGRANT

We used the funds we had collected throughout the academy to arrange for a celebratory get-together and dinner at the J.W. Marriott Star Pass hotel in Tucson. It was a five-star luxury resort and made for a fitting venue to conclude this once-in-a-lifetime challenge and accomplishment.

Annie and I dressed up for the event and walked together down the hallway toward the conference room, which had been prepared and decorated for the occasion. While I greeted classmates and instructors, Annie was approached by a woman. They briefly introduced themselves. Then the woman asked my wife, "So, is your son graduating as well?" My wife had a broad smile on her face and told the inquiring mother, "It is my husband who's graduating." The woman smiled. End of conversation. I didn't notice it at the time. When Annie later told me about it, we had a hearty laugh and thought it was the most memorable part of the evening.

During dinner, we watched a video our class counselors had put together. And of course, the footage included a still frame right at the moment where the Taser probes hit me. Yelling out in agony with a bizarre facial expression, half leaning, half falling forward, all perfectly preserved in a frozen frame on the big screen. Not a pretty picture, but of great entertainment value.

The next day, we went to Tucson Symphony Hall for the public oath ceremony. It was a beautiful day. Friends and family of all recruits filled the seats of the symphony. We marched into the room under thunderous applause from the audience and all the struggles were forgotten. I felt like a million bucks. At 41 years old, I had overcome the physically and mentally exhausting 20 weeks of a U.S. law enforcement academy and was about to be sworn in as Deputy Sheriff. The national anthem was performed by one of my classmates. Speeches by council members, command staff of the department and a video message from the Sheriff of Pima County, who was not able to attend in person, followed. We were seated on stage. Then a judge from the Pima County Superior Court came to the podium. We rose from our seats and raised our right hands. Repeating after the judge, I proudly said, "I, Thomas Peine, do solemnly swear, that I will support the Constitution of the United States, and the

Constitution and laws of the State of Arizona, that I will bear true faith and allegiance to the same, and defend them against enemies, foreign and domestic, and that I will faithfully and impartially discharge, the duties of a peace officer, to the best of my ability, so help me God."

Following the oath, we were called up individually to receive our badge from a Bureau Chief, the second in command of the department, right after the Sheriff himself. Badge in hand, we made our way down a set of stairs into the auditorium and right in front of the stage. Once each of us had received our star-shaped badge and were lined up, previously designated family members or friends were asked to step forward. Annie came up to me and had a huge smile on her face. I handed her the brand-new, shiny sheriff's star, and she pinned it onto my shirt, right over my heart, and sealed the whole act with a kiss. My brother-in-law took a shaky picture of the whole caboodle. I was officially Deputy Peine.

My classmates and all the other members of the department—and, in fact, this profession—had become very special people to me. They were my family. Together we had suffered and endured because we helped each other. We would always help each other. For these people, I was ready to lay down my life.

5

FIELD TRAINING

We were sworn-in, certified peace officers. But the selection and evaluation process was not over yet. Following the academy, we had to prove that we could use what we had learned in theory and during practical exercises in real-life situations. For that purpose, we had to go through and pass 12 weeks of field training. The time was divided into three separate phases, each lasting four weeks. During Phase 1, we would accompany our assigned Field Training Officer (FTO) during their shift. They would show us how to handle certain calls and involve us by assigning tasks to us. We would write our own reports and handle smaller incidents as we progressed. There was still a weekly test and a board review at the end of each phase to determine if we had passed. Should we fail, we would be given the opportunity to repeat a phase once. If you failed again, you were dismissed from the department. During Phase 2, we would begin to handle calls as the primary deputy with the help of our FTO and increasingly gain independence. The FTO and district we worked in would change with each phase. Finally, there was Phase 3, during which we'd handle all calls ourselves and the FTO would simply observe. With few exceptions, they would not even answer our questions, as we had to learn to function as a solo Deputy Sheriff. Once we successfully passed all three phases and the accompanying evaluations, we would receive our first assignment to a patrol district.

The night following graduation day was my first time working on the streets. At 10:00 p.m., or 2200 hours, as we would say, I reported to the San Xavier district on the Southside of Tucson. It was an area with higher crime rates than the other districts. Gangs would go about their business in neighborhoods and business areas. Smugglers would roam the vast desert areas to the South. From Old Tucson Studios, to the Desert Museum, to airfields, farms, trailer parks, gated communities, and shopping malls, this district had it all.

I parked my car in the lot of the district office and stayed in my seat for another few minutes to gather my thoughts. This was it. I was about to do real police work. Half a world away from where I first caught "the bug" and well over 20 years later. I got out, locked my car, and keyed up on the mic of my handheld radio to use my training designator for the first time on a live, operational patrol frequency.

"Fox 4-6."

"Fox 4-6, go ahead."

"Fox 4-6. 10-41."

"Good evening, sir. 21-56."

The dispatcher had acknowledged that I had started my shift and closed the radio call by announcing the time in military format. The letter "F" or Fox, which is short for Foxtrot from the military spelling alphabet, stood for "field training unit." A two-person unit comprised of the trainee and their FTO.

I entered the district office and looked for my FTO, Gabriel Cortez.

"Are you Peine?" came from across the briefing room.

"Yes, sir!" I responded.

"Why aren't you answering when I call your designator? You are Fox 4-6, correct?"

"Yes, sir. I'm not sure. I didn't hear you calling me."

Oh my, off to a good start, I thought. Deputy Cortez went into an explanation of how important it was to listen to the radio. He added that I should turn on my radio on my way to work, so I would know what was going on by the time I got to the district office. He asked if I was ready to go and we went back outside to the parking lot. "You want to drive?"

he asked. "Yes, sir," I responded confidently. Yes! This was so cool. I was ready, ready, ready! I threw my gear into the trunk of Cortez's patrol car and took a seat on the driver's side. He sat down in the passenger seat. It seemed almost surreal. I was seated in a police car, in full uniform, armed and about to the patrol the streets of Pima County.

"Ready?" Cortez asked.

"Yup," I responded.

"Well, let's go then."

Rolling through the exit gate of the fence surrounding the district office, I slowly made a right-hand turn and took the Ford Police Interceptor onto the streets. Cortez looked at the screen of the laptop computer that was mounted in front of the dashboard and between our two seats. "There's a call for a runaway juvenile that's been holding for a few minutes. Come up on the radio for it," Deputy Cortez instructed me.

Each district was divided into patrol beats. This particular call was in Beat 2. It took us about 15 minutes or so to drive out there. I rolled into the neighborhood and stopped the car a few houses down from the caller's address. This was a safety measure, as we didn't know what would possibly happen. Yes, it was originally called in as a runaway juvenile, but things could change. Or it could be a ruse to lure us into an ambush. You would never know. We got out of our car, walked a short distance on the sidewalk, and up to the front door of the caller's home. Deputy Cortez rang the doorbell, and both of took a step back and off to each side of the door. We had learned that we had to make sure to not stand in what was referred to as the "fatal funnel." If someone opened fire from within the residence, the bullets coming through the wood of that door would certainly hit whoever was standing in front of it. The ballistic vest we all wore underneath our uniform shirts was not something we could simply rely on. Besides, who said a potential shooter inside would aim for our chest? So, step to the side.

No shots were fired, and a friendly, though seemingly distressed, woman opened the door. She was relieved to see us and immediately began telling us a story about her 12-year-old son who had not come home. She said she thought that he was at a neighbor's house, but the adults there weren't home yet. The mother was very upset and explained how her son's behavior had become increasingly disrespectful. His absences from home were getting longer and longer, and she wasn't having it anymore.

We went to a house across the street she had pointed out and rang the doorbell. One of us on each side of the front door, we waited. As the door was not answered, Deputy Cortez loudly banged against it and said, "This is the Sheriff's Department! Diego, we know that you're in there. Come to the door and talk to us." After some noises inside, the front door opened, and a boy emerged in the doorway. "Are you Diego?" It was, in fact, the missing son. Deputy Cortez had a stern but friendly conversation with the boy. He struck a fatherly tone with Diego and explained how his mom was seriously concerned about him. Diego learned that he would have to listen to his mother and be home at the time set by mom. Otherwise, he would run in danger of being arrested for running away from home. Having to explain a lackadaisical attitude to a judge in juvenile court was no laughing matter, Cortez continued. His words had an impact on Diego, and he agreed to come with us back to his family's home. Once there, his mother was upset, but Cortez explained what he had told Diego and that he had agreed to be more thoughtful and respect his mother's instructions. He explained how it would be better to not issue a juvenile court referral for Diego and for her to give it another go with him. She agreed, and we wished her a good night, leaving Diego in her care. It was my first call, and I had already experienced how having a good sense for what is the right thing to do was something incredibly important. It determined if the people we served would respect us, and also how deep an impact someone's— often poor—choice would have on their future.

Overall, it was a pretty uneventful shift, and we returned to the station at approximately 0400 hours. It took me the entire remaining two hours to write my four reports to Deputy Cortez's liking. At 0600 hours, I walked out to my car in the parking lot. The sun had risen. I was exhausted, but I had survived the first night out on the streets of Pima County.

"Fox 4-6."

DEPUTY WHILE IMMIGRANT

"Fox 4-6, go ahead."

"Fox 4-6. 10-42."

"Good night, sir. 06-08."

Two days and one shift later, back at home, I managed to sleep a few hours during daylight. That took some getting used to. Reluctantly, still tired, I sat down at the dining room table. A disheveled copy of the Arizona Daily Star lay on the table. After fixing myself a strong cup of coffee and a slice of toast loaded with strawberry jam, I looked for the local section and froze when my eyes came across this article:

> *6.14.2006*
> *Deputy in 1st day on job before shooting:*
> *Injured man's relatives dispute officers' version*
> *by Alexis Huicochea, Tucson, Arizona*
>
> *A deputy was only four hours into his first shift with the Pima County Sheriff's Department when he and his field training officer were sent out to a hit-and-run call.*
>
> *But the Pima County Sheriff's Department said the incident escalated to a life-or-death situation, leaving the deputies no choice but to fire their weapons, hitting a 21-year-old man several times and leaving him hospitalized. The deputy in training had just graduated from the Pima County Sheriff's Basic Training Academy Friday before beginning his shift Monday with his field training officer, a seven-year veteran, according to a Sheriff's Department news release.*
>
> *The suspect was hit several times but was able to make his way out of the trailer park and became involved in another hit-and-run accident before crashing into brick wall of a back yard at East Irvington Road and South Aleppo Drive, near South Campbell Avenue, the release said.*

TOM PEINE

> *After the crash, the suspect led officers on a short foot chase until he was caught right around the corner,* Barkman said in the news release.
>
> *The suspect, a Tucson resident, was taken to University Medical Center to be treated for multiple gunshot wounds, and he is expected to survive,* Barkman said."

A deputy from *my* class? In the academy, we received a class on drugs and drug-related crimes. At the beginning of the class, the instructor asked who in the class had never smoked marijuana or been present when marijuana was being smoked and for that recruit to raise their hand. The purpose was to identify if anyone in the class needed to be exposed to the smell of burnt marijuana, so they could testify to their observation in court if needed should they ever come across that odor in the field. One hand rose. It was this particular deputy. *And he got into a shooting?* Things had turned very real, very quick. As they had told us: It's not a matter of if, but of when.

Together with my FTO, we discussed the incident that night upon my return to work and also used it to run possible scenarios, trying to identify all the different ways to react under the described circumstances.

During the days following the unsettling event involving my classmate, I began to feel a little more comfortable in my deputy skin working the same district as Tuttle had been; however, it was not quite all downhill yet. Like the night we drove down Ajo Way when the two tones for a priority one call came over the radio speaker in the patrol car. Following the two beeps, we learned about a domestic violence incident that had turned physical. A woman had been threatened by her husband. He had pushed her onto the bed and slapped her in the face, according to the 911 call. Cortez looked at me and said, "That's us. Let's go!" The victim must be in terrible fear, I thought, and listened as other units came over the radio to advise they would respond too. I had missed to key up quick enough. It was always the first unit to respond on the radio that would be assigned the call. But we were a Fox or training unit. So, once we'd get there, we were likely to take over so I could get exposure to as many situations as possible. Flipping the switch on the Omnitrol in the center console brought on the unmistakable whale of an emergency siren and filled the entire car with its howling sound. The desert outside was illuminated by red and blue flashes. "Fox 4-6. 10-76, Code 3," I advised the dispatcher over the radio. This would tell her that we were en route to the caller's location, and we were using lights and siren to expedite our response. I could feel the adrenaline building as we raced down the desert roadways. The siren blared through the dark of the night and scenarios of domestic violence kept buzzing around in my head.

"Peine!"

"Yes, sir!"

"Where the fuck are you going?"

"Uh, to the 10-16 Physical, sir."

"Of course, you are. What direction are you headed right now?"

"Uh, East, sir?"

"Nope!"

"Oh! West?"

"No, you are not going West! Goddamn it, Peine! Turn it off. Pull over and figure out where the fuck you are and where you need to go!"

I could not believe I had just done that. Thoroughly embarrassed and confused, I turned off the lights and siren and pulled over onto the dirt shoulder. From the side pocket in the driver's side door, I pulled the Pima County street atlas and with nervous fingers opened the page for the alphabetical street listings. I was troubled by the fact that I had become that flustered from driving to a high priority call, a call where someone really needed us to get there quickly. It took me a few minutes to get my act together, find the address, locate it on the map, and figure out how to get there. Once I had a better idea of where I was and where I needed to go, I turned around and headed toward the incident location. No lights, no siren. Other deputies had already made it to the scene. When we got there, all parties involved had already been separated, and the investigation was well under way. My lesson learned: Keep your shit together! Don't lose your head just because it's a priority call.

A few days later and a little while into our shift, we had already handled our first two calls and were roaming through Beat 1. From a side street, we came up on Valencia Road, just west of Tucson International Airport. My FTO said this would be a good spot to look for some traffic violations. We would use our interactions with the vehicle's occupants during those stops to look for signs of potential criminal activity or identify someone who may have a warrant for their arrest. There was virtually no traffic on our street and very few cars on Valencia. Cortez instructed me to just sit at the traffic light and turn off my headlights, though this T-intersection was illuminated by streetlights. We sat at the light, blacked out, and let the signal cycle through several times. A red sedan approached the intersection. The signal had just cycled again and showed green for us. I stayed put, continuing to observe the oncoming car. Across the intersection, I could see the red signal for the sedan. We sat in our car, not moving, and waited for the sedan to stop at the light. Much to my surprise, it did not even slow down, simply blew through the red light. I gave Cortez a surprised look and was momentarily rendered speechless. Cortez threw up his hands and yelled, "What are you waiting for?" That jolted me back into cop-mode.

Turning on my headlights, I put the patrol car into gear, made a turn onto Valencia, and then turned on my overhead emergency lights. The sedan had already gained some distance, and I had to put the pedal to the metal to catch up with it. That's when I learned that a few seconds of indecisiveness can cost you dearly. As we came closer, I turned my siren on as well. Cortez grabbed the radio mic from the center console and called out our traffic stop with location and plate information for the car ahead of us. The vehicle slowly pulled over to the right and came to a stop on the shoulder. I turned on my take-down lights on the roof of my car and directed my spotlight at the interior of the sedan.

Cortez went to the passenger side, and I approached on the driver's side. My eyes were trained on the driver and his every move. The window had been rolled down and cigarette smoke wafted out. When I reached the b-pillar of the car, I addressed the driver. "Sir, put your hands on the steering wheel where I can see them." He complied, and I felt a slight sense of relief. The two occupants of the car were the driver and passenger, men in their late twenties. My eyes quickly scanned the interior and did not notice anything suspicious or dangerous. The driver was blinded by all the lights coming from the patrol car and now my flashlight. Moving things along, I said, "Are you aware that you ran a red light back there?" "What?" came the prompt and surprised sounding response. "Yes, Sir. I will need to see your driver's license, registration, and proof of insurance." Cortez was standing next to the passenger, also keeping a watchful eye on everything that was going on inside this vehicle. The area surrounding us kept flashing in red and blue reflections from our light bar.

As the driver was fidgeting with his wallet and said something unintelligible to the passenger, I thought I had noticed a reflection in the light cone of my flashlight coming from the floorboard on the driver's side. When I moved the light beam through the legs of the driver and toward his floor mat, I saw a silver object partially tucked underneath the driver's seat. It was the grip of a chrome-plated pistol. "Gun!" I yelled out loud and drew my Glock from its holster. As I punched out my weapon, pointing it directly at the driver, I took a step back toward the front of the car to not create a crossfire situation with my FTO. "Don't move!" I yelled at the driver. From the other side, I heard Cortez in his finest command voice yell at the passenger. With his gun only about a foot away from the passenger's head, he barked, "If you move a hair, I will blow your fucking head off!" Both driver and passenger seemed perfectly frozen in place. My heart was racing. I heard Cortez say, "Get him out." My eyes thoroughly trained on the driver's every move, I said, "Slowly get out of the car! Keep your hands up where I can see them!" Slowly and carefully, the driver opened his door. With his hands above his head, he stepped out of the car and mumbled something about having no idea what this was all about. Through the now open door, I glanced at the driver's side floor and could clearly see the chrome-plated gun. I instructed the driver to walk to the back of his car and face away from me. A few cars drove past us and slowed down, curiously watching as I was pointing my pistol at the young man. "Put your hands behind the small of your back!" While the driver faced the dirt shoulder, I stepped up to him, and as he brought his hands against his back, I holstered my weapon and grabbed his right wrist. My left foot placed against the inside of his left foot, I pulled it outward to spread his feet further apart and force him into a somewhat unstable position. Just like I had trained hundreds of times, my handcuffs ratcheted around his wrists. Giving the driver a slight tug from the cuffs, I had him lean into me. Now that he was off balance, I quickly patted him down for weapons, but did not feel anything that concerned me. Confident that he was "clean," I had him sit in the backseat (or cage) of our patrol car.

This whole time, my FTO stood and held the passenger at gunpoint. Now it was his turn. The passenger was made to exit the car and then handcuffed and searched as well. We kept him outside against the trunk of the sedan, so the two would stay separated.

After I took a deep breath, I walked around the sedan to the open driver's side door and carefully picked up the weapon I had seen a few minutes earlier. It was huge! As a matter of fact, I had never seen a handgun this big. As I walked to the back of the patrol car to unload and secure it, I noticed the markings on the side of it. "Desert Eagle - Israel Military Industries" it read. That was a monstrous weapon, a .50 caliber handgun. It had a hefty weight to it. A round was chambered, and a fully loaded magazine inserted. The ammunition was equally impressive. My FTO had advised over the radio that we had two individuals detained and that they were "10-32 with a handgun." That radio call prompted two other deputies, one of them a K-9 unit, to stop by.

We interrogated both vehicle occupants and were told they had "just been driving around." Cortez said, "They were in a titty bar." He laughed when I asked him how he'd know. When he pointed out the fact that they both had glitter on their faces, I was educated how the dancers in the clubs would put it onto their breasts. Never having stuck my face in between a nude dancer's breasts before, the experience had true educational value.

DEPUTY WHILE IMMIGRANT

The things I had to learn. When asked if anything illegal was inside the vehicle, the driver shook his head and said, "Nuh. Go ahead and check." Said and done. I walked over to the K-9 Deputy and asked if he could let his K-9 partner check out the car. Probably not shocking, we found two baggies of marijuana and another bag containing a small amount of a crystalline substance, which, upon further testing, turned out to be crystal methamphetamine or simply "meth." To tie a bow on the whole bust, the passenger turned out to have an arrest warrant. Both were arrested on a variety of charges, plus the warrant, and the car was impounded.

Though I was slightly overwhelmed by the ungodly amount of paperwork this arrest had caused, I was very proud. Proud that I had spotted the gun and kept my FTO and myself safe. Proud that I had found some real criminals and taken them off the streets, at least for now. Not so proud of the fact that Cortez later told me to be more aware of where I put a person I was about to place in handcuffs. He critiqued my decision to have the driver face the shoulder of the road and me standing with my back exposed to the roadway. If it had come to a fight, the driver could have pushed me into the street. A car with their friends could have driven by and fired at me without me being behind cover. Yes, I certainly hadn't thought of those aspects. Rookie mistake, got it. Next time, I would make sure to be on the same side as my partner, behind the cover of my patrol car and take care of business there. It was a situation I would flash back to many times over while being on patrol in the years to come. It was clear that my FTO was not only my instructor, but my partner.

"Fox 4-6."

"Fox 4-6, go ahead."

"10-95 with two. 10-76 Code 1-15."

"10-4. 01-21."

A few days later, we patrolled Beat 2 again and were dispatched to a rescue follow up. That is the type of call where the initial response is of a medical nature, but either the circumstances appear potentially suspicious at the time the call was taken or medics requested for us to respond. Typically, law enforcement responds to these calls to ensure no crime has been committed or to take appropriate steps if the matter is in fact deemed suspicious in nature. We were advised that Rural Metro Fire Department was en route. From the call text on our laptop, we learned that the female 911 caller was hysterical and said that her husband fell out of his bed and was unresponsive. The caller refused to follow CPR instructions and advised she would prefer to wait for the ambulance.

It was not a high priority call for us, as the medical need was obviously more urgent. When we arrived at the home from where the call had originated, the fire truck and ambulance had just arrived. I saw the crew make their way into the house. We parked on the dirt shoulder and followed them inside. It was a smaller home, and the inside had become very busy. There were the medics, who disappeared into a back room, the fire captain, three family members, and us. Cortez pointed at a young man, maybe 17 or 18 years old, who stood in the living room with another man in his early twenties, who turned out to be the brother, and a woman, who I figured was the initial 911 caller. The woman was very tearful, sobbing, and was being soothed by the older of the two young men. I approached the teenager my FTO had pointed out, introduced myself, and explained that I needed to talk to him to collect some initial information. We took a step away from the others, and I learned how earlier he had heard his mother, the woman who was being consoled by the brother, scream from the bedroom. When he went to see what had happened and looked through the open door of the guest bedroom, he saw his father lying on the floor next to the bed. He said his mother ran into the kitchen and went straight for the telephone to call 911. She told her son that she thought his father was dead.

Out of the corner of my eye, I saw the fire captain come out of the guest bedroom, which was just down a narrow hallway to my left. He looked at my FTO and shook his head. A simple gesture that would mean so much more to this family. None of the family members seemed to have noticed. Cortez signaled me to come over to him. I asked the young man to hold on for a minute and went to the hallway, where Cortez stood next to the fire captain.

DEPUTY WHILE IMMIGRANT

"The medics are done. They can't do anything for the guy. Looks as if he has been dead for a little while. Maybe a half hour or an hour. There's been a history of heart problems. Go with the medics to let the family know." There it was. One of those moments I had dreaded. I thought to myself, "The family must know. The mother told her son she thought his father was dead." Still. It was the first time I had to break such tragic news to anyone and had no idea how to go about it. In the academy they had explained how there is no easy way to break such news, even if family members or loved ones would know what was about to be said. My heart was racing and the whole scene turned surreal, as if I was standing there and only observing it all.

The fire captain and I walked into the living room. We looked at each other, and he seemed to have noticed the giant lump that had formed in my throat. Without further ado, he went ahead and called for the two sons and their mother to gather in the living room. Addressing the mother in a gentle tone, he said, "Ma'am, your husband has passed away. We couldn't do anything for him. My condolences." Before anything else could be said or done, the woman turned pale and her knees gave in, sending her into a forward plunge. I rushed in and together with her son managed to catch her, preventing her from falling to the floor. We gently laid her on the sofa in the living room. She was unconscious. Alerted by the fire captain, the medics came over from the other room and tended to her.

Through the living room window, I saw two more cars come up the driveway. Other family members who had been called by the sons were arriving. It was about to get even busier inside this little house. The front door opened and as the newly arrived saw the mother lying on the sofa, being cared for by paramedics, they seemed to grasp what had occurred. A storm of tears, whaling, and sobbing broke loose. The whole situation turned extremely emotional. The sons kept calling out, "Dad! Dad!" The family switched to Spanish.

I walked back over to the hallway, which led to the guest bedroom. We had learned that the parents had separate bedrooms for quite some time already. The door to the bedroom was pulled to, and through the crack

I saw one of the medics packing up his gear. My FTO looked at me and said, "Now what?" It was that typical question indicating that I would take over from here.

The only dead person I had seen up to that point was my father-in-law, at his wake. But he was embalmed, and it was an Irish wake. Things go a little differently during an Irish wake compared to a very subdued and somber German funeral, I had learned. Though there were still a lot of tears, the whole event was a pretty lively affair—even loud at times—involving an extended circle of family and friends who would consume copious amounts of adult beverages. People would tell anecdotes from my father-in-law's life, including funny or awkward situations and the whole room would break into laughter. It was as if he was still in the room, not just his body. It was a new experience for me, and I was fond of it.

This, of course, was entirely different. The deceased was not embalmed. I didn't even know the person, nor did I speak his family's language. The relatives were still in a complete uproar over the unexpected death. And here I was, supposed to conduct a death investigation.

We entered the guest bedroom. The deceased was lying right next to the bed on his back. He was heavy set. On his bare chest, the sticker contacts for the EKG the medics had taken were still attached. He was wearing only his underwear. His lips had a blueish gray color. His eyes were only half closed, and it appeared he was staring into nowhere. I was torn between curiosity and fascination on the one hand and the eerie awareness that I was standing next to a corpse. But there was not a lot of time for emotion. My training kicked in, and I began to focus on my investigation. Turning to the medics, I asked who had declared death and learned that it was a doctor from Northwest Hospital at 0236 hours. My eyes scanned the room. Was there anything noteworthy, anything that seemed unusual? Did anything appear out of place? What kind of medications were present? When were they last filled and was that consistent with the remaining count of pills? Then I took my field camera I had brought along and took pictures of the body to document how we had found the deceased. With him lying there in front of us, I told my FTO, "I don't see anything unusual." Cortez shook his head and mumbled something that sounded like "rookie." He knelt down next to the dead man and carefully lifted the corpse's arms and legs, visually inspecting them for anything suspicious. Then he asked me to assist him in turning over the body to take a look at the back side. With a bit of inner hesitation, I put on the exam gloves I always had in the back pocket of my pants. We pulled the body over onto its left side to get a good look at its back. I took a few pictures, and we laid him back down the way he was. "One last thing," my FTO said. "The head." He wanted me to check the head for possible injuries hidden underneath the hair. Once again, I felt that lump in my throat. "Come on, Peine. I don't want to be here all night," Cortez said with a slightly frustrated undertone. I knelt down behind the dead man's head and carefully ran my fingers through his hair to feel across the shape of his skull. "What am I looking for?" was a question I asked just to say something. "Well, if someone smashed in his head you'll notice," was his stoic response. All I felt was the man's cold scalp and hair.

Earlier, we had requested the Office of the Medical Examiner (OME) over the radio to come and retrieve the body. We were advised that it would be about 45 minutes for them to get there. Once we were finished with our exam of the body, we took a blanket from the bed and draped it over the body. Then we left the guest bedroom, closed the door, and went back into the living room to inform the family of the next steps. The firefighters and medics had already left. Family members had gathered around the widow to provide comfort to her and each other.

It ended up taking about an hour for the OME guy to show up. He brought along a gurney with a purple cloth and a white plastic body bag. The three of us headed back into the small bedroom, where I learned that my FTO and I would need to help with the removal of the corpse. Until this moment, it had never occurred to me that we might need to assist with something like this. But of course, there was nobody else who could. Certainly not the family. Mr. OME wanted to get things done. He had two more calls in the queue after this. He turned the body bag inside out and placed a white linen sheet over it. "We'll just place him on top of the sheet," he said.

We each took positions around the dead man. I stood at his left. Cortez took the other arm, the OME guy had the feet. "On three." Then he counted loud, "1, 2, 3." I had fastened my grip around the wrists of the deceased. Just as I began to lift, I looked at the other two men and the whole scene turned into a slow-motion movie. Both of them had this terrified look on their faces and pressed a long "Nooo!" out of their lungs. Too late! I gave it a good tug and instantly felt and heard a snapping noise coming from the wrist I tightly held on to. My colleagues looked at me with an expression of disbelief. "What just happened?" was the thought running through my mind, sending instant chills of repulsion down my spine. I had no idea if I had just broken his wrist or was it something more benign, like the joint had simply cracked? All I had was the reaction of the other two men in the room with me. "Come on! Move him onto the sheet," the OME investigator said. Things moved along. I had no time to absorb or further think about what just happened. While we tucked the body into the bag and zipped it shut, the OME investigator explained that the wrists of a dead person are a weak spot. He told me that when lifting a dead person, especially if they've been dead for more than a few minutes, you want to grab well above the wrists or even underneath the shoulders if possible. I felt not only stupid but was sorry that this had happened. It was certainly not my intention to mishandle this man's body, yet I had, and I mentally added it to the list of things I would be careful to never do again.

We opened the door to the hallway and were approached by the older son. He wondered if it was possible for the family to see their father one more time before we took him out of the house. We briefly looked at the OME investigator and he said, "Of course. Give us a minute." We went back into the room, opened the body bag, and then draped the purple cloth all around, so as to hide the white plastic bag underneath. A few minutes later, and after we all agreed that the deceased looked presentable, we opened the door and stood off to the side. The family came in and tearfully said their goodbyes. After a short while, they all went back to the living room. The oldest son came back and was very appreciative. He thanked us for allowing this to take place in the close family circle and while their father was still at home. We nodded and the OME investigator said, "Of course." I then helped him carry the deceased down the stairs near the front door and loaded him into the SUV.

This is how I sometimes ended up in deeply personal situations, where I often felt like an intruder, yet I had a job to do. It was calls like this one that taught me to have and show empathy, while still remaining professional and in charge of the situation.

The situations I ended up involved in obviously varied widely and it would go beyond the volume of a single book to describe them all, but there were some that really stood out. There was the intoxicated man, who had been drinking with his friends all day until finally his judgement was so clouded that he got into an argument with his drinking buddies. The argument turned heated until, ultimately, punches were exchanged. A neighbor called 911, and we responded to separate the agitated combatants. The heavily intoxicated man, who we had identified as the instigator went in and out of consciousness and when awake, alternated between cooperative and belligerent. Due to his serious level of intoxication, he was transported to Kino Hospital. But as he was so unpredictable, my FTO decided I should ride in the ambulance to help out in case he would become violent with the medics. During the ride in the back of the ambulance, with no windows other than the ones in the back door, I became motion sick. Then drunk-guy decided to try and start a fight with the medic and myself. When we rolled up to the ER at Kino Hospital, I was seated on the man's legs, holding down his feet with my hands. The paramedic partially sat on the guy's face, which had kept his belligerence to a minimum. While that wasn't part of my official training, it certainly taught me to appreciate improvisation.

Given my professional background, a well-mannered and respectful approach had become second nature when dealing with strangers.

However, there were days where that kind of conduct failed to have the desired effect on the individuals we were dealing with. One night we had stopped a group of young gang members, all between 14 and 16 years old. Other deputies joined us for backup. In order to keep a better eye on everyone and to establish control of the situation, Cortez told me to make them all sit down. I looked straight at them and said, "Sit down!" Nothing happened. "Sir, I need you to sit down!" which I delivered louder than the first time for emphasis. Again, they just stared at me but failed to sit down on the curb. My FTO, who had observed my futile attempts to use my version of command presence, explained, "They don't understand you when you talk like that." Then he turned to the group of male teenagers and barked a loud, but perfectly clear, "Sit. The fuck. Down!" They dropped their butts onto the curb immediately. Cortez smiled at me and said, "See? You need to speak their language." Yes, being able to adjust my style of communication toward the more drastic ends of verbal exchanges was something I had not adjusted to… yet.

Then came the day where we drove on Ajo Way again. Over the radio, the dispatcher advised of an off-duty officer with the Tucson Police Department (TPD), who had noticed a stolen car. The officer had just come off his shift, where one of the last things he looked at was the description and license plate in a stolen vehicle report on his computer screen. These shortened versions of reports were known as "Be on the lookout" or BOLO. After work, he had stopped at a gas station to fill up his private vehicle, when he noticed a vehicle matching the description from the BOLO drive up and park in front of the store. The driver walked into the convenience store. A short while later, the driver came back out, got back into the stolen car, and took off going westward. The off-duty officer decided to take action and got into his own vehicle. Following the stolen car, he called 911 and reported to our dispatcher where they were going. As he was outside of city limits when he made the 911 call, it had automatically been routed to our call center. They ended up in a neighborhood not too far from Ryan Airfield, on the southwest side of Tucson. The off-duty officer parked his car around a street corner from where the suspect had parked the stolen car and had then disappeared into a trailer home. TPD advised they had several officers en route. A group of their car theft detectives were headed that way as well. We attached ourselves to the call, together with another deputy and a K-9 deputy, who came from farther away.

Upon arrival in the neighborhood, we joined the off-duty TPD officer and received a first-hand briefing with vehicle and suspect description. Over the next few minutes, several marked and unmarked TPD cars arrived quietly. They all lined up behind us, maybe 80 yards away from the stolen car and the trailer where the suspect had last been seen. The TPD officers, as well as a Detective Sergeant who had arrived, put together a plan of action with us. We learned that TPD had their helicopter with the call sign "Air One" on its way. They would assist in the apprehension effort.

A tactical maneuver of surrounding the trailer from all sides with an approach to the front and multiple marked police cars to show a strong presence, was quickly agreed upon. When we heard the helicopter at a distance, we all jumped into our cars and drove up to the trailer. I was so tense at that moment; I could not feel any nervousness or fear. All I felt was an incredible focus on the task at hand. As soon as the first two cars had turned the corner, everybody sped up and quickly set up in front of the house. The whole scene was now a display of red and blue emergency lights from all the marked police cars. The front of the house was lit up daylight-bright by all of our take-down lights and spotlights. Then suddenly, the unmistakable, loud chop-chop-chop of the helicopter cut through the night. I could feel the sharp snapping sounds of its rotor blades in my stomach. The crew turned on an incredibly bright search light and began to slowly circle over the scene. Through the public address system of one of the marked cars, the occupants of the trailers were told to step out of their home with their hands up. All of our guns were trained on the front side of this residence.

After a few seconds, the front door of the trailer slowly opened and a man who looked to be in his 50s appeared. Everybody began to yell simultaneously, "Hands! Hands! Hands!" The man quickly brought up his hands over his head and was ordered to step outside. Another, slightly younger man came out and a young girl, who looked as if she was not much older than 14 or 15 years. TPD officers and Detectives rushed up and took them back behind the police cars. As agreed beforehand, Cortez, another deputy, and I were going to clear the inside of the trailer. They made me the point man, but it didn't go quite as well as it was supposed to. It was extremely tight inside the trailer, and Cortez later told me that I had failed to properly communicate. He said communication between those who were searching a place was paramount for everyone's safety. This was not the movies. No stealthy, quiet combing through a house. We were loud, made our presence known with constant "police" calls, and systematically checked out the entire trailer. The place was a mess on the inside. There was trash everywhere; the carpet was stained beyond color recognition, and everything had a musky, moldy, and smoky smell to it. Empty cans of Bud Light seemed to be everywhere. There was a small TV screen with a porn movie flickering on the screen. The bedrooms had clothes, bed linens, and sleeping bags strewn about. After a few brief minutes, we were done and declared the place secure.

I stepped back out into the busy scene outside the front of the trailer. The city officers had turned off all of their extra lights to illuminate the front of the trailer, but some of the red and blues were still going to indicate an active crime scene. TPD detectives were separately interviewing all three people who had come out of the trailer. Suddenly, there was a lot of commotion to my left. Someone took off running toward the main roadway where we had staged earlier. Everybody was just looking on and one of the detectives said, "We have a runner!" Cortez and I took off after the guy, passing all the TPD officers who curiously observed the scene. Thanks to my long legs, I gained quickly on the runner and left my FTO behind. In my earpiece, I heard Cortez advise over the radio, "10-80 on foot. Going eastbound into the desert area." About 20 to 30 feet ahead of me, the suspect ran across the road, jumped across a drainage ditch, and into thick desert mesquite underbrush. I kept running after him, not noticing anything around me, but solely focused on the running bad guy ahead of me. When I crossed the street, a patrol car came to a screeching halt a few feet off to my right. Our K-9 deputy and his partner. As I jumped across the ditch, I could hear the suspect hustling through the underbrush, breaking branches in the process. It was pitch black, when suddenly everything turned daylight bright. The helicopter pilot had overheard the action on the radio and returned. Now I was totally fired up. The K-9 handler came up from behind me and yelled in my direction that he would fan out to my right. Over the radio, the pilot gave us an update on the suspect's location as we continued to race through the underbrush. Off to my right and maybe thirty feet or so ahead of me, I heard loud yelling but couldn't make out what was being said. More yelling, then the sound I remembered all too well from the academy. A sharp pop and subsequent moaning let me know that someone had deployed a Taser. Within a few seconds, I caught up. The helicopter overhead illuminated the area around us and revealed the K-9 deputy who held his Taser in his extended right hand. The bright light of the helicopter search light made the copper wires coming from the Taser sparkle. The suspect was on the ground after taking a brief 50,000-volt ride. The dog was barking incessantly, and other officers and deputies joined us. The K-9 Deputy briefly looked in my direction and yelled against the helicopter noise, "Go ahead! Cuff him!" I moved in on the suspect on the ground and ordered him to turn over onto his belly. Fortunately, he did as he was told. I pulled the handcuffs from the back of my duty belt, but failed to simply slap them on, as we used to say. It was a fidgety, time-consuming process and when I tried to double-lock them, I noticed the tremors in my hands, preventing me from quickly fitting the handcuff key onto the tiny indentation on the side of the cuffs to keep them from ratcheting ever tighter. Finally, it worked, and I brought the suspect to his feet. The K-9 deputy came over and handed me the Taser cartridge with the wires wrapped around it. The probes were still inside the man's back.

    We slowly made our way back through the brush toward the roadway, where an ambulance was waiting. Cortez came up and told me to remove the probes from the suspect's back. The guy was okay with that, as he just wanted them out and to be done with it. He looked at me and, with a tone of defeat, breathlessly said, "I'm done, man. I'm not going to do anything stupid." We partially rolled up his shirt to get a better look at the embedded probes. As I had learned only a few weeks earlier, I put on a pair of exam gloves, stretched the skin of his back and quickly yanked out both prongs. "Thank you!" he said while a TPD officer exchanged my cuffs for a pair of his. I nodded in his direction and took the probes and the expended Taser cartridge back to our patrol car. They would need to be packaged and turned into evidence.

When I returned to our patrol car, the young girl who had emerged from the trailer was seated in the back. Cortez came over and said to interview her and make sure we had her name, address, date of birth, and other pertinent information. I opened the back door and asked her to step out. When she stood up, I asked her to turn around so I could take off the handcuffs. "How old are you?" I asked her. "Nineteen," she responded. She said her driver's license was in her back pocket. The handcuffs around her wrists were at their tightest setting, yet her wrists were so small and skinny, with a little bit of wiggling she could have probably simply slipped out of them. She was skin and bones and, concerned for her well-being, I asked, "How much do you weigh?" She laughed and said, "Yeah, I know. I'm really skinny. We call it 'the crack diet.'" After jotting down her information and getting her story, she was allowed to leave. A friend came by a few minutes later to pick her up.

Each day, I was evaluated using a list of 30 performance categories. Each category allowed a grade between one and five, with one being the worst and five being the most exceptional grade the trainee could receive. Each day my interactions with citizens, my radio traffic, behavior toward the FTO and/or other deputies, my driving and obedience of traffic rules, as well as a host of other things were graded. By the end of my work week, there was a brief multiple-choice test on a variety of topics and finally, by the end of a phase, there was the "End of Phase Test." The End of Phase Test was accompanied by the phase board. That board consisted of the shift supervising Sergeant, my FTO, the FTO Coordinator, who was a member of the academy staff, and of course myself. All of these tests and examinations had to be passed to be able to continue in the process. After four weeks, I passed the test and the phase board approved my progression to the next level.

From San Xavier on Tucson's Southside, I moved on to the Rincon District on the Eastside for phase two. While in Rincon, we had monsoon rainfalls, and I spent countless hours at roadblocks, explaining to drivers why it was not safe trying to drive through raging floodwaters with a Chevy Malibu and three kids in the back.

There was also the memorable experience of a family who had called 911 after their adult son had attacked his father at the family home. When we arrived, we learned from the mother that her son, who was in his late twenties to early thirties, had been diagnosed with bipolar disorder. He had delivered a few heavy blows to his father in a fit of rage. The father's face showed the physical signs of the blows received. We found the son in the backyard, where he was pacing back and forth. He was yelling out loud and appeared terribly agitated. My FTO tried to get through to him and said that we would not risk getting hurt in a physical fight or—worse—getting him injured in the process of detention, as he would have to answer to a judge for his physical attack on his father. When faced with the option of taking an electric ride courtesy of Taser, Inc., he submitted to our custody.

Approximately halfway to the Pima County Jail, our arrestee threw a hysterical fit in the back of our patrol car and claimed to have trouble breathing, accompanied by chest pain. We pulled over with his behavior continuing. As neither of us was a medic, we had to call an ambulance to our location. This episode eventually landed us in the emergency room of the closest hospital to have our arrestee evaluated further. Paramedics were not comfortable giving him a clean bill of health at the scene. While in the ER, tied to his bed, our arrestee threw yet another fit. Unfortunately, it was in the presence of a sturdy, middle-aged, experienced ER nurse, who told us she was from Michigan. She attempted to tend to her patient nicely and explained to him multiple times that he was safe and there to receive care, despite our presence. The episode ended with a barrage of verbal insults and slurs yelled by the arrestee and likely audible well beyond the confines of the emergency department. Though warned by the nurse not to test her patience and to stop putting other patients in fear, he continued his rage. With a nod in our direction, the nurse calmly took a syringe and drew a dose of a sedative which, upon closer examination, had a massive needle mounted on top of it. She called it the "bad boy needle." Minutes after receiving his injection with a needle that likely could have pierced an elephant hide, our arrestee became calm. He apologized profusely to the nurse and to us, adding an offer of lifelong friendship. Everyone respectfully declined. That was the day I learned not to question or mess with ER nurses.

Shortly before leaving Rincon to move on to my final phase in the Foothills District, I was parked near Sabino Canyon, filling out paperwork about a call we had just wrapped up nearby. My FTO was busy going through my field training handbook, making sure we had covered all the subjects we were supposed to during this phase. Deputy Reynolds, my FTO, asked me a question that triggered the memory of a funny incident a few days back. Unfortunately, I had just taken a big gulp of water from my jug as the heat had been incessant the past few days. I tried to contain the uncontrollable urge to laugh out loud because none of the water had made it down my throat yet. The awkward look from my FTO, who noticed something was amiss with my facial expression following his seemingly innocuous question, "broke the camel's back." My laughter forced its way outward and made me spew the contents of my mouth throughout the interior of my FTO's patrol car. The dashboard and inside of the windshield was covered in a fine layer of droplets of water and possibly some saliva. Still laughing and wiping some of the water from my nose and chin, I tried to get a grip. Deputy Reynolds's puzzled look painted his struggle to comprehend what had just happened all over his face and will stay with me to the end of my days. If there would ever be a need to define what someone who had just experienced a "What-the-fuck?" moment would look like, this *had* to be it. I cannot begin to describe the level of my embarrassment, especially in light of the fact that there was truly no good reason for my sudden outbreak of comic relief. I looked at him and simply said, "I am so sorry. Sorry! Please, don't ask. Do you have a towel in the back?"

My final phase in Foothills went very well. I felt confident and was encouraged by Deputy Mitchell. She performed her role as expected, which was mainly to be an observer and evaluator. I recall only one occasion where I knew backup to be farther away, and I "broke" her observer role by asking, "Could you be my backup?"

She gave me a few more pointers and tips to add to my toolbox, but otherwise encouraged me to follow my instincts and use my ability to talk to people as much as I could. Finally, there was the end.

This line of work began to feel more natural. I thought of my first few calls back on Tucson's south side. The experience of walking up to a scene, and everyone there either walking or running towards me, erupting in a cacophony of statements about what had happened and whose fault it was. Or the awkward silence when everyone present automatically looked at me and waited for my decision or instructions. Even a seemingly simple scenario like a traffic collision could be very stressful. (Yes, cops call this everything but an "accident." There is no such thing as a traffic "accident." The rationale for this is the perception that the term "accident" implies something happening by chance, when in reality, 99 % [Caution: Made-up statistic!] of the time it is someone who is at fault and the incident occurred because of that particular person's erroneous behavior or action.) I arrived at the tangled mess of cars and agitated drivers, who are being instructed by unseen advisors on the other end of the phones they're holding to their ear. All of this surrounded by ongoing traffic, adding more agitated drivers upset about the inconvenience this crash scene created, and the dangers of someone getting hurt by passing cars or add-on crashes. Add-ons are collisions caused by the disturbance of traffic flow from the initial crash (or rubber necks). My personal record while investigating one crash were three add-ons. Especially in the very beginning, all of this created the excruciatingly unfamiliar burden of deciding on the next steps, when I was not entirely sure myself about what to do at that moment. But with the growing volume of calls I responded to I gained the necessary experience, which turned the shouldering of that burden into confidence that I knew what to do or would be able to figure it out with the help from other deputies.

During my final week in field training, I learned that I would be going to the Rincon District to start my career in patrol, only to find out two days later that decision had been reversed. I was to start out my duty as a solo deputy right here in the Foothills District. Too bad, I thought. During a brief visit to the District Commander there, I was given the opportunity to pick a patrol car from the pool of vehicles out back and found myself lucky. A Crown Victoria was in decent shape and was only five years old. Of course, all of that had to be reversed. By the end of my final day as a trainee deputy, I had been assigned to the Foothills District - day shift and my patrol car was parked in the back of the lot. "Report back here Sunday morning—0600 sharp," the Sergeant instructed. I took the keys for the car from him and—with the urgent warning not to engage in any kind of law enforcement activity on my way home—I was allowed to take the vehicle home for some TLC.

For the first time, proud as can be and feeling strangely alone in this police vehicle, I put my hands onto the sticky steering wheel and drove home to Vail in my 1999 Ford Police Interceptor with 132,000 miles on the odometer.

6

ROOKIE DAYS

How do I describe the feeling I had when I realized I finally made it? To drive to work for the first time, engaging in my dream job after a journey that had lasted more than 20 years, putting me into the southwestern United States just north of the border with Mexico, passing a rigorous selection process, enduring and successfully completing a law enforcement academy, and last but not least, being given the okay to be on my own after 12-weeks of field training, was exhilarating. I was Deputy Sheriff Peine. On my own, ready to serve.

Of course, my training period was not over completely. There was roughly a year of probationary period left. A time during which I could have been fired at any time or as it was so eloquently phrased "without cause." But that was not in the forefront of my mind. On this, my first morning on the streets as a cop by myself, I just wanted to do well. Doing well in that context meant not screwing up so badly that someone got hurt or me leaving work knowing I had left some kind of unexplainable mess behind or that I had thoroughly embarrassed myself or the department. As we all know, to make a mistake, an error, as a police officer can seriously mess up someone's life. So, I thought to myself, *put your head on straight. Eyes and ears wide open. Be aware of your surroundings and listen to those with more experience.*

I had spent the better part of Saturday, my day off, attempting to clean the patrol car I had been assigned. The Sheriff's Department had assigned me a vehicle, as was customary. Deputies took their patrol car home every day after work. It made a lot of sense, given the size of the county, that it was beneficial for us to be seen on the streets even on our way to and from work, and it also gave us a sense of ownership. After giving my patrol car a manual wash and applying some wax, it looked… cleaner. The official markings and wrap were seriously weathered and had begun to peel off in places. The paint underneath the door handles had come off, revealing the sheet metal underneath. Yet, the interior was worse. Using regular household cleaner, I removed five buckets of disgustingly dirty water, which changed in color from black to gray, but never reached the clear level. Finally, I took some Armor All, applied it to the dashboard and disinfected the cage with a bleach solution and then Lysol. Vacuuming took about a half hour and only revealed the completely worn-out carpets and upholstery, all the way down to the metal in some places. Then, I put my gear into the car, lots of gear. Our personal protective equipment (PPE) bag, first aid kit, camera case with camera, extra forms, raincoat, traffic cones, et cetera. On the passenger seat, I put up a newly purchased seat organizer. A place for the most commonly used forms, an extra set of handcuffs, flex cuffs, my "haz can" (a metal clip board with a compartment to store completed paperwork), and extra ammunition. When I left the driveway of our house that morning, I left behind my wife and son, who saw me off to patrol on my own for the first time, and an oil stain.

It was Sunday morning at approximately 5:15 a.m. with virtually no traffic on the Interstate. It took me about 40 minutes to get to my district on the other side of town. When I got off the highway and into the district, I used my new radio designator for the first time to sign on for the shift.

"1-1-4-2."

"1-1-4-2, go ahead."

"Good Morning, 10-41."

"Good Morning, sir. 05-56."

Without any calls holding on the screen, I drove to the district office to see the shift supervisor. There were three more rookies from my class who had started that morning. The sergeant simply wanted us out on the streets and said there was no need for us to "hang out at the office." So, to the streets we took. With a sense of excitement and still feeling a little odd not having an FTO seated next to me, I pulled out onto the streets and let the dispatcher know that I was available to take any calls that would come in.

"1-1-4-2. 10-8."

"1-1-4-2 at 06-15."

I made a left turn onto Ina Road, and the sense of being by myself, being able to rely on my own judgement, dealing with people the way I wanted to deal with them, was very powerful. If we were not involved in other activities and enough people were available to deal with priority calls, we were tasked with traffic enforcement. So, I followed a car in front of me and ran the license plate. Minutes into my first shift ever, I had potentially struck gold. The plate returned expired, and I requested a confirmation over the air. The expiration was confirmed. It doesn't sound like much, but I had already seen how minor offenses and the traffic stops resulting from it had led to much more significant matters. When the car made a right turn on Orange Grove, I called out a traffic stop and turned on my overhead emergency lights. I didn't even need the siren, as the driver immediately responded and pulled over to the right curb. Once again, I felt the pressure of doing this on my own, complete with responsibility for all outcomes, decisions, and risks involved.

Though I had done this plenty of times during field training, I went over the procedures—and possible threats—in my head again. Who else might be in the car that I was not aware of? Was the driver a dangerous felon already planning his escape—or worse: an attack on me? How far away was my next backup? As I put my car in park and got ready to step out, I observed the driver in the car ahead of me. Nothing seemed suspicious at this point. He simply sat there waiting for the things to come. Still, my heart was racing. I noticed another patrol car driving by in the opposite direction, most likely one of the more senior deputies keeping an eye on what I was doing. That felt reassuring. I opened my door and stepped out. Walking up to the driver's side of the vehicle in front of me, I tried to discern if there was anybody else inside the car. When I came closer, it seemed the driver was the sole occupant. The memory of that big Desert Eagle I found during one of my early traffic stops briefly popped into my head, triggering a quick glance at the rear seat as I reached the c-pillar. Clear. The driver had already rolled down his window and was digging in the center console. What was he doing? I stopped just shy of the b-pillar and addressed him.

"Sir? I need you to stop doing what you're doing and put your hands where I can see them."

"Oh! Oh, yes! Of course," came the prompt response.

"Sir, my name is Deputy Peine with the Sheriff's Department. I stopped you because your plates seem to be expired."

"Oh, gee, I had no idea. Sorry."

"Let me see your driver's license, registration, and proof of insurance, please."

"Sure, I was just looking for the insurance thing," he responded and turned his attention back to the center console, his hands disappearing from my sight. I grabbed my gun, flipped down the safety hood of the holster and drew my weapon, but held it down alongside my right leg.

"Sir, I need you to keep your hands where I can see them," I said, more sternly this time.

"Oh, no no no. I know, I just wanted to see…"

"Are there any guns or weapons inside this vehicle?"

"No. Why would I have a gun in the car? No, no guns," he nervously responded.

"Okay, go ahead. Take a look in your center console." He seemed okay, I thought, and, without him noticing, holstered my weapon.

He rummaged for a few more seconds and then said, "I can't find it. I must have left it at home."

"Is the vehicle insured, sir?"

"Oh, I'm sure it is."

"But you're not certain?"

"Well, Officer, see, my wife usually pays for it and… but I wouldn't really know. She wouldn't miss something like that."

DEPUTY WHILE IMMIGRANT

"Okay, okay. Stop looking now. Let me have your driver's license and registration, then."

He handed me the expired registration and his driver's license.

"Thank you. Stay in your car. I'll be right back."

Walking back to the patrol car was always one of the more vulnerable parts of a traffic stop. Especially now, as I did not yet have any real sense of who I was dealing with. Sure, my gut feeling said that he was probably going to be okay, but I lacked the experience. The driver seemed nervous, but it was probably more because he got pulled over, nothing else. As I walked back to my car, I quickly looked over my shoulder when I was about halfway, just to make sure he was still sitting where he was supposed to sit. Back in my car, I ran his name and date of birth through the Arizona Criminal Justice Information System (ACJIS) to see if there was a warrant for his arrest. That check returned negative, no warrants. The data coming back from the Motor Vehicle Division (MVD) was a different story. His driver's license had been suspended about two months prior. Oh, wow! My first ever traffic stop all by myself and I caught a guy who was driving on a suspended license.

Back on that particular day, fresh out of the academy and field training, "flying solo" for the first time, full of anticipation, and ready to prove I knew what I was doing, I thought *that was cool!* They said, you'll always remember your first solo call. And sure enough, an otherwise seemingly mundane task of traffic law enforcement, with its rather paper-intensive aftermath, had become my first call. While consequential for the person caught, it was "nothing to write home about" from a law enforcement perspective. That said, looking back at the situation today, knowing how deep an encounter with law enforcement can cut, I no longer think of it as something "cool." It was the sheer excitement of the first call, the first solo act of enforcing the law, that made it feel that way. Immobilizing someone's vehicle and stapling a hole into their driver's license is not cool.

Meanwhile, back on that day, my brain was racing. I would…wait, wait, wait. I had to gather my thoughts and run through one of the many checklists in my head. I had done all of this before. Deputy Reynolds, my

FTO back in the Rincon District, seemed to have some sort of invisible radar when it came to finding suspended drivers. So I'd had my share of experience when it came to suspended or revoked licenses. To be 100 % sure, I figured I'd run the driver's information over the radio. That way, other deputies could hear it as well and would know that I'd be tied up here for a few more minutes.

Once the dispatcher confirmed the suspension, I requested a case number and a tow truck. In Arizona, when someone is caught driving on a suspended or revoked license, the vehicle they operated was, as we called it, taken to "car jail" for 30 days. If the owner was someone other than the driver, they could get it back earlier, but that was not the case here. Had I thought of everything?

I returned to the driver in his car, still watchful that nothing suspicious had occurred. It should be all okay from here, I thought. However, an uneasy feeling remained. When I reached his door, I asked him to step out and come to the back of his car. He was shorter than me and sloppily dressed. In maintaining a safe distance from him, I tried to stay ahead of things, just in case he decided to do something stupid. By the trunk of his car, I explained that I had found he was driving on a suspended license and told him that he was under arrest. In his apparent surprise, he began to talk at rapid fire speed. He admitted and explained that this was his only way to get to work and a lot more information, which didn't really matter at this point. He had been driving without a valid license and that was it. I explained to him that there was no need for him to go to jail, but instead I would issue a citation and would release him, as long as he would sign the form promising to appear in court. He said that, of course, he would do so. But his reaction became way more concerned when I told him that his car was being immobilized and taken to a yard at the tow company, where it would have to remain for 30 days. Now he began to gesture wildly and got louder. He tried to negotiate with me, saying his wife could come by and drive the car home. Of course, none of the options he offered were a possibility under the law, and I told him so. After a few upset minutes, he resigned himself to the inevitable fact that he'd have to leave his car behind. I asked him to remove his belongings from within the vehicle and to call his wife for a pickup. Then, he signed the citation and other paperwork. His wife came about 10 minutes later in a different car, and I saw them gesturing in the car as they drove off. That definitely did not look like a friendly conversation.

From there, it was more of an administrative act for me. My tension subsided. I double-and triple-checked all my paperwork, handed the necessary copies to the tow truck driver, who arrived about 20 minutes later. My first traffic stop, first arrest, first vehicle immobilization, and all that within the first five minutes of my time out on the street. When I ran into my classmates later on, they wanted to hear every detail. How did you find out? Was he cooperative? Did you remember to inventory the vehicle? The senior deputies were more concerned about having a "Traffic Nazi" on the squad now. I assured them it was coincidence, and that I would focus on responding to calls for the rest of the day. The remaining eight hours went by as you would expect for a Sunday morning, in a low-pressure kind of way.

The next few days were still filled with getting used to the new feeling of being by myself. The senior deputies were generally very helpful and regularly showed up to my calls, asking if I had thought to do this, asked for that, filled out such-and-such a form. Though annoying at times because it was a constant reminder of how much of a rookie I still was, it was also very reassuring. We all looked out for each other.

Toward the end of my first week as I drove to work one morning, still on I-10 going westbound, I heard a deputy in our district call out a traffic stop. Then, in short order, came his next call to advise that the vehicle was continuing on Ina Road westbound. Through the speaker of the radio, I heard his siren wail in the background. The next transmission said they were entering the Interstate going eastbound. He was still in pursuit. But then he got on again and advised, as was required by rules and regulations, to provide additional information, including their speed. The deputy said they were going 35 mph on the Interstate. Each time he keyed up, you could hear his siren blaring in the background.

Other deputies joined and advised they were ahead of him, setting up at different on and off ramps. The pursuing deputy described that the car in front of him was continuing, still not stopping, going at various speeds, sometimes as low as 25 mph, then again speeding up to 45 mph. Units ahead of him advised they were ready to deploy road spikes in order to deflate the pursued vehicle's tires. I briefly considered setting up at one of the upcoming off-ramps myself, but they were still several exits ahead of me and most of them were already covered by other deputies. If necessary, however, I could join at a moment's notice.

The sergeant came on the radio and asked for traffic conditions. It was early in the morning and there was barely any traffic in the eastbound lanes, which is exactly what the deputy a few miles ahead of me described in his radio response. The sergeant then approved the spike's deployment. We could potentially be dealing with a heavily intoxicated person, who simply failed to react appropriately to the lights and siren behind him. Or it could be a dangerous wanted person, who was trying to come up with a plan while they're driving down I-10. There were a lot of bad scenarios going through my head and it felt like a good call to not risk having this whole scenario leave the Interstate and enter residential streets again.

Still going westbound, I was glued to all the radio chatter, wondering what was going to happen next. Then the pursuing deputy said they were coming up to the next on/off ramp and deputies who had set up there confirmed they saw them coming up to their position. They told the pursuing deputy to slightly fall back, so they wouldn't accidentally spike his tires as well. Then the radio went quiet for a moment. With the next transmission, a breathless deputy keyed up and with his mouth way too close to the mic announced, "Vehicle has been spiked. They're slowly continuing eastbound." Then the familiar voice of the pursuing deputy came back on the air. "Looks like they're stopping. Yes—vehicle has come to a complete stop in the number two lane, just east of the on-ramp. High-risk stop!" A high-risk stop was a standardized procedure in these types of cases where the occupants were called out of their car at gun point and from a distance. They were then taken into custody and the

DEPUTY WHILE IMMIGRANT

vehicle would be searched. The Interstate would be completely shut down by following deputies, so all of this could happen in as safe a manner as possible. Radio silence was ordered by the dispatcher.

After a very short time, too short to go through a whole high-risk stop, I thought, the original deputy keyed up. "Everybody stand down! It's two number fours. We need a Japanese interpreter." Just as all that happened, I drove past the scene on the other side of the Interstate. I saw the deputies walking around a small passenger car, a few women of Asian appearance, and several patrol cars behind them. Then the roadblock on the Interstate and the stalled traffic behind that. The sergeant barked into the radio and ordered the involved deputies to get everybody off the roadway "ASAP" and open the traffic lanes again.

For reference: The description of ethnicity, which can be an important part of the description of an individual, is encoded for radio traffic. A "number four" stands for a person of Asian ethnicity. The occupants of the spiked vehicle were visitors from Japan, who had come to meet friends studying at the University of Arizona in Tucson. They took their friend's car and when the initial deputy wanted to conduct a traffic stop, did not know they were required to pull over to the right shoulder. Confused by the noise and the fact that the patrol car stayed behind them, they slowed down, sped up, and then simply fell into a state of mild panic. When the tires deflated after being spiked, they finally stopped and got out of their car. It quickly became clear that they didn't mean to evade the deputy, but simply didn't know what to do. They were very lucky that nothing worse had happened and would have a story to tell for years to come. On our side, the story would also have quite the aftermath. For days to come, we went over the requirements of a pursuit and over the definition of when someone was actually trying to flee. It was explained—and reiterated—what other ways this whole incident could have been resolved and brought to a much less dramatic conclusion.

On another afternoon, my shift in the Foothills district had been going on for maybe a half hour. Prior to driving out into my "beat," I had stopped by the district office and turned in some paperwork from the previous day. I was still in that phase of excitement every morning I drove in and showed up for work. It was the excitement over who I would be able to help that day, what kind of scenarios I might encounter, and what dangers might lurk around the seemingly calm corner.

Ethan, a classmate of mine, and I were assigned to the same beat. As I drove away from the district office in my '99 Ford Police Interceptor (aka Crown Victoria) with peeling paint toward residential areas to the north of the district, I glanced across the computer screen to see what types of calls were coming in and who they were assigned to. Not a big task with only four active calls on the screen, none of which sounded too challenging.

Then the two-tone signal indicating a priority call broke the radio silence.

"Foothills Beat 3, copy Code 18-03 10-31 at 1234 W Ina Road, The Foothills Apartments. Units responding advise."

A car theft in progress! Ethan beat me to the punch, keyed up, and by simply stating his radio designator, he became the lead deputy on the call. Next, I called out my designator, "1-1-4-2," and was added to the call. I made a U-turn and was near the apartment complex within two minutes. Ethan had already positioned himself at a street corner and stood by for me. We had not responded with lights or sirens. First of all, there was no need to as there was virtually no traffic at 6:30 a.m. on a Sunday morning, and we also did not want to announce our presence and alert the bad guys to our close proximity. Updates broadcast over the radio indicated that the suspect had broken into a sedan and was still in the parking lot.

The apartment complex and its parking lot were surrounded by a 4-foot landscape wall. Ethan took the lead and we slowly and quietly rolled through the main entrance, which was on a side street, into the complex, making a left turn. A small dark sedan turned around the corner of the first building, coming directly at us. Ethan came on the radio and said, "That's him! Fan right." He veered to the left and I to the right in an attempt to block the suspect's exit and potentially use our vehicles for cover. The distance between Ethan's car and mine was about the width of a car. From the corner of my eye, I saw Ethan had turned on his overhead red and blue lights. I did the same to signal the driver of the vehicle to stop. A firework of scenarios went through my head. The car in front of us came to a stop, as did we. Would we need to conduct a high-risk stop? No, they might not be the people we're looking for. But it's a car theft, a felony. So, in order to be cautious, we should treat it as a felony or high-risk stop with guns drawn.

Before I could finish my thoughts, the sedan's engine revved, and the car came barreling toward us. The driver took the vehicle right through us, in between our patrol cars. The gap was so tight that Ethan's vehicle was scraped on the passenger side by the sedan's side-view mirror. As he passed in between our police cars, I could see what looked like a male driver, but nobody else inside. In the rear-view mirror, I saw the car go through the exit and make a left turn toward Ina Road. Ethan backed up toward the exit and I made a rapid three-point-turn in the parking lot, following him out of the complex. Ethan provided an update over the radio.

"Suspect vehicle has fled and took off toward Ina. He struck my car!"

Both of us turned on our lights and sirens to pursue. As we pulled out of the parking lot, the stolen car sped toward the traffic light. We were on a quiet side street and Ina Road was a major traffic artery on this side of town. Traffic was very light that morning, and the lights showed a red signal for us. Without ever slowing down or the brake lights coming on, the stolen car dashed across the intersection and continued southbound. With clearly noticeable excitement in his voice, Ethan radioed the update.

"Suspect just blew a red light on Ina continuing southbound."

Other units broadcasted their location, and that they were headed our way. During each transmission, you could hear their sirens in the background. I noticed all the radio traffic, but who was responding and from where did not register in my brain. I was solely focused on Ethan's car in front of me. The suspect quickly pulled away from us as he sped down a residential road. A quick glance at my speedometer showed 55 mph. We were flying through these streets and thank God nobody was out and about. A few hundred feet ahead, I saw the car go over a hill top. Now he was out of sight and, not seeing anyone on the sidewalk or any other vehicles, Ethan and I accelerated more. We flew over the top of the small hill, briefly went airborne, and then slammed back onto the pavement. Once we cleared the top, there was no sign of the stolen car. It had vanished. The long stretch of road ahead of us was void of any traffic.

"1-1-4-2. We have lost visual of the suspect vehicle. Still going southbound."

We slowed down to 20 mph and turned off our sirens. Calling out every cross street we passed to continuously indicate our location, we scanned every driveway, every parked vehicle and every side street. Then, down a small residential side street, we saw what looked like our suspect car pulled over to the side of the road. We quickly turned into the street and raced toward the sedan. When we got there, we saw the car had pulled diagonally off the road and was sitting partially on the sidewalk and partially in a front yard. The driver's side door was open, and the engine was still running.

Ethan and I jumped out of our cars. I drew my weapon from its holster and for the first time experienced the tunnel vision they had told us about in the academy. All I saw was the stolen car with its door open. Fanning out, both of us pointed our guns at the car and loudly yelled, "Police! Get out of the car with your hands up!" No response. Though it seemed obvious that the driver had taken off, I vividly remembered a scenario from the academy. A driver had taken off on foot, while a second person had remained in the vehicle lying down across the rear seats. As we had pursued the runner, the guy who had been hiding in the backseat took a seat on the hood of my patrol car and shot us with his finger gun. Scenario over. With that in mind, we conducted a brief sweep of the vehicle's interior. It was empty. The gravel laid out in the front yard kept us from seeing any clear footprints indicating where he could have run. As Ethan looked around the area, we noticed access to a large wash that ran behind the houses. Washes or dried out riverbeds were known as a popular getaway route and both of us ran toward it. Ethan turned around and said, "Stay with the car. I'll see if I can find him." With that, he took off into the dusty river bed and its underbrush. Over the radio, I heard other units arrive nearby, setting up a perimeter to keep an eye out should the suspect emerge elsewhere in the neighborhood.

The setting up of a secure perimeter was called "setting up quads," as in quadrants. A deputy not involved in the call would pull over his car, get a map out, and look at the incident location. Anticipating possible escape routes and taking into account the time since the suspect was last seen, that deputy would then call out intersections for which units near the incident location would come up on the radio. Once assigned a quadrant, the deputies would position their patrol car at a point near the intersection and go "high vis" or highly visible. It made for an obvious police presence and visually contained the search area. If done right, the suspect who emerged into a main roadway would always clearly see a police car with its lights turned on, forcing them to hunker down or make a run for it.

I got on the radio.

"1-1-4-2. 1-1-3-6 is pursuing the suspect on foot. I'm staying with the victim's car."

As I stood there next to the stolen car, I could suddenly feel my heart pounding and noticed how my brain was in overdrive. All kinds of procedural details went through my head in an utter mess. What to do next? A patrol car pulled up to my location. On the hood of the car, it had an extra set of stickers spelling out the word "Supervisor." It was Sergeant Silva, our shift supervisor. Sergeant Silva was somewhat similar in appearance to The Hat. A hulk of a man, a good 6 feet tall, solid muscle, SWAT operator, and one mean look on his face. He is actually a great guy and very supportive, but at the time my academy experience was way too recent to notice that. The sergeant stopped his car next to me, rolled down his passenger side window and said, "What you got, Peine?" Out of my mouth came a jumble of words, a half-assed description of the suspect and then… nothing. My mind went blank. I just looked at the sergeant. His building frustration was palpable. Whatever I had just said did not really make any sense. He got out of his car, looked over the roof of his vehicle straight at me, and I could see the veins on the side of his neck bulging. Then he yelled at me, saying, "Peine, you need to unfuck yourself! Your brain is working at a million miles per hour and your mouth can't keep up with it." That was probably the most observant statement anyone could have made at that point. Rather than getting intimidated, much to my own surprise, it snapped me out of mumbo-jumbo-confusion mode back into cop mode. I started over and told him what we had observed once we arrived with the stolen car. How we did not really get a good enough look at the suspect to be sure of his appearance and where Ethan had gone. The sergeant said, "Thank you! Much better. Call Forensics and stay with the car. Let the people in the house know what's going on in their front yard and let them know it's okay." Then he took off.

A short while later, a civilian pickup truck stopped on the other side of the road, and I prepared myself for the typical "Nothing to see here. Move on, please." The window rolled down and the woman in the driver's seat signaled me to come over to her. Maybe she had seen something useful? As I came closer, she held up a badge, and I noticed her holding a radio in her right hand. "Hi. I'm Detective So-and-so. I was on my way to run some errands when I heard you guys chasing the 18-03 suspect. Any idea what direction he went?" I gave her a quick briefing on the situation, and she decided to take a drive through the neighborhood to see if she noticed anything or anyone unusual.

Putting on my patrol gloves, I turned off the stolen car's engine and called for a forensic unit to respond to my location in order to process the vehicle for fingerprints and other possible evidence. I walked over to the front door of the home and rang the doorbell to let the homeowner know what was going on.

After a prolonged search of the area, a suspect and a potential accomplice, who he may have called to help him get away, were apprehended. I never saw him as I was busy with processing the car, organizing a tow truck, filling out forms, and making notes for my report. Ethan came back frustrated, as he had not been able to be part of the apprehension. After approximately two hours, all of this was history, and we moved on to handling the more mundane calls for service.

It was a strange back and forth between routine, slow parts of the shift, and then suddenly all hell would break loose. I had conversations with neighbors over whose dog supposedly pooped into the other's front yard and then five minutes later I'd be dealing with the worst kind of individual society had to offer at gun point.

After my first weekend, which was a Wednesday/Thursday combination, I went back to work on Friday (now called "my Monday"). As every morning, I drove on I-10 westbound toward the Foothills District. Coming up on the Ajo Way exit, there was a sudden loud bang from underneath my vehicle, then a grinding noise, followed by a rapid increase in RPMs of my engine. I immediately took my foot off the accelerator, which calmed down the engine. Then, when I tried to continue and put my foot down on the accelerator again, the engine howled loudly, but no acceleration—nothing. Just howling. I was just rolling on the Interstate, continuing to slow down. Nothing happened when I tried to put the car into second gear. Back in "Drive" and applying the accelerator resulted in more engine howling. I resigned. Turning on my overhead emergency lights, I slowly pulled over into the breakdown lane. The engine stalled. Keying up on the radio, I said, "1-1-4-2. My vehicle is 10-85. I'll need a 9-2-6." In plain English, my car broke down and I needed a tow.

To make matters worse, my battery died in short order, and the mirrors twirling around the lights underneath the red and blue plastic cover on the roof of my car went from rapid to slow to crawl to finally stopping altogether. No power, no emergency lights. My sergeant called and wanted to know what had happened. I explained, and he sent another deputy to the county's car shop, where I had to leave my vehicle behind to give me a ride back to the district. A few days later, I learned my car would be retired. The transmission had blown out from under me as the material had simply tired after almost 140,000 police miles. They say police miles count double because of what these cars are put through. The following car had just under 100,000 miles on the odometer, and I was hopeful it would last longer than a few weeks.

One day, I was assigned to the northern part of the district, which was significantly more rural in nature, houses on larger lots, vast desert areas in between developed neighborhoods, a golf resort in between. It was late morning, and the heat had become quite significant already, hovering around the low 100s. Priority tones rang out over the air and the dispatcher announced a suicide attempt in my beat. I picked up the mic and took the assignment. The call had just come in with the caller reporting he had found the victim in the garage with a gunshot wound to the head. Deputy Reynolds came up on the radio as well. I was relieved not to be alone on that one. It still felt good to have someone else there to keep an eye on things.

When I came close to the turn off into the neighborhood, I switched off my siren and pulled up in front of the house. It was a nice single-family home on a large lot in this cul-de-sac of maybe six or eight houses, all of a similar size. At first glance, I saw an SUV parked in the driveway, facing the garage. The garage door was open, and a person laid slumped over in the center of the garage toward the back wall. A man was standing near the SUV, talking on a cell phone. The front door to the home was open. In the rearview mirror, I saw Jordan Reynolds pull up his patrol car behind me. Rural Metro Fire Department was already on scene, and I saw their personnel in the driveway and, more importantly, in the garage with the body. There was always a sense of comradery with them. During a regular shift, we would often meet them several times as they'd respond to the same incident. Unfortunately, they knew little about crime scene management and were concerned only with aiding the person in need. In a joking way, we kept referring to them as the EDS or Evidence Destruction Squad, because we often had more bloody footprints coming from firefighter boots than anything else at a crime scene.

I stepped out and asked Jordan if he could talk to the guy in the driveway. He nodded. The Fire Captain approached me and told me how they had arrived about a minute or two before us. The man in the garage was dead, he said. We walked over to the garage, while he told me the family had found the deceased. Mindful of my entering a crime scene, I looked at the scene in the garage. The dead man was properly dressed. He was lying parallel to the back wall, on his face, and turned away from me. Taking a few steps further to my left and angling my approach so I could begin to see the other side of his body, I continuously scanned the room and the body's surroundings for anything that might stand out to me as out of place or possibly connected to what had taken place here. Look beyond the obvious, they had told us in the academy.

By now, I had seen a fair number of dead people. It was part of our patrol routine. If someone was found dead or had died in the presence of someone else, we were called to make sure no crime had occurred unnoticed. The investigation of a death had become part of my toolbox. Seeing and dealing with a dead body was no longer something that affected me emotionally, the same way it did early on. After seeing it more or less regularly and having to deal with investigative aspects surrounding a person who had died in their bed, someone who had blown off most of their head with a shotgun, poisoned themselves with the exhaust from their car, died in a car crash, or any other variety of causes of death, I had learned to "deal with it." Dealing with it, I would come to find out years later, meant to disassociate from it and put it away. Put it away in an area of memory only accessed during trial or other kinds of case reviews. I had learned to put it aside, to supplant it. In addition, I had learned to turn my initial curiosity into investigative vigor. Asking questions, looking for explanations, evaluating statements under the circumstances present at the time an event occurred, had become activities I found deeply satisfying. My years of working in enterprise sales, which requires a good deal of investigative work itself, had proven very helpful. I knew how to talk to people and make them feel comfortable when answering my questions. The only difference was that now I "sold" investigative services to protect my community.

Evidently, the man had fallen forward. He was lying with his head in a bed of cat litter, which itself had been placed on a black trash bag. The cat litter had a bright red color and blood had spilled past it onto the spread-out plastic. "We put the gun over here," the Fire Captain announced and pointed to a small revolver on a step near the interior door. "It's a .22. Went in, twirled around at high speed, and turned his brain to mush. No exit wound." What a picture to paint, I thought. And, of course, they were firefighters and medics. They were not concerned with the preservation of the scene and evidence. They had trampled all over the place, touched or moved things. And a strange scene it was. It looked as if the deceased had taken every precaution to not cause a mess.

I thanked the Fire Captain and his crew. He asked if they were okay to leave, and I said I'd catch up with them later if I needed any additional information. Jordan came back with a roll of crime scene tape and roped off the driveway. He had not spoken with anyone yet, as he had to keep the neighbors from coming too close and witness what they didn't need to see. The dignity of the deceased was something we were responsible for now that we were here. I got on the radio and called for OME to respond and pick up the body. It would take a while for them to get there, and it didn't hurt to ask for them early on. Jordan said he'd take pictures of the scene when he finished roping off the place. Then I went inside the home and called out, "Hello?" The answer came promptly, "Yes, over here." The home was immaculate on the inside. From the appearance of furniture and interior design, it seemed the people living there were well off. Following the voice, I ended up in the kitchen, where I met with a woman and a younger man, maybe in his late twenties, early thirties. In introducing themselves, I learned the woman was the wife of the deceased and the man was his son. In separate conversations with each of them, I learned that the deceased had suffered from cancer. While the mother and son had left the house to run an errand, he apparently prepared the setup in the garage. The son described how they came back, rolled up the driveway, and he had used the remote control to open the garage door. As soon as the garage door began to rise, they heard a gunshot and through the ever-increasing opening, he saw his father fall forward. It seemed they had come back earlier than anticipated, which led to mother and son witnessing their father's violent moment of death. I felt terrible for them.

The emotional burden of victims, relatives, friends, or witnesses was something I had not yet been able to handle well. Nor would I truly ever be able to. It was the suffering, the misery of those left behind that stuck with me most often. Sure, I joined in on the gallows' humor that was ever present at the scene of a violent crime. The kind of cynical, dark humor used by all involved to cope with what humans should otherwise not need to see or deal with. But the sorrow, the feeling of loss, despair, and helplessness is what frequently got to me. It often felt like being sucker punched. It was the people and their struggle to understand what had happened, their struggle to cope with the inevitability of a tragic event. It was them who would often "visit" me at night when I lay down to rest.

Yes, it was easy in this country to take your own life. Straight forward, just put a gun to your head, easily available at your local neighborhood gun store. No license needed. For home and self-protection as most people would say. Over the course of the coming years, however, I would have to witness the result of their destructive power used by their owners against themselves countless times. It was easier to advocate for gun rights and to satisfy the urge felt by so many to execute their constitutional right to arm themselves, than to deal with the larger question of why a free, civilized, highly developed society in the 21st century saw the need to arm themselves to the teeth. The question would come up again and again. I never had a problem with gun ownership, especially as I had already owned one before I became a cop. But coming from Europe, the unexpected ease of obtaining a firearm, and the right to openly carry a weapon almost anywhere in the state (concealed carry without a license became legal in the following years) was outright scary. In this job, nothing was left to my imagination. Time and time again, I had to witness how the use of firearms had resulted in deformed, damaged, and destroyed bodies and lives, often enough self-inflicted.

There was another case that ended deadly during my first few months in the Foothills district. That one started out as a domestic violence call.

TOM PEINE

It was at a gas station where I met with a woman, who tearfully explained and described her ordeal of dealing with a physically and mentally abusive husband. That day, he had tormented her again and for the first time, she had found the courage to call for help. Having fled from her house, she ended up at the gas station, where there were other people, offering her a sense of relative safety. Her husband, according to her description, had gone off the deep end this time. She was simply too scared to return home. She told me, while intermittently looking over my shoulder, how he would probably be roaming the streets in his pickup truck looking for her. We agreed for her to stay with a friend. As part of my investigation, I drove over to their home to see if I could interview the husband, but he and his car were indeed gone.

As I had broadcast his license plate over the radio, a sergeant in the area had noticed the car in traffic and attempted to stop him for questioning. The car took off on him. It ended up driving across lanes into a desert area, where it crashed into a Palo Verde tree. I arrived within a minute of all this, and we found him dead behind the steering wheel. It was not the impact of the tree that had killed him. He had put a Glock handgun in his mouth and blew his brains all over the interior of the cabin. Little pieces of his skull bone were stuck against the inside of the windshield. I couldn't help but feel sorry for someone like him. Other deputies were more cynical and considered it a problem solved. What demons may have possessed someone to do the terrible things he had done to his wife and to himself? Nobody seemed to really care. Alleged perpetrator dead, problem solved.

And then there were other firsts. Like the case in Beat 5, where I had to arrest a 10-year-old for attacking her mother with a pair of scissors. Placing a child in handcuffs, no matter how they behave, was one of the worst experiences to have. It was all justified—but still.

It was not all doom and gloom, though. Some calls would leave me shaking my head. Like the one where someone had called in vandalism by neighborhood youth. Upon arrival, the homeowner showed me the remains of three or four raw eggs that had been smashed in his driveway.

DEPUTY WHILE IMMIGRANT

Yes, he had called 911 to report that his driveway had been egged. Why this was even dispatched, I'm not certain. I asked him if he had a garden hose and then hosed down his precious driveway. Problem solved.

Or the situation where I was called in as an interpreter for the first time. Other deputies were dealing with a depressed, pregnant woman who had expressed her intention to commit suicide. Then suddenly she had stopped talking with the deputies and switched to a language they did not speak: German. They called me over the radio for assistance. Upon arrival at the house, I learned from fellow deputies they had checked her papers and she was indeed German. I went into the bedroom, where I found her lying on the bed, sobbing. Without "warning" and in plain German, I addressed her and asked what was going on. She was completely stunned and unable to respond. She just looked at me and tried to put together in her head what she was looking at and what she was hearing. Still with an undertone of disbelief she asked, "Sind Sie Deutscher?" (Are you German?) In response, I explained my being German/American and why I had been called out here to help. That puzzled look by Germans when they would encounter me in my official capacity as Deputy Sheriff, paired with my native Westphalian German, was something I would experience on several other occasions in the years to come. The situation with this young lady resolved smoothly. My ability to have a calm conversation with her in her native tongue led to her agreeing to be transported for further psychiatric evaluation and help.

On a different occasion, I was asked to relieve a deputy who had been assigned to University Medical Center (UMC) to guard an arrestee while he received treatment, following a shootout with another deputy. The suspect had been shot in the leg by the deputy and was currently undergoing surgery at UMC. As the individual had been arrested at the scene, someone had to be with him at all times because he was in our custody. In addition, there was evidence to be retrieved as the projectile fired from the deputy's gun was still inside the suspect's leg. The currently assigned deputy was coming up on the end of his shift and still had to write his report.

TOM PEINE

Upon arrival at UMC, I was in the emergency department trying to figure out where I had to go to relieve my coworker. After a few minutes, I ended up outside an area of a set of operating rooms sealed off from the public. I rang the little doorbell next to the access doors, and a short while later, a nurse came and said, "Oh, the other deputy is already waiting for you." I was led down a hallway and into a room next to the operating room (OR). The nurse instructed me to remain in the specific area inside the OR she would point out to me. Should I intend to go anywhere else in the OR—or need to move from the designated area for any reason—I had to ask for approval by the surgeon first. Then she helped me put on a sterile gown, shoe covers, and gloves. Everything went on top of my uniform. Within minutes, I was roasting. She said, "You'll get pretty hot in there." And she was not kidding. The operating room was heated to Floridian summer levels. The other deputy looked at me with a broad smile on his face. "I must have a lost three pounds just from standing here," he said and walked out the door I had just entered through. There were two female nurses and a doctor performing the surgery. The patient was covered in green sheets. Only one of his legs was visible and had been partially propped up. The thigh had been cut open, and the doctor was wearing special magnifying glasses to have a better view of the obviously delicate work he was performing on the patient's vascular system. A large pool of blood had formed on the floor of the room, underneath the operating table. That must have occurred earlier, I thought, as it didn't seem to be bleeding enough now. Most strikingly, rock music was playing from speakers in the ceiling.

The doctor, who was humming along, said, "Have you ever watched a surgery?"

"No, I never had the opportunity," I responded truthfully.

"You can come a little closer if it doesn't bother you. I'm working to fix this guy's leg," the doctor said, and I stepped in a little closer. However, I also tried to maintain an appropriate distance. I was there as a guard and not a medical apprentice. The doctor's work was fascinatingly intricate. How he was able to successfully navigate his way through the tangled mess the suspect's leg had turned into was beyond me.

"Hey, can you do me a favor, Deputy? Can you talk to your buddy who shot this guy and send him out to the range for some extra practice?"

What? Did he seriously just say that? Did he mean to say what I thought he said? Our conversation remained minimal afterward. He finished up about 90 minutes later, and when the patient was pushed into the wake-up room, I was relieved by a Corrections Officer. I returned to my district and had to share my experience with the guys from my squad.

Last but not least, there was one of the more infamous incidents of my time in Foothills. Far north and past the next incorporated town of Oro Valley, there is a beat which consists of the area surrounding a then small, unincorporated community called Catalina. The northern boundary of that community was the border to the county north of us, Pinal County. Especially during weekends, I was sometimes the only Deputy up there. If backup was needed, I had to make that call early enough, because it would take my coworkers some 20 minutes, depending on where they were coming from, to head up my way and assist me. It was the classic Deputy Sheriff situation where you had to "think on your feet" to survive and handle potentially critical situations with vigilance and foresight.

This particular call was a very low-key kind of affair, however. I was near our little substation, located along the main strip through this growing community, when the dispatcher called my designator. They sent me to a "Check Welfare" call. Checking on someone's welfare was one of those regularly occurring calls. It sounds deceivingly unexciting. Yet, you'd never know what you would walk into. These calls could range from a neighbor's concern about not having seen the person next door for several days, to someone being concerned about a child's appearance, or a friend who had just received a phone call from a buddy of theirs and the person on the other end sounded incoherent or suicidal. People called from out of state, out of country, or from next door to the location in question.

My call concerned a property just west of the substation. The description was about someone who had not been seen for a while and the man would not answer his phone either. I pulled over onto the dirt shoulder of the state highway and called the reporting party to gather as much information as I could about the person they wanted me to check on. Then I called the individual my caller was concerned about. He didn't answer the phone. It just so happened that the home of the person I was supposed to check on was right around the corner. I drove back to the area behind the substation, where there were a few trailer homes. One of them belonged to the person my caller was concerned about. While it had only been two days since they had last spoken, it was unusual, as they would typically talk several times a day.

Thick dark clouds built up over my head as I drove up onto the dusty lot in front of the home. Nobody was outside and I could not see anybody near the property. I got out of my car and looked around back, to no avail. Then I walked up to the front door and loudly knocked, announcing myself: "Sheriff's Department! Come to the door!" I took two steps back and to the side to wait. Nothing happened. I tried knocking again and then listened to hear anything. Nothing. It was dead quiet, with "dead" being the word of concern. Grabbing the knob of the front door, I turned it and found it to be open, which was not all that unusual out here. People would often leave their homes or cars unlocked. I opened the door wide and called out for anybody inside, again identifying myself as Deputy Sheriff. Still nothing. Then I carefully turned around the open front door in a semi-circle from left to right to get a good view of the interior as far as I could see from out here without entering. As I came about halfway, I noticed a person lying face down inside. It looked like a man. At that point, I laid my right hand on my handgun and called out again. Maybe the person was only unconscious or heavily intoxicated. I resisted the urge to simply rush in, as I didn't know if anybody else was inside. It remained silent. Could I trust the obvious scene? To be sure, I drew my service weapon and stepped up the stairs and into the trailer. Ah, dang it! I forgot to tell my dispatcher what was going on here and that I had entered the trailer. Quickly, I grabbed my lapel mic and advised over the radio that I had found a person down and was about to clear the trailer.

DEPUTY WHILE IMMIGRANT

I took a step forward and addressed the person on the ground. "Sir, can you hear me?" Then I gave the bottom of his shoe a slight tap with my boot. No reaction. I quickly looked into each of the rooms inside the trailer to make sure there was nobody else inside and then returned to the man on the floor. Now, standing closer, I noticed the waxen appearance of the man's skin and the grayish color. From the back pocket of my pants, I pulled a pair of exam gloves. My gun went back into its holster, and I squatted down next to the man's body to confirm the obvious. In touching the skin on his neck to see if I could find a pulse, the cold sensation I felt through the latex covering my gloved finger gave proof that he had been dead for some time. Now that I was even closer, I could see that lividity had built on the left side of his face, the side that was touching the floor. The purple discoloration was blood underneath the skin that had pooled following gravity once the heart of the deceased had stopped pumping. A medical telltale sign of death. Rigor mortis had already passed, so he must have died some time ago, yet I did not notice any obvious decay yet. The weather had been cool in recent days and had slowed the otherwise rapid decomposition of the body we would regularly encounter in this heat-prone part of the country. I got on the radio.

"1-1-4-2."

"1-1-4-2, go ahead."

"Code 900. Could you start OME, please?"

"10-4. Code 900 at 12-31. I'll notify OME."

12:31 p.m. would be noted as the official time this person was pronounced dead. In obvious cases like these, there was no need to call for medics. As Deputy Sheriff, we were entitled by law to pronounce a person dead.

Then began my routine investigation of the scene. As an investigator with OME was on his way, I decided to take pictures of the body once he was there. It would make the process easier. I went back outside to my car to grab my camera. My stomach growled. Yes, several months into my duty as Deputy Sheriff, I had grown so accustomed to the sight of a dead person that it no longer fazed my sensation of hunger. Was that a good thing? The camera was in the trunk of my patrol car. I decided to put it down on the kitchen counter inside the trailer and then eat the sandwich I had brought along for lunch just outside the front door of the trailer. Nothing inside would be disturbed and nobody could come back later and blame me for sitting in my car while "the body and all the evidence inside the trailer" were unmonitored. Stepping back into the trailer, I placed the camera case on top of the kitchen counter. Carefully stepping over the legs of the dead man, I stepped back outside to eat my sandwich. OME shouldn't be more than 20 minutes out, I thought. As soon as I stepped outside, the heavens opened their flood gates. The dark clouds over my head had turned into a near-black color. Suddenly, there were impacts all around me. Bean or gravel-sized hail was falling all around me. It was a massive downpour that turned everything white, seemingly in an instant. In a reflex, I stepped back into the trailer and, taking another bite from my sandwich, watched the onslaught of nature on my surroundings. Still chewing on my turkey sandwich with fresh lettuce, I turned around to walk over to the kitchen area. The body! I was standing inside a trailer home, eating my sandwich next to a corpse. There was no odor, though. The body was still intact, and the place was otherwise reasonably clean. What was I supposed to do? Stand there, sandwich in hand, and wait for the hail shower to pass? No, no. I was hungry and just because there was a dead man lying on the floor, I wouldn't lose my composure. And I was much friendlier when, a few minutes later, the OME investigator showed up and we went about our business.

    The first few months in the Foothills district provided for a lot of valuable lessons. Many more calls and incidents happened that would go beyond the frame of a book chapter to cover them all. The fact was that I was well on my way to becoming a regular member of the squad. However, the daily commute of ninety minutes or longer was something I dreaded. So, I decided to see if I could get transferred closer to home. In my written request for transfer at the time of the upcoming shift change (three times a year, promotions, shift assignments and possible district transfers would occur simultaneously and department-wide), I laid out an efficiency case. Every day, I put a significant amount of mileage on my patrol car driving from the Southeast of Tucson to the Northwest. Command staff appeared receptive and eventually confirmed that I would transfer over to the Rincon district (the district in which I lived). Obviously, that got me very excited and on the day prior to the anticipated shift change, while I was back in the Foothills District office, I ran into our new District Commander, who had started his new assignment there only a few days prior. I thought I'd say "thank you" for supporting my transfer request and greeted him. He was receptive and friendly. After initial hesitation and trying to locate my name on the invisible org chart in his head, the commander looked at me and said, "Peine, right? You wanted to go to Rincon?"

"Yes, sir. That's what I was told would happen."

"Yeah, no. You'll report to Green Valley tomorrow at 2200 hours," he said.

I was stunned. *Green Valley?* That was a retirement community. And midnight shift? "Yes, sir. Of course. Who do I report to over there?"

7

ON THE BORDER

The first night I drove into my new work district, still reeling from the unexpected development and certainly a tad upset, it immediately became clear what a difference the shortened commute would make. The Green Valley District bordered Rincon's rural Beat 1, where I lived, and was much closer than the northwest side of Tucson. From our driveway to the district boundary, it was a mere 15-minute drive. Green Valley was an unincorporated community of some 20,000 inhabitants, located approximately 40 miles north of the international border with Mexico and 20 miles south of Tucson. With more than 70 % of people living there being over the age of 65, the median age identified in census statistics was 72. It was a place where any kind of noteworthy activity on the streets would cease around 8:00 p.m. Germans would refer to this as "folding up the sidewalks at dusk." This is where I would patrol from 10:00 p.m. to 6:00 a.m. every day of my work week.

I drove to the district office and met my new squad: two other deputies and a sergeant. Sergeant Cross was a veteran and, for once, someone older than me. He was the salty, stereotypical kind of sergeant, hardened by years of experience as a deputy, detective, undercover investigator, and patrol sergeant. The hash marks on his uniform sleeve, indicating his long years of duty for the department, reminded me of a crosswalk going up the side of his arm. The Green Valley District office was distinctly different from Foothills. The squad briefing room was neat and clean.

Each deputy had a postbox with an etched nameplate in front of it. It all seemed much more organized, newer, and cleaner. The main difference, however, was the much, much lower call volume. Our patrol area was vast and consisted mostly of uninhabited desert wilderness. There were only two other noteworthy settlements. Located to the south and either bordering Santa Cruz County or the Republic of Mexico were Amado (population approximately 300) and Arivaca (population around 900). Both of those locations were known hubs for drug and human smuggling. Coming from Green Valley, it could take thirty minutes or more to get to Arivaca with lights and siren. The area was remote, often leaving us without either radio or cell phone coverage. And then there was the main highway going north-south, Interstate 19. It was the main connection and transit route between the state of Sonora, Mexico and Arizona, easily recognizable and unique because it was part of a test project in the United States where distances on the signs were marked in kilometers. It also lacked mile markers, but instead had kilometer markers. At night, there were typically no state troopers on the freeway, otherwise responsible for everything happening on the highway, often leaving the initial response to emergencies on this roadway to us.

The first event I remember happening down there involved the U.S. Border Patrol (USBP). Our sergeant called another rookie deputy, also newly assigned to the district, and me on our cell phones. A USBP agent had pursued a fleeing vehicle, suspected of smuggling drugs. The pursuit ended in a shootout, and he wanted us to go down to the Amado area and find the USBP scene supervisor. We should tell him that we had been sent by our sergeant to get a look at what had happened, see the evidence, and learn as much as we could from observing the scene. "Observe and learn. Don't get in the way," he instructed us. I thought that it was really cool to be able to see something like that.

Daniel Parker, the other deputy, and I drove up to the scene on the eastside of I-19. There were a lot of marked USBP vehicles and several unmarked cars. We parked our patrol cars on the side of the street, near a cattle fence, and walked up to the first car asking for the scene supervisor.

DEPUTY WHILE IMMIGRANT

It felt empowering to simply walk up to a crime scene with all these federal agents and to gain access to the scene and basic information about what had occurred simply by asking. You may say, "Well, of course. You're a cop." But that was still, a few months in, a new normal, a new situation. It felt special to be able to do that.

As we came closer to the main scene of the incident, lit up only by the high beams and take-down lights of USBP patrol vehicles surrounding it, I noticed a strong odor. The whole area smelled like skunk. The supervisory agent met us, and we explained our reason for being there. He politely gave us a brief summary of what had occurred and said we could look around if we wanted to. We were then hooked up with another agent at the scene, who walked us around the two involved vehicles.

The perpetrators had driven a Chevy Suburban with extremely dark tinted windows. Now that we were next to the SUV, I realized that this was the source of the smell. The agent who was with us opened the back door and we instantly stood in an overwhelming cloud of marijuana odor. The whole back of the car was filled with bales of marijuana. Yes, I said bales. At this point, I had seen joints and plastic sandwich bags of marijuana, mostly weighing in at a few measly ounces. Now, I was looking at hundreds of pounds of it, pressed into bales, in the back of an SUV. The agent said they had estimated it to be some 500 pounds. Whoa!

Right behind the Suburban, sat an unmarked, black Dodge Challenger. The vehicle had two slim light bars against the inside top of the windshield, which were alternating red and blue, dowsing everything around us in this familiar color pattern. The headlights also flashed alternatingly, and additional emergency lights had been mounted inside the vehicle's grill. I loved this car. It looked aggressive and very bold. Then I noticed the bullet holes in the windshield. Our chaperone agent explained that his colleague had attempted to conduct a traffic stop to investigate the Suburban. It was likely that he had smelled the dope or otherwise had a suspicion about the vehicle and its occupants. When he activated his lights, the Suburban took off, and a pursuit began. It ultimately ended up in a pasture, in front of a cattle gate the Suburban had crashed into. The driver had backed up, hitting the front of the Challenger that had stopped right behind them. In a panic, the driver apparently tried once again to crash through the gate and got stuck. At some point shots were fired in both directions. The pursuing agent was not hit. I'm not sure if one of the occupants of the Suburban was hit or not, but I seem to remember that one of them sat handcuffed in the back of a USBP patrol car nearby. We briefly met the agent who had pursued the SUV. He was bitching about his brand-new undercover (UC) car, which he had been issued only two days prior. He was fine.

So, this is what they called a quiet patrol district. True. But it was also the area where the powerful and vicious Mexican drug cartels conducted their business. It may have seemed quiet on the surface, but the cartels were ruthless in the pursuit of their interests and protection of their "goods." Now, I understood why our Sergeant had sent us out here. It was his way of teaching us to be vigilant, careful, and smart. What we had seen and heard at this scene taught us more than an hour of our Sergeant telling us to be on guard when doing our job out here. Humbled and with a heightened awareness, Daniel and I left to get back to our patrol duties.

A week or two later, Daniel had pulled over a car on the southbound on-ramp to I-19 in Amado. It was maybe a half mile as the crow flies from where the shooting had occurred weeks earlier. The driver of the car ended up having a suspended license and, given the remote location and the time of day, it would take a while for the tow truck to come all the way out here. I decided to join Daniel and be available as backup if needed. It took me some 15 minutes to get to where he had stopped the car. With his patrol car sitting behind the offender, he was talking to the driver by the trunk of the police car. The wrecker had been called already, and the suspended driver of the car was in the process of calling a friend to be picked up here. Fortunately, he was a local, and it didn't take too long for his buddy to arrive and take him away. We had some time to shoot the breeze. It was a cold desert night, and it seemingly took forever for the tow truck to arrive. After an hour of waiting, Daniel looked at me and said, "You think it's okay to call Comm and check on the tow?"

"Absolutely!" I said, thinking that an hour was certainly plenty of time to wait. "I got it," I offered and went back to my car.

"1-1-4-2."

"1-1-4-2, go ahead," Sophia, the dispatcher on our frequency, responded.

"Do we have an ETA for the 9-2-6?"

"I'll check and advise."

But then something happened. Something I had experienced only once before. Unbeknown to the dispatcher, her radio key got jammed and she was still broadcasting. This is called an "open mic" and is every dispatcher's nightmare. She thought she had released the key and the line was down. Not so. I could hear her breathing and then, apparently talking to herself, she said, "Oh, the 9-2-6. Just hold your pants, would you?" Then some humming a song and more breathing, paired with the sound of her fingers hitting the keyboard when typing. All of this went out over the air, audible to all deputies who had turned to this frequency. Then I heard someone yelling in the background, "East 1 open mic!" The last I heard Sophia say was, "Oh sh—" then the frequency was cleared, the speaker fell mum.

I flipped open my phone and called Communications (or Comm), our term for the dispatch center.

"North 1. This is Emily."

"Hi Emily! It's Tom Peine, 1-1-4-2. Can I speak to East 1, please?"

"Sure. Hold on."

A few moments of silence.

"East 1. This is Sophia."

"Hey Sophia. This is Tom. 1-1-4-2. I'm still holding my pants out here and wanted to see if you had heard back from the tow company."

"Oh my god!" she laughed out loud. "I am so sorry. I didn't mean it in a bad way."

"I know. I know. Just couldn't resist and had to call to give you some grief."

"I understand," she was still giggly. "The tow should be there in the next 15 or so."

"Alright. That's all I wanted to know. Thanks. Talk to you later."

This would follow me around for a while. When we came back to the district office, the Sergeant and the third deputy on shift asked, of course, how long we had been holding our pants out there. I learned that an open-mic situation could certainly be funny at the expense of the deputy in the field.

Encounters with USBP were frequent down here. Especially during calls that had a higher degree of risk involved, USBP agents would often come to assist or stop out with us to make sure we were okay. There were several occasions where I came upon one of them while engaged in a traffic stop and I joined them as backup. It felt good to know that we would have each other's backs.

Patrolling the Green Valley district involved a lot of driving. Being responsible for such a vast area, most of it uninhabited, could be challenging. Yet, the citizens who lived there expected us to respond to their emergencies just as expeditiously as we would anywhere else. Coming through the Amado area one night, I came through what one may consider the center of this community. In a dirt lot across the street from a few stores and near a well-known steakhouse that had an entrance shaped like a giant cow skull, three buses were parked. This was at a time where there were several hundred thousand people apprehended each year, after they had tried to illegally cross the US-Mexico border, in USBP's Tucson sector alone. It was an eerie scene. The three buses looked just like the ones Greyhound was using at the time. But on the side, it said "Wackenhut" instead. In our cop humor, we sarcastically referred to them as "Whack 'n Fuck." They were a USBP contractor, tasked with transporting the masses of apprehended border crossers to the nearest USBP processing and detention center. In front of the buses, kneeling or sitting in the dirt, were probably about a hundred people. Most of them looked disheveled and dirty, some with torn clothes. There were men, women, and children. Walking around among them with clipboards, occasionally asking a question of one of the people on the ground, were

DEPUTY WHILE IMMIGRANT

USBP agents. It was a busy scene, but calm. No more running.

These were the people who had sometimes traveled thousands of miles across Central America to make it to the US-Mexico border. They had paid a guide, called a "coyote" to bring them across. Sometimes they were being picked up on the US side, but often they were left to fend for themselves and find their own way. Female border crossers were especially vulnerable and frequently ended up getting raped. If someone in a group led by a coyote got injured or became sick, they were simply left behind, often to die. USBP agents weren't sure if there were still coyotes among the captured. It was difficult to discern who was a smuggler and who was simply an undocumented alien (UDA). In talking to one of the USBP agents, I learned that this night "someone must have opened the floodgates on the other side." The cartels would often do this to overwhelm USBP agents and tie them up for hours on end and then use the opportunity to push through big drug loads transported by vehicle. Also, it was winter and illegal crossers had a much better chance of surviving the treacherous journey. Death from exhaustion and heat was very common during the summer months. The agent said, "This is the third set of buses we're about to fill. A fourth is en route." He estimated they had about 120 to 150 seated in the dirt right there. Then he stoically added, "We may reach 1,000 tonight."

I couldn't help but notice and acknowledge to myself how lucky I had been. An immigrant myself, I had married an American, which rendered my situation incomparably different. Once we decided to move to the U.S. permanently, back in 2000, we were already married. All I had to do is turn in half a forest worth of paperwork and forms, and pay roughly $2,000 for all sorts of fees and dues. I was summoned to the U.S. General Consulate in Frankfurt a few weeks later to present some original documents, be interviewed, and go through a medical exam. The interview took place through the glass barrier of a service counter and lasted all but 2 minutes. Afterwards, I had to walk to a doctor's office nearby to undergo a medical exam, including a blood test and an x-ray to prove that I was free from tuberculosis (TB). A few years later, I started the process of naturalization to become a U.S. citizen. While I was sworn in a citizen in Tucson, we still lived in Boston at the time I started the process. I spent hours and hours and a few thousand dollars more at the offices of what was then called the Immigration and Naturalization Service or INS. Waiting for my 5 minute or so interviews, I sat among people from all over the world. Individuals from Africa, Asia, Europe, including a few fellow Germans. Interesting enough, when I went through the medical screening of the Sheriff's Department's selection process approximately two years later, I tested positive for the presence of the TB virus (By the way, one can carry the virus but not be infectious). Knowing that I had tested negative upon entering the U.S., I reengineered that it was most likely-and ironically-during all those hours of waiting among people from across the world at the INS office in Boston that I picked up the virus. Consequently, I had to undergo a fairly aggressive pharmaceutical treatment for nine months, monitored by the Pima County Public Health Department. The treatment included a notice that I should not be alarmed when I notice my urine changing color to a disturbing deep orange. That was an anticipated side effect of the medication and no sign for alarm. So yes, I did it all by the book dictated by my circumstances at the time-and it made me TB-positive.

These people were driven by either fear, desperation, or desire. And for those reasons, they risked everything, life and limb. If they did not have enough money to pay the cartel-controlled smugglers, they would often end up carrying drug loads strapped to their backs. Doing so two, three, or more times would "buy" them a ticket with the coyote. I had to get back out on patrol again, but thoughts of that particular scene with all those people sitting in the dirt lot stayed with me for a long time. How privileged I was.

It was one of those nights that was otherwise utterly boring. We had all but three calls for service so far. At around 2:00 a.m., I pulled up on the I-19 on-ramp at Canoa Ranch, parked slightly below eye level, still on the ramp, and blacked out. The agent said they might try to push a drug load through and could haul it north on the Interstate as we spoke. By

DEPUTY WHILE IMMIGRANT

2:30 a.m., two vehicles had passed my position, both of them compact-sized cars. I gave up and drove back to Green Valley to see if I could find anything up there.

All of this reminded me of the time when we had moved into our new house in Vail. During construction, there were a number of illegals involved on all building sites in our community. Interesting enough, one of our new neighbors was a USBP agent and at times came by to check on the building progress of his house. He told us about a day where he swung by in his marked USBP patrol vehicle as he was on his way from Sonoita back to the main station in Tucson. He described how as he drove into the neighborhood, he could see construction workers run into the desert and toward the nearby Interstate as soon as one of them had spotted his car.

On one of my "weekend" days, I met our neighbor from across the street. He told me how he had been watching TV the previous night and fell asleep in his Lazy Boy. He was awakened by a noise and, still reclined in his chair, tried to figure out the source of the noise. When he looked over at the patio windows, he noticed a man peeping through the glass. They noticed each other at about the same time and were both startled. My neighbor said he could see him run off through the moonlit desert landscape toward the highway. It was likely that it was a UDA, looking for a place to sleep or some water and food. In the early days of this remote neighborhood, when only a few houses were occupied, we saw them come through, walking toward the Interstate, which was to our north. Time and again a USBP helicopter would circle over or near our house in search of the illegals. As more and more houses were finished, and owners had moved in, the activity died down. Paired with the eventual emergence of landscape walls around everyone's property, the risk of being discovered before they could reach their pickup point had increased significantly and it had become too dangerous to come near our neighborhood.

It was easy to pass judgement on those labeled with the acronym UDA. Many people simply saw them as law breakers. And they were. Yet, that quick general judgement fell short of acknowledging the much more complex reality. We also had to take into account the incredible draw this country created with all its riches, its rule of law, stable society, and relative lack of constant, unimaginable cartel violence or civil war. Why would anyone otherwise make this terribly dangerous journey? There was plenty of wealth to share and most Americans readily accepted the all too pleasant "side effects" of cheap laborers, who were capable and willing to do the jobs most U.S. citizens would not consider for themselves. The temptation of this glamorous world right in front of their geographical nose was real. The lure was only intensified by the fact that a lot of farmers, contractors, and landscapers offered them jobs hundreds of times more lucrative than those they could find at home. They didn't mean to harm anyone. All they wanted was a piece of the pie for themselves and their families. The crimes were typically committed by those who already lived here, legally. For most UDAs it was too dangerous to risk being discovered and get arrested, which would also dry up the money flow for their loved ones at home in Guatemala, Nicaragua, Mexico, or elsewhere.

One cold night, while on patrol, returning from Amado back to the Green Valley area, I noticed a person sitting on an I-19 guardrail. Knowing already who I was about to encounter, I slowed down, pulled over onto the shoulder, and got on my radio.

"1-1-4-2. I-19 northbound. I'll be out with a Code 81. Start BP for one."

"1-1-4-2, 10-4 at 0-4-53."

As I got out of my patrol car and walked toward the man, he was blinded by my take-down lights and shielded his eyes with his left hand. He looked tired and cold. It was about 5:00 a.m. "Good morning, sir." All he had with him was a green backpack and the smell of someone who hadn't had a chance to shower in several days. He slowly raised his head and looked at me. "I'm done," he said. "Just take me to Border Patrol," he said with a noticeable Spanish accent. He was out of water, food, and most importantly, he was cold and exhausted from his treacherous journey. While he had come a long way, he had reached the end of his rope. I asked where he was going, and he said his goal had been to get to Los Angeles. What's in LA? His family. Wife, three daughters, his house and job. "What kind of work do you do?" I was curious to know and learned he was a tile layer.

He was very cooperative, and I asked if he wanted to sit in the back of my patrol car where it was much warmer. Only condition: I would have to give him a thorough pat down to make sure he wasn't carrying any weapons. He agreed and about two minutes later, was seated in the back of my car, soaking up the warmth from the heater. While I ran a wants-and-warrants check on him, I learned he'd been living in the U.S. for almost 20 years, got to know his wife in California and started a family. We kept talking, and I wondered why someone like him would risk everything to go back to Mexico, knowing fair well that he'd have to illegally cross the international border and make his way back to LA. He looked at me and his whole posture turned into that of a defeated man. "My mother passed away. I had to go and help arrange her funeral. I'm glad I went, and that I was able to say my goodbyes." Just for a second, put yourself into his shoes.

"1-1-4-2."

"1-1-4-2, go ahead."

"Do you have an ETA for BP?"

It took a few moments, and the dispatcher came back on air.

"1-1-4-2, ETA for BP is 45 minutes to one hour."

In my head played Sergeant Cross's voice asking me why I spent an hour or more tied down on the side of the Interstate, unable to respond to any other calls while waiting for federal law enforcement, who most likely were just now dealing with the exact same issue, only on a much larger scale. This was one guy. His wants-and-warrants check came back negative, and he was staring out the rear window into the cold desert night. At this point, given my location, the time of day, our staffing situation, and the fact that I was dealing with a single, highly cooperative individual, who for all I could tell did not pose any kind of threat, there was not much else I could reasonably do.

"1-1-4-2, 10-4. Cancel BP. I'll be 10-8."

"1-1-4-2, 10-4. 10-8 at 0-5-0-8."

I gave him $10 and told him that on the other side of the Interstate was a McDonald's. There he'd be able to get a hot coffee and some food in his stomach. He looked back at me in disbelief and became teary-eyed. "Graçias. Thank you, sir. God bless you." I opened the back door to let him out. We shook hands, and he started walking on the shoulder toward the off-ramp in a distance. He turned around twice and waved. Yes, it was a different story when you met a UDA in person. When it became up close and personal.

A few weeks later, just on the other side of I-19, I sat at a traffic light. It was an intersection where, across from a Safeway store, the road to Amado turned off south and met with Continental Road of Green Valley. As was typical for this area at around 1:00 a.m., there was no traffic whatsoever. So, I sat at the traffic light and had lowered my headlights. The signal kept cycling through and I fooled around on my notebook computer installed in my car, when from my right (or south), I noticed a set of headlights coming toward the intersection. I turned my attention toward the lights. As the vehicle came closer, I was able to see that they belonged to an old Ford F-150. The light turned green for their street and the driver slowly pulled into the intersection, when he suddenly noticed my police car. It was an adult driver wearing a cowboy hat, and another person sat next to him in the passenger seat. The truck slowly continued through the intersection and drove past me to my left onto Continental Road. The entire time he drove around the front of my car, the driver looked straight at me. Now that was odd. People would certainly look at a cop car sitting in an intersection, especially at night and sparsely lit, but this was different. His eyes were glued to me. I instantly knew in my gut this was wrong. Not sure what it was, but this was wrong, and he was up to no good. I picked up my radio mic, when all of a sudden, the truck sped up and blasted up Continental Road. Aroused from my torpor, I quickly made a U-turn, turned on my headlights, and followed him. Just in time to see the vehicle make a right turn onto La Cañada. Through my open window, I could hear his tires squeal as he sped around the corner.

"1-1-4-2, I have a blue and white colored, older model F-150 speeding away on La Cañada going northbound. I don't have a plate yet. Unprovoked flight."

As soon as I had finished my transmission, I turned on lights and the siren. That guy was hauling ass! Adrenaline pumped through my veins, heightening all perceptions and sensations, as if all my senses had been hooked up to an amplifier. The sergeant came up on the radio and asked for traffic volume and speeds. I had not called a pursuit yet, but he wanted to be sure.

"No other traffic. Speeds coming up on 60."

At that very moment, I saw the truck, which was about 50 yards in front of me, suddenly veer left, through the raised median, tearing through cacti and other plants. It left debris in the roadway, caused a huge dust cloud and was now driving on the other side.

"Vehicle has just gone through the median, now going on the wrong side of the road. Still northbound."

The Sergeant keyed up again, "Terminate. Terminate."

It was his order to stop the pursuit, which meant I had to shut down the lights and siren and pull over to make it clear to the pursued driver that I was no longer following him. It had become too dangerous. Just as I reached down to flip the toggle on the Omnitrol and turn off my lights and siren, the truck's brake lights came on brightly and I rapidly gained on him. Then he turned off into a driveway. I passed it and used an intersection ahead to flip a U-turn. As I turned onto the opposite side, now going south, I noticed red and blue lights coming from behind me. That must be Daniel, I thought. I could see the pickup truck just ahead. It had pulled into a church parking lot or driveway. As I came up to the vehicle, I noticed people running everywhere. From the bed of the truck, a tarp had flipped over. People were still jumping out and running into the desert and further onto the church property.

"1-1-4-2, I have several runners. At least eight. I'm at St. Francis in the Valley."

Daniel pulled up in his patrol car behind me. I had jumped out of my car and made my way around the driver's side of the truck. With my weapon drawn and pointed at the open driver's side door, I quickly, but carefully, circled around to the front, making sure nobody was inside the cabin. I got a clear view of the interior and yelled out loud in Daniel's direction, "Clear!"

I holstered my gun to take off after those fleeing, when I saw two men step out of the desert and back into the parking lot. Once again, I drew my pistol and yelled at them, "Hands! Hands!" Nothing. They kept coming toward me, hands extended out in front of them, as if begging for mercy. They didn't understand. "Manos arriba!" They stopped and brought their hands up in the air. With the few Spanish words I knew, I tried to make sure they were unarmed. "Armas? Pistolas?" They shook their heads. I gestured for them to lower themselves onto their knees. "Abajo!" They followed my commands, but instead sat down. Daniel came over and put both his pairs of handcuffs on them. Once he brought them over to the pickup truck, I went into a small courtyard of the church. I holstered my gun again and used my flashlight to illuminate all corners. In the far left corner stood a woman. She was shaking and had buried her face in the palms of her hands. She stood at an angle, partially facing the wall, and was obviously terrified. If it would not have been such a tense moment, it could have been funny. I came closer and addressed her from a distance. "Policia!" She turned around and I could see that she was crying. "It's okay. Come on over here. Vamos aqui," I said in a softer tone, gesturing with my hand toward my left, where our patrol cars were parked near the entrance. She trotted toward me and I led her toward our cars and the pickup truck. The sergeant had arrived as well. All in all, we gathered 12 people in and around the church. They had no idea where they were and simply gave up. Using plastic flex cuffs we had in our patrol cars, we tied their hands to make sure nothing unexpected would happen. The sergeant, who spoke Spanish, asked if anyone was injured. That was not the case, and we called USBP to respond to our location. Daniel and I walked around and gave all of them some water we always carried in our cars. We didn't know if the "coyote" was still among them but would leave that investigation to the federal agents. Three of them responded and ended up requesting one of the "Whack 'n Fuck" buses for transport.

The most tragic incident involving UDAs happened only a few days later. It was in the wee hours of the morning and all of us were at the district office to complete reports, lock away evidence items seized earlier that night, and for a hot cup of coffee. I had just finished dictating a report over the phone when the radio silence broke. The announcement blared over the speaker of the radio installed in the briefing room.

"Green Valley, copy Rescue Follow-Up."

A Rescue Follow-Up was a call that was medical in nature initially, but the fire department had requested our response. I walked over to the radio, keyed up, gave my radio designator, and accepted the assignment. The fire department had responded to the Canoa rest area on I-19 for a call about a woman who had badly injured her foot. Two men were with her as well. It was not clear how she had been injured or what the role of the two men was.

We ran out to our cars and took off with lights and siren going south on I-19. Trying to anticipate what we might encounter, I ran possible scenarios in my head. While en route, we received radio updates informing us that there was no immediate danger at the rest area. Medics had considered calling for a helicopter to transport the injured woman. However, they felt, given their remote location, it would take too long for the helicopter to arrive and instead decided to transport the patient to Tucson by ambulance. The two men who were with the woman had assisted her and were not a threat. A few minutes later, the ambulance passed us in the northbound lanes racing toward the regional trauma center, Tucson University Medical Center (UMC).

When we finally arrived at the rest area, the fire truck was still there with one of the two men. He was Latino and in his mid-thirties. The other man was on board the ambulance to accompany the young woman to UMC. The witness' English was limited, but here is what we learned from him. He and the couple had made their way to Nogales, Mexico over the course of roughly three weeks. That night, they had decided it was time to cross. Once on the U.S. side, they boarded one of the slow moving, almost crawling freight trains. After a while, the train had slowed down to less than walking speed and almost stopped somewhere in the desert, but nowhere near Tucson, yet. Curious as to what was going on and not sure where they were, the younger of the two men had jumped off to get a better glimpse of what was going on up ahead. His girlfriend, tired and exhausted from the strenuous journey, had somehow ended up with one of her feet dangling in between the buffers of their train car and the train car in front of them. Just at that moment, the train came to a full stop. The cars were still moving and pushed toward the engine. While the young woman's foot was still in the void between the two buffers, the gap suddenly closed shut with the entire weight of the train car and all the subsequent cars behind it. While telling the story, the man became tearful and kept repeating that she was so young and didn't deserve this. He described how the woman, with her foot crushed in between the buffers, screamed in pain. The engine was too far away for anyone to hear, and at that point, they were still scared to be discovered as well.

Eventually, they were able to free the woman and laid her down on the ground. She had passed out and the two men began to fear for her life. Looking at the bottom of her leg, they couldn't see her foot anymore. Obviously, she was bleeding profusely. Using part of the young man's shirt, they created a makeshift tourniquet and applied it to her leg. In the distance, they could see the lights of the rest area on I-19 and decided to take her there. They took turns carrying the woman on their backs, walking down what turned out to be Elephant Head Road. They turned northbound on the Frontage Road until they reached the Interstate rest area. From there, they were able to call for help.

Daniel had retrieved his camera and took pictures of the man and an area on the pavement where there was a big blood stain. The fire captain said the two men likely saved the young woman's life by quickly applying the tourniquet. The man did not have any identification on him and, given the story he had just told us, I got on the radio and requested a USBP agent meet us at the rest area to determine what would happen to him. About 15 minutes later, the agent arrived and began his investigation.

DEPUTY WHILE IMMIGRANT

After talking to the fire captain and having learned from the witness that the woman's foot seemed to have been severed, we decided to drive out to the train tracks in an effort to find the incident location. Once there, we wanted to try to see if we could find the woman's foot. According to the fire captain, they had determined she was only 19 years old, and we wanted to do everything we could to help her. The USBP agent told me he would take the witness into custody and then gave me the man's personal information. I called Sergeant Cross and told him about our plan. He agreed with the caveat that we would have to stay 10-8 (In Service) and be available for emergency calls as there was otherwise nobody else to do so. We agreed and got into our cars. I keyed up on the radio and let the dispatcher know about our plan.

Driving down the Frontage Road, I imagined how the two men had carried the woman all this way, bleeding, clinging to life. In the darkness ahead, I saw the reflection of a street sign and then turned eastbound onto Elephant Head Road. It was a small, deserted roadway leading toward the mountains. No street lights, just leading into the pitch-black night. A few moments later, we came upon a level crossing, no barriers. I parked my patrol car on the dirt shoulder. Daniel stopped right behind me. The witness had described that they had been walking north and eventually came upon the crossing with a roadway. The train had started to roll toward Tucson again. Switching on our flashlights, Daniel and I walked southbound on the tracks. Stepping from tie to tie, we were looking for blood on the gravel. Given the witness' description, it should be easy to find. I had taken a large plastic Ziploc bag and had tucked it in the back of my pants. If we found the foot, I would have to have some kind of container to put it in for transport. I planned how I would have the sergeant meet me on my way back with ice from the cooler at the station to preserve as much of the tissue as possible. We had walked for about 5 minutes or so when my phone rang. It was one of the medics who had transported the woman to UMC. They had been informed about our search effort.

TOM PEINE

"Is this Deputy Peine?"

He mispronounced my last name, as was common, and instead said something like "Pynee."

"If you are still looking for the girl's foot, you can disregard. When they looked at that mangled mess here in the ER, they determined that... You know the bloody mess at the bottom of her leg? Yeah, that was her foot. You guys can stop looking."

I tried to picture the severity of the woman's injury and was grossed out by the thought. I looked at Daniel and said, "We can 10-22. They have her foot at the hospital. Or what's left of it."

Next, I called the sergeant to tell him what I had just learned. He instructed me to drive to Tucson and talk to the patient and her boyfriend. Get their information and story. Then come back as soon as possible.

It took me about a good half hour to get to the hospital. Firefighters had given me a jacket that belonged to the woman, so I could return it to her. It took me a few minutes to locate her and what turned out not to be her boyfriend, but her newlywed husband inside UMC. The woman was awake, her husband by her bedside. She was crying quietly, and the two were holding hands. I was approached by a nurse and learned that the doctors had just informed the young woman that they would have to amputate the bottom of her leg just above the knee. Good grief! I felt terrible. The USBP agent had called me on my way and told me that one of his colleagues was on his way to UMC to determine the husband's status. If he was illegal, as was to be expected, and given the circumstances, he said the husband could probably stay with his wife until after the surgery. But then he'd have to be picked up. Anyway, an agent was en route to meet with me.

I returned the woman's jacket, got her story, and also noted her husband's account. Wishing her all the best for her recovery, I left to drive back down to Green Valley. It was an emotionally crushing experience to see this young woman and her husband. All their dreams. They had risked everything. How would she deal with her missing limb back in Mexico? In the academy they had told us about these incidents that get to you. "You have to push it aside," they said. "Look at the case. It's a case you have to handle." That was what I was trying to do. Make it a case.

Of course, while they occur more often in this district than elsewhere, we didn't only handle incidents involving illegal border crossers. There's one in particular, I remember well. We responded to a residential area maybe around 11:00 p.m., in reference to a "Suspicious Activity." Daniel and I arrived at the incident location at the same time. The 911 caller met us outside his house, on the sidewalk of this residential street. Alongside the curb, a van, which we later learned belonged to his son, was parked in front of the house. The gentleman had a concerned look on his face and said he had called as soon as they had made the discovery, which was around the time he and his wife had said their goodbyes to some friends who had come over for drinks. He described how, standing on the sidewalk still chatting with their friends, he noticed damage to the back window of the van.

We walked over to the parked vehicle and immediately spotted the cracked back window. In the reflection of the flashlight, you could see a greasy facial imprint on the glass. Little pieces of skin and a few hairs were stuck to it as well. Then there was some blood splatter, a dent in the metal of the door a little below the window, and what looked like the impression of a bicycle tire. The most disturbing part, however, was a large blood pool on the pavement, right near the rear bumper of the van. Evidently, a bicyclist had hit the back of the van with a great deal of force. As I took pictures and listened to the reportee's statements, Daniel had walked up onto the sidewalk. "Hey, Tom. There's a blood trail over here!" he exclaimed and started walking south on the sidewalk, following the trail he had found. I quickly tossed the camera into the trunk of my patrol car and ran up to him. Where the beam of his flashlight hit the sidewalk, I could clearly see the red blood drops. It looked as if someone had sprinkled them there. It looked so perfect. The trail went on for some time, but then suddenly curved to the right, off the sidewalk and into a cul-de-sac. We were getting close. Ultimately, it led toward a single-family home, up the driveway, and ended in front of a closed garage door. We walked from the driveway on a small paved path to the front door. A light could be seen back inside the house. I banged my fist against the front door and rang the doorbell. "Sheriff's Department! Come to the door!" Then both Daniel and I stopped to breathe and listened. Nothing. I pounded on the door again. "Police! Anybody inside?" I leaned against the door with my ear and listened for any kind of noise indicating that someone might be inside. Again, nothing. We shined our flashlights through the front windows, and what we saw was even more troubling. There was blood on the floor inside the house. A trail that seemed to lead to different rooms. Daniel climbed over the back wall to look inside from a different angle and see if a door or window was open. He said there was more blood in the kitchen, but no way to get in. Nothing was unlocked on the front side either, and the garage door was shut as well. I called the sergeant and explained what we had found, asking if he would authorize forced entry into the home. There was a real possibility the injured person was inside, desperately needing help. The sergeant gave his okay.

I hung up and looked at Daniel. "He said we can go ahead."

Then I keyed it up on the radio. "1-1-4-2, we are going to force entry through the front door."

Daniel and I looked at each other and nodded. But then, something unexpected happened. Daniel drew his Glock pistol to a low-ready position (meaning his arms were extended, and the muzzle was pointed to the ground at a 45-degree angle). Then he slowly raised the gun and, pointing it in the direction of the door lock, he said, "I've always wanted to do this."

At that moment, the sergeant's car pulled up in front of the house. Wide eyed and with clinched teeth, I said, "What are you doing? Put the fucking gun away!"

Daniel had a puzzled expression on his face, but fortunately, holstered his weapon in a smooth and fast motion.

The sergeant walked up right behind me. "What are you waiting for? The tall guy has the best leverage. Give it a good kick," he said and pointed at me.

Daniel looked at him and said, "Can I do it?"

"Sure. Just stop talking and start doing!" Just to be sure, I hissed a quick, "Just kicking! Kick the door. Near the lock."

"I know. I know," came his annoyed response.

I smiled at the sergeant and was relieved that he didn't seem to have noticed Daniel's little Rambo episode.

It took him two or three kicks to get the right spot, and the door gave way with a loud crack. We drew our weapons and announced ourselves with loud calls of "Police! Anybody inside?" and quickly entered the home. We still did not know what we were dealing with. Was it really what it seemed like at the initial scene? Or was something more sinister going on? What if he was inside, but didn't want to be found because he was a wanted felon? What if it was not an accident but had been caused by someone purposely and that someone was now inside this house? The victim could be seriously disoriented from the hit against the head and think someone was trying to break into their house. It would be worse if he or she had access to a firearm. Going into each room, we searched the residence for our victim, but didn't find anyone. There was a blood trail leading from the interior garage door all the way to the kitchen. In the kitchen was more blood and a bloody towel in the sink. From the kitchen went another blood trail to the bathroom, where there was more blood. I wondered how much blood someone could lose without passing out. Where was the victim?

I looked at Daniel and said, "I'll take pictures of all this. Why don't you check with the local hospitals and see if anyone with facial lacerations has checked in recently? Maybe the victim called 911 as well. Have Comm check with the fire department." Then I went back to my patrol car that was still parked at the initial scene with the van. I drove it over to the victim's house. When I came back inside to take pictures, Daniel told me he had been successful. A middle-aged man had checked into Kino Hospital and had been treated for facial lacerations. Deputies with the San Xavier District were already on their way to get a statement from him. I took several pictures of the front door and the damage we had caused. We would have to document everything and submit it to the county, because the victim had the right to be reimbursed for the repair. Then we secured the door as best we could and blocked it from the inside. We left the house through the garage door and let it close behind us.

When we received the callback from the San Xavier deputies, we learned that the victim had been riding his bicycle down the street and began to manipulate his iPod while listening to music. He had looked down at the device and missed the parked van on the side of the road and hit it at full speed. The impact was so forceful, the victim, now lying behind the van, lost consciousness. When he awoke, he picked up his bicycle and walked to his home down the street. He called a friend to come over and then tried to attend to his wounds. Upon arrival, the friend immediately realized the severity of his injuries, put him in her car and drove him to Kino Hospital for treatment. The friend told deputies she was on her way back to the house and it would be okay for us to leave. It was a lengthy report with a lot of paperwork due to the damaged front door.

A few months later, when shift change was coming up once again, the sergeant approached me and asked how I liked working down in Green Valley. Being honest, I told him that it was nice to be closer to home, but that it was boring at times. I felt I was quickly losing the little experience I had gathered during the first few months, simply because the call volume was so low. He was wondering if I would be interested in transferring to the Rincon District. Interested? Absolutely! I would love to work in Rincon. It was my home district. While it was considered a slower district as well, it was not as slow as this. And I did not necessarily need to work in an area where deputies were racing from one call to the next to come home with a sense of fulfillment at the end of the day. It had a busier metro beat, two rural beats, and then Mt. Lemmon in the Santa Catalina Mountains, which had two deputies permanently stationed near the village on top of the mountain. "Do you need me to put in a request?" I asked with hard to mask excitement in my voice. "No, that's okay. I'll take care of it." Shift change was just around the corner, and I couldn't wait to tell Annie when I came home in the morning. In a few weeks, I'd roll the patrol car out of our driveway and be in service. Fabulous!

But before that could happen, there were a few more shifts to cover down in Green Valley. No need to get carried away. Focus on the job at hand. In our attempts to come up with some sort of activity, Daniel and I focused on the Interstate and certain known hot spots throughout the district. Whenever the sergeant gave his okay, meaning that we had enough deputies on duty, we were allowed to "go play." This resulted in a traffic stop on the Interstate for Daniel one night. I wasn't too far away and joined him as backup. When I rolled up behind his patrol car, he had just returned from speaking to the driver of the SUV. Through the open passenger window of his patrol car, he told me there were two women in the front seats and an infant in a car seat in the back. He had stopped them for a minor infraction, but he said the women seemed nervous. I asked him if it would be okay for me to talk to them while he runs the usual checks on their licenses. "Sure. Knock yourself out," he responded.

Carefully walking up to the SUV on the passenger side, away from what little traffic was on this stretch of freeway, I made my way toward the front of the vehicle, and pointed my flashlight inside. The light beam did not quite make it through the rear windows, which had a very dark tint. That was not necessarily unusual in an area where daytime temperatures would go well into the 100s during summer months. I could see that something was being transported in the cargo area but was not able to make out details. I stopped at the rear passenger doors and asked for the rear windows to be rolled down so I could look inside. I did not receive a response, but the windows were lowered. My flashlight illuminated a small child in a car safety seat, wearing a cute shirt with some Disney character on it. The child looked at me with droopy eyes. Why were they driving around with an infant at 3:00 a.m. in the morning? Then I reached the passenger door.

"Morning, ladies. Deputy Peine with the Pima County Sheriff's Department. Where are you guys headed today?" I asked.

"We already told the other officer. Back home to Tucson," the driver answered.

"Where are you coming from at this hour?"

"Oh, we were camping."

"Camping? Okay. Where at?"

"I don't know. Some place down near Amado."

"Isn't it a bit cold still to go camping?"

"Yeah, that's why we left."

"I see. Where in Amado was this?"

"Just near town. I'm not sure exactly."

"You just came from there. Can you describe it?"

"No, I'm sorry. Not really. I'm not good with maps and stuff."

"I understand. What's in the back of the car?"

"Just camping stuff."

"Okay. Just hang tight. My colleague is just running some checks on your license and will be right back. Everything okay with your license, ma'am?"

"Oh, yeah. Everything's fine."

I walked back to the passenger side of Daniel's car and said, "Yeah, I see what you're saying. Something's not quite right. They can't say where they're coming from. They decide it's too cold for camping and then return to Tucson at 3:00 a.m. with an infant in the car? Her answers were really short, and they do seem nervous." Daniel nodded and said he'd request a K-9 deputy to assist. He got out and came around to the passenger side, approaching the SUV again.

"Ma'am, would you mind letting me take a look in the back of your vehicle? I just want to make sure there's nothing illegal inside." Daniel asked the driver.

"Of course. Go ahead. It's open."

"Are there any drugs or anything else illegal inside this vehicle?"

"No, sir, nothing."

"Please step outside the car and onto the side here with Deputy Peine, while I check the back of the car. It's for my safety. You can leave the child in the backseat."

Both the driver and passenger got out, but chose to the take the infant out of the seat and carry him for the duration of Daniel's activity in the back. I saw Daniel open the hatch and shine his flashlight inside.

"Wow! What's all this?" he asked. I couldn't see what he was looking at from where I stood.

"What do you mean?" the driver tried to clarify.

"What's in all these coolers and tubs? Can I look inside?" Again, the woman gave her permission.

"It's just food. Yeah, go ahead."

While Daniel was rummaging through the cargo area of the SUV, another patrol car pulled up behind us. It was the K-9 deputy. I briefly asked the women to stay where they were and walked over to the dog handler. "Dang! Were you flying?" I wondered. It was unusual for anybody who was not assigned to the district to make it down there in less than 30 minutes. He laughed. "No, no. We were in the area on Stonegarden deployment, when I heard your call on the radio. What've you got here?"

Stonegarden was a special deployment, allowing deputies to work overtime hours paid for by federal grant money. It was a special deployment to look for and interrupt possible smuggling activity along the border corridor. I filled him in on Daniel's stop and explained that he had just been granted permission to look through the back of the vehicle. Daniel came back to join us and share his observations.

"This is really weird. The back is filled with coolers and plastic containers loaded with food. I mean tacos, bread, rice, lots and lots of bottled water. You could easily feed 20 or 30 people with all that."

The K-9 deputy smiled. "They're setting up a stash. Where were they going?"

"Tucson.," Daniel said.

"Uh, bullshit. They're not going to Tucson. Let me see if they let my dog in the car."

The cartels would set up stash sites or hidden camps for their drug runners to replenish. Along certain smuggling trails, stashes were hidden or driven out to meet with those who had carried the heavy loads on their backs across the border. They had often tracked for hours on end through heat, dense underbrush, and sandy soil. It was part of the logistical aspect of the smuggling operation of illegal drugs from Mexico into the United States.

The two women standing in the breakdown lane started to look concerned. The K-9 deputy walked over to them and talked for a while. Then he came back and asked us to bring the two women to the back of our patrol cars while he'd let his dog search the car. The women joined us, and we made small talk, while the other deputy got his dog out of the car and led it over to the SUV. First, he walked the dog around the outside of the vehicle, then he took the leash off and it disappeared into the vehicle interior. The dog seemed excited, panting heavily and his tail constantly wagging. That guy was having a lot of fun in that car, I thought. I saw how it jumped onto the backseat and a few seconds later, the deputy stepped in closer to the open backdoor. He gestured for us to come over. Once I could see inside the back of the SUV, the K-9 stood on the backseat, tail wagging excitedly, and "digging" on the upholstery. The handler looked at us and said that something would have to be underneath the seat for the dog to react so strongly. His dog was, in fact, frantically going through his digging motions as if he was trying to go straight through the bench. He was leashed up again and brought to the back of the SUV, where the deputy waited and also kept an eye on the two women and their child.

Daniel rattled and manipulated the rear bench of the SUV, and, to his surprise, it gave way easily. Underneath the seat, right where the small child sat in his safety seat, was an AR-15 assault rifle, two semi-automatic pistols, and ammunition. Alarmed by this unexpected find, we turned the vehicle inside out for other potential contraband.

After all was said and done, the driver was arrested. And the passenger and child were picked up by a friend. Child Protective Services (CPS) was notified of the situation. The SUV was impounded, and everything processed by a Forensic Technician who had responded to the scene as well. All this was the result of a simple traffic stop and the tangled,

DEPUTY WHILE IMMIGRANT

nonsensical response to a few open-ended questions. What truly bothered me about this whole thing was the child being exposed to all of this, being put in this situation, made part of this dangerous activity.

It was the last of the more noteworthy incidents I was involved in out there. Ready to return to more populated areas, I moved on from Green Valley and hoped to gain some desperately needed experience. The following weekend, I was transferred to Rincon.

8

RINCON

Working in the same district I was living in meant a lot to me. This was my "home turf." It felt more like protecting my own community, even though it was a massive area to cover. The district had four beats. All the way to the north were beats three and four. The latter was the area of and around Mt. Lemmon, consisting of a large part of the Coronado National Forest. Therefore, yet another kind of police would occasionally be involved. The National Forest Service, as part of the Department of the Interior, had Rangers patrol the area. Two, to be exact. The mountain rose 9,157 feet above sea level and driving up the main access road made for an impressive ascent from the desert valley into a coniferous forest, which typically received some snow cover during the winter months. That was just enough to operate what was probably the southernmost ski lift in the entire United States. The views from high up on the mountain range down into the desert valley in the ever-expanding city of Tucson were breathtakingly beautiful.

Beat 3 was what we referred to as "metro," because it was the most densely populated part of the district along the foothills of the Catalina Mountains and bordering the city of Tucson to the south.

Beat 2 was already much more rural and included Redington Pass through the Catalina and Rincon Mountains to the east.

Finally, there was Beat 1, which is where we lived. It went all the way from Old Spanish Trail to the north and Kolb Road to the west to

Cochise County to the east, and Santa Cruz County to the south. You could easily drive for 45 minutes to an hour and still be in Beat 1. Vail, our home community, was an unincorporated area located to the southeast of Tucson. For the next three and a half years or so, that would be my area of assignment.

My first shift assignment was for midnights again, working from 10:00 p.m. to 6:00 a.m. It was a fantastic feeling to simply drive onto my neighborhood street, get on the radio and announce my being in service and available for calls. However, when I was assigned to work in Beat 3 for the shift, it meant that it would take me approximately 30 minutes to get to my assigned patrol area. So, I left early and signed on once I got close to the metro area.

It was still in the early days of being a member of the Rincon District staff when I drove up the long stretch of Houghton Road going north. It was shortly before 10:00 p.m., and I was about to sign on for duty in a few minutes. I glanced at the call narratives on the screen of my laptop to get a sense of what calls were being worked. Before I passed a large Fry's grocery store in Rita Ranch, dispatch broadcasted an "Assist Other Agency" or AOA. It came from TPD and informed us that they requested our help with the pursuit of a vehicle going southbound on Houghton Road. They were coming straight at me.

The dispatcher announced the whole thing in a very monotone, nothing-out-of-the-ordinary kind of a tone. I keyed up on my radio and took the call. "Do we have any additional 10-43 from TPD? What's going on and why are they asking for help? Are they requesting road spikes?" A lot of questions, but I was trying to make up for virtually no information as to what was going on.

Each patrol car was equipped with a set of road spikes. That's a piece of equipment largely made of a collapsed, accordion-type piece of rugged plastic, spiked with tiny, hollow metal tubes. The device was kept rolled up in a duffel bag in the trunk of my car. If needed, I could remove the whole contraption from its bag, and grab it by a specially marked red handle. I'd then remove the two Velcro safety strips, and we'd be ready to go. Once the target vehicle is in sight, I would then throw the rolled-up contents forward with all my might, only holding on to the red handle. That jolt would cause the spikes to partially unfold across the roadway. Then a quick yank on the piece still in my hand and the accordion-like structure of the collapsed road spikes would fully unfold, ideally across the full width of the lane. The sheared plastic was loaded with metal thorns mounted upright across the plastic grid. Once the target vehicle drove over the spikes, they would penetrate the tires and disconnect from the plastic grid to remain inside the tire. As the spikes themselves were hollow, they slowly released the air from the tires. So much for the theory.

After some time, I received a response from Comm.
"1-1-4-2? That's affirmative. TPD is requesting spikes. They are three to four miles from your 10-20."

Wow! All that right at the beginning of my shift. And there was that hammering pulse again. I always intended to remain calm and collected. But somehow it wasn't working out that way. At least not yet. So, as usual, my heart was beating up a storm, and I could see how all that running prior to and during the academy was smart physical preparation for this kind of stress. I chose the exit of the grocery store, which was about to close, to set up with my spikes and advised Comm accordingly. There I was able to cover the entire width of the lane, which would have been nearly impossible elsewhere. There was a raised and vegetated median as well, making it harder for the fleeing vehicle to cross over into the opposing lane. In addition, I would use my patrol car to block the entry/exit to the parking lot, preventing uninvolved civilians from getting into the middle of things. My tactics were squared away, I thought and pulled my patrol car across the exit of the store to block it. I turned on my red and blues, and traffic in the parking lot came to a halt. Curious shoppers stopped with their shopping carts in the middle of the parking lot, magically mesmerized by the flashing emergency lights.

A mental checklist for the use of road spikes went through my head at lightning speed. In opening the driver's side door, I thought, "Three to four miles, they could be here any minute." In all the excitement and adrenaline rush, I forgot to unbuckle and provided a humorous performance free of charge for the onlooking shoppers in the parking lot. Suicide by safety belt. Funny. With a still pounding pulse and a blushed face, I depressed the seatbelt buckle and sprinted around my car to the back. The trunk flew open. I grabbed the black duffel bag with the road spikes, unzipped it, and took out the spikes. For a second, I paused and listened for the sirens of the approaching police cars. Updates were broadcast over the radio.

"Occupants of the suspect vehicle were approached at a gas station by TPD officers in civilian clothes. They are suspects in drug and gang-related activity. The driver threatened one of the officers with a handgun and then took off from the gas station. TPD initiated a pursuit, during which several shots have been fired at the pursuing officers and their vehicles. Nobody has been injured yet."

I still didn't hear anything indicating they would be closing in on my location. After I removed the spike set from the duffel bag, I found the safety goggles and a protective glove (the spikes have a sharpened tip). One glove? Where was the second? Safety protocols shot through my head. Throwing my training and the instructions overboard, I put the glove and the scratched up goggles back into the bag and picked the spike set back up from where I had set it on the ground. There I was, a set of road spikes in hand, standing at the side of the road, looking north. I tried to make out any emergency lights in a distance but couldn't see any. Then I keyed up on the radio.

"1-1-4-2. Ready to deploy spikes."

For a while, nothing happened. I just stood there, ready to throw the spike strip across the street, spectators who could hardly believe their luck behind me. The whole time, I was wondering if there would be enough room in between the suspect vehicle and the pursuing TPD cars, so I could quickly remove the strip without inadvertently spiking my fellow officers. The description said the suspect vehicle was a dark Ford Expedition. Lots of cars passed my location. When they noticed my police car in the driveway, two "rubbernecks" almost caused a collision because the driver felt an urge to check out what was going on. I already talked about that magic power of the emergency lights.

Then another radio call.

"1-1-4-2?"

I responded, "1-1-4-2. Go ahead."

"TPD just advised they already passed your position. Air One is following the group as well."

What? Excuse me? Not a single police car had come by since I took up my position. No helicopter noise from TPD's Air One. But they have passed my position? I was baffled. Totally stunned. But okay, if that's how it was going to be.

"1-1-4-2, 10-4. Nobody has passed my position, but I'll pack it up then."

It took a while to fidget with the spikes strip, but eventually I managed to put it back in the duffel bag and threw it all into the trunk. Just as I slammed it shut and walked around to the driver's side door, it happened. With lots of siren noise and at great speed a black Ford Expedition and a convoy of four or five TPD cruisers raced past my position and continued southbound toward the Interstate. Fabulous! Inter-agency communication at its best, I thought.

I jumped in behind the steering wheel and joined the pursuit. Or rather, I tried to. Using the radio in my car, I notified Comm.

"1-1-4-2, the vehicles just passed my position. I've joined the pursuit. We're going southbound on Houghton."

Comm simply acknowledged, "1-1-4-2, 10-4."

With the pedal to the metal, I tried to catch up to the TPD cars in front of me. There was a surprising amount of traffic at this late hour, and I raced past cars that had pulled over for the pursuit convoy a few seconds ago. I was closing in on the TPD cruisers now. As we came up on I-10, the pursuit turned onto the freeway toward El Paso. A look in my rearview mirror revealed that more patrol cars had joined the party. Then I heard over the radio that another Deputy was already part of the pursuit and was now the second car behind the suspect. Good news!

That way we would receive firsthand updates from the tip of the pursuit. We were not able to talk to TPD directly using our standard radios and therefore relied on updates their dispatch center relayed via phone to our Communications Center.

On the Interstate, the speed increased. A look at my speedometer showed 110 mph, about as much as my car could muster. It was all fine and well for the guy who grew up in Germany and learned to drive on the Autobahn, where there was no speed limit. But for the American drivers all around us, it was a different experience altogether. Civilian vehicles we passed seemingly stood still. My siren screamed through the night. A familiar voice came through on the radio speaker. It was Ryan. He was the Deputy at the top end of the chase and gave an update, saying that they were leaving the Interstate at the Vail exit and continued northbound. As I was not that far behind anymore, the exit came up quickly and we all left the freeway. We flew north toward a set of buildings that was considered the center of Vail: a feed store, a gas station, a church, and the local middle school. Finally, I could see the top group of police cars. But I could hardly believe what I saw happen next. Maybe 200 yards ahead of us, the red warning lights at the railroad tracks going straight through Vail began to flash. Slowly and unrelentingly, the barriers of the crossing began to lower. The blasting noise of the train's horn, which I was sure could raise people from the dead, cut through the air, overpowering even our sirens, and announced the approaching freight train. The first three or four cars behind the suspect made it across. But the rest of the whole pursuit convoy came to a screeching halt right there. I was the second car in front of the barrier when the train thundered by. Our red and blue lights were reflected on the side of the passing train cars. I got out and banged my flat hand against the roof of my car. Damn it! *How much bad luck could you have during one call?* As I stood there and tried to come to grips with my streak of bad luck, I looked behind my car and saw another four patrol cars behind me. The guys behind the suspect kept providing updates via radio, after we let them know that we had been held up by a train.

DEPUTY WHILE IMMIGRANT

Finally, the last train car came into sight and shortly after it passed, the barriers rose again. My tires squealed, and I barreled right past my son's school. We decided to split into two groups, because the suspect had two possible escape routes from where the pursuit was going. As you might already expect by now, I ended up on the "wrong" route and once again had to try to catch up with the rest of the group.

A new update came over the air. It was my sergeant's voice, and he sounded excited. "Suspect vehicle spiked at the Rincon Market. Vehicle continues westbound toward Tucson." Once the tires were deflated, the whole pursuit was going to slow down significantly, I thought. At that moment, I passed the roadblock at the Rincon Market and noticed Sergeant Stefanopoulos on the side of the road, packing his spike set back into the trunk of his car. A short distance ahead of me, I saw the flashing emergency lights of several patrol cars. It was the actual pursuit I had caught up with, and I was closing the distance quickly. Another radio call, "Suspect vehicle continues westbound, now driving only on its rims. Speeds have slowed to 25 to 30 mph and dropping." Now I was close enough to see the suspect vehicle. It was a completely surreal scene, better than in any movie. Seeing something like this on a screen as opposed to live were two completely different things. The Ford SUV drove toward Tucson on this winding roadway, traveling at maybe 30 mph, on a stretch of road with no street lights. The tires had completely disintegrated and had come off the rims, leaving only the bare metal to drive on. The pavement was illuminated by the spray of orange and yellow sparks caused by the Ford's metal rims cutting gouges into the pavement. It looked as if someone had affixed fireworks to each of the four rims, now spewing colorful displays into the night. Then I noticed that I was vehicle number four behind the suspect. Close enough!

We suddenly slowed down to a crawl. The SUV slowly pulled over to the left shoulder and eventually came to a complete stop. We fanned out our patrol cars behind the suspect vehicle and jumped out. I ran around the back of my car to get to the passenger side and behind the engine block to use it for cover. I drew my gun and with my arms lying steady on the hood of my car, I aimed at the passenger side window. The glass was heavily tinted, and I couldn't see anything on the inside. Several times, I had to lower my weapon because other officers would run across my line of fire to get closer to the suspect vehicle. A wild cacophony of orders was yelled at the suspects. "Hold your hands up out the window! Do it now!" Nothing happened. The commands were repeated, but again, nothing happened. The SUV just sat there, windows rolled up, invisible interior. Our sergeant, who minutes ago packed up his road spikes at the Rincon Market, came running toward my position. Some of the TPD officers shot pepper balls at the back window of the Ford Expedition. Pepper balls were fired from a paintball gun. But rather than being filled with marking color, they contained the same oleoresin capsicum we had in the spray cans on our duty belts. However, they did not do any damage to the glass of the vehicle's rear window.

A brief discussion between TPD and the Sheriff's Department ensued. Our sergeant decided to deploy a specialized shotgun he carried. It had an orange-colored stock to mark it as a less-lethal weapon that would fire bean bags instead of regular shotgun ammunition. A bean bag is a small cloth bag filled with a granulate. The cloth projectile could hurt but would not kill a person hit by it. Hence, this type of ammunition was referred to as less lethal. It would, however, leave a nasty bruise and could knock the wind out of the targeted individual. More commands were yelled in the direction of the suspect vehicle, while Sergeant Stefanopoulos got in position with the bean bag rifle. Maybe the vehicle's occupants would change their mind and come to terms. This whole time, I kept my Glock trained on the passenger side window of the Expedition. A TPD officer knelt down next to me. He was huffing and puffing and then laid his rifle on top of the hood of my car, also pointing it at the suspect vehicle. Without looking over at him, I briefly asked, "Are you alright?" He responded, "Yeah, I'm okay. Thanks. Hopefully, this doesn't end in a bloodbath."

There was my pulse again. For the first time, the thought briefly crossed my mind that today could be the day I might have to shoot someone. Pictures popped in my head of the passenger door opening and a gun being pointed at my fellow officers and deputies. I imagined my right index finger smoothly pulling the trigger back. A shot rang out! The mental picture in my head disappeared as rapidly as it had formed.

Sergeant Stefanopoulos had fired his shotgun. With a loud thump the bean bag hit the rear window of the Expedition and then shot straight up into the air, only to hit the ground with a thud near the SUV after a brief but impressive flight. The rear window was completely intact. No damage whatsoever. The sergeant quickly acknowledged, "Wrong angle!" and loaded another round into the gun. Boom! The rear window burst into thousands of little glass shards. Now, for the first time, we could see the occupants of the SUV. Somebody yelled out loud, "Three occupants in the vehicle!" Pepper balls followed. The doors opened, and I looked for the hands of those getting out. Any guns? Everybody started yelling wildly, "Hands up! Hands up!" "Get on the ground!" On the passenger side, two women emerged. From where I was at, I could not see what was happening on the driver's side. TPD officers called the women closer to them, then rushed forward, cuffed them, and quickly brought them to one of the surrounding patrol cars. The tactics of all of this didn't look like what I remembered from the academy, and I thought it looked pretty awful from a safety perspective. Various officers yelling sometimes conflicting commands, instead of one officer being in charge. People running across the line of fire, etc. It was pretty messy.

From behind the array of police cars, I could hear a dog bark. A K-9 handler had arrived and was ready to deploy his partner. It appeared that they had not taken the driver into custody yet. Then, I heard someone giving the K-9 warning, but the dog was never deployed. A few short moments later, the driver was in custody and escorted back to the patrol cars. All that was left now was to clear the suspect's vehicle. Nobody knew if there was still someone hiding inside. Worst case scenario: armed and hiding. Add to that the possibility of that person being very frightened at this point and you have a very volatile combination, I thought to myself. After another dog warning, I saw a Belgian Malinois shoot toward the suspect's SUV and disappear inside. After a few seconds, I could see the dog stand on the back seat, wagging his tail. The K-9 officer walked up to the car and took his dog on the leash again. Myself, another deputy, and two TPD officers cleared the vehicle, just to be on the safe side. Finally, Ryan yelled out toward the phalanx of patrol cars behind it, "Vehicle is clear!"

As scary as it had been at times, this was right after my taste. It felt exhilarating to take down a violent and dangerous criminal. And it also felt comfortable to go about this kind of work as part of a much larger community of law enforcement officers, who had each other's backs. I had become a full member of that community.

A different and significantly less exciting aspect of working in the Rincon District was the response to alarm calls or 10-90s. A "10-90" was dispatched, when a house alarm was activated, and the monitoring company called 911. The triggering of an alarm could occur in a variety of different ways. The most common way was that a sensor in the house equipped with an alarm system was tripped. That did not necessarily mean a break-in had occurred. Loud thunder could trip a glass break sensor on a large window. The homeowner failed to properly close a door, which was flung open by a wind gust. The dog or cat would trip a motion sensor that was not calibrated accurately. The cleaning person forgot the code to disarm the system. I could go on for some time, but you get the idea. Then there were the panic alarms. Some of the systems were equipped with a panic alarm, which could be triggered via the control panel of the alarm system or by using a fob the manufacturers offered as an add-on accessory. The calls were then dispatched with different priority codes. A panic alert was dispatched at significantly higher priority than a regular sensor trip. Statistically speaking, the vast majority of dispatched 10-90s were false alarms. Meaning the system was triggered, but there was no actual intrusion. The vast majority, however, did not mean all of them. There were several alarms during my tenure, which resulted from an actual break-in. If we found an open door at a residence upon arrival, we would call for backup and then clear the interior of the home jointly.

DEPUTY WHILE IMMIGRANT

One of these many 10-90 calls sent me to a large, multi-million-dollar home not too far from Sabino Canyon. I came up on the guard shack of this gated community. The security officer smiled and waved his hand as I drove through the gate he readily opened for me. I returned the gesture and made a mental note to include him as a potential witness should I find something amiss at the incident location. Driving past some of these mansions, each with a shiny luxury sedan or SUV parked in the driveway that cost three or more times my annual salary, was a sight to see in its own right.

The residence in question was a large, contemporary villa perched on a hilltop. It was located at the end of a short cul-de-sac, and there was no good spot to park my patrol car nearby. Typically, we would try to park our cars one or two houses down the street and walk the rest of the way. But here, that would place my vehicle a significant distance from the incident location and didn't feel quite right. Still, I parked a short distance away from the main entrance and driveway and walked up to the front of the house. As I reached the edge of the driveway, I saw that the large front door, which had some ornate, custom cast iron work attached to it, stood open a few inches.

"1-1-4-2. I have an open door. 10-78."

If the door stood open, I would have to clear the interior of the home and could not do so by myself. I walked up to the garage, posting myself in a position from where I could observe the open door. I stood with my back to the wall and waited. It took about 10 minutes for one of the senior deputies to arrive. He parked his car behind mine and walked up to me. "Anything?" he asked.

"No. I saw the open door, big house, and called for backup right away," I responded.

"Okay. Let's get it done," he answered.

"1-1-4-2. We're about to clear the residence. 10-35," I advised Comm. While searching a place, we would typically request radio silence in case we encountered somebody and needed to get on the air quickly, without someone else tying up the frequency for their traffic stop.

"1-1-4-2, 10-4. East 1 is 10-35," Comm responded promptly. And with that, the airwaves fell silent.

We walked up to the front door with our guns drawn. Each of us hugging one side, I pushed the door open. It opened into a large hall with marble floor and then continued into an open living room that was situated slightly lower and connected by two sets of three stairs to the right and left. A super-sized, floor-to-ceiling panorama window offered a breathtaking view across the lower-lying hills all the way to the side of the Catalina Mountains. The hallways led further into the home on both sides.

"Police! Anybody inside?" I yelled.

"Police! If you're inside, come out now or call out so we can hear you!"

No response. I looked at the other deputy.

"This place is huge. Fucking death trap. You go left, I cover your six?" I suggested.

"Sounds good. Let's go," he confirmed and, moving diagonally across the doorway, he disappeared inside.

I followed him and walked up to a large support pillar to the left of the entrance. He had taken a position of cover from where he could look down a hallway to our left. I covered the living room and a hallway to our right. To do this right and truly safe, we would need at least five deputies. But the only other deputy available was in Beat 2 and the sergeant would have to come from the district office. We decided to continue without additional help. Keying up on my radio, I called Comm and told them to lift the limitation of radio traffic, as it would take us a while to clear this massive place. The dispatcher confirmed, but the air remained quiet. Everybody got the message.

It took us a little over 10 minutes to clear the whole place. Several bedrooms, an office, a separate entertainment room with theater seating, a billiard room, a small library, kitchen, laundry, guest bathrooms, master bath, closets. I'd say roughly 5,000 square feet. We didn't find anyone or anything that looked suspicious and advised Comm accordingly. We relaxed, holstered our weapons and, standing in that glamorous living room with a view, we looked around one more time.

"Did you see this here?" the other deputy asked me. He walked over to an area accessible from the living room. There was a giant walk-in safe. The solid, thick steel door was swung open. Inside was a lounge chair, a fancy-looking humidor full of fine cigars, and the walls were lined with wine racks. "Must be some Chateau La Very Expensive," I said with a fake French accent, and we both started laughing. Looking at the big, wide-open door of the safe, I said, "Did you check behind?" His eyes widened. "Nope," came his concerned answer. Given the angle from our position, there was no way to check quickly without exposing ourselves. Our guns came out again, but my partner, staying behind the door using it as cover, had to pull on the interior handle of the heavy door with some force. It finally started to move and both of us moved around it quickly to get a look behind it, guns pointed at the empty space. Nothing. "Good catch," my partner said. Just as he said that the safe's door, still moving, closed with huffing noise and once snug, produced a clicking noise. "That didn't sound good," I offered. We failed to open the door again, and it appeared there was some sort of auto-lock mechanism that had activated. "I hope they have the combination," said my partner. We both grinned nervously. Usually, we'd make sure to leave a place exactly the way we found it. So, this was not as it was supposed to have gone. However, we felt we were okay, as we didn't know the door would close shut on us and at the same time it was out of concern for our safety that we had moved it in the first place. Still, it was an uneasy feeling, and I was afraid we might get a complaint. We left through the front door, pulling it shut behind us. The other deputy left, while I dropped a business card with our case number and a note that we had entered the home into the mailbox. Fingers crossed.

Yes, this was the area where traffic stops could involve more exotic vehicle makes such as Bentley, souped-up Audis, BMWs, Mercedes, and the only Lamborghini I ever pulled over.

Things went pretty easy for a few weeks and nothing too crazy happened. That was exactly what began to worry us. When there were prolonged periods of no major calls, it felt as if something was brewing. And the longer it took to brew, the worse it would get in the end. Unfortunately, our concerns would soon be confirmed. I had just cleared from assisting another deputy at a domestic violence call and drove down a narrow, winding residential road to get back onto River Road. Priority tones rang out over the radio. "Rincon Beat Three, copy shots fired. Shots fired at the intersection of Swan and Sunrise. Units responding advise." Oh my, here we go! A deputy responded on the air with, "I'm 10-60," which meant she was in the vicinity of the reported incident location. Comm advised the caller had told them she had heard several gun shots coming from a vehicle as it approached the intersection. The car in question was now gone. Other units began to respond. Then another priority call. "Attention Rincon Beat Three. 10-50 at Swan, south of Sunrise." A car crash with unknown injuries. Now we were hopping, I thought and grabbed my mic to take the crash. Before I was able to key up, Sergeant Stefanopoulos got on. "Sierra 2-8-4. I'll take the crash. Swan, Calle Barril." He was a lot closer than me. I was still on River Road, headed west toward Swan. The deputies near the intersection kept providing updates, stating that they were unable to locate the suspect vehicle. One of them had stopped out with the 911 caller and was getting information from her.

When I came up on the intersection of River and Swan, I set my signal to turn toward the incident location. Sergeant Stefanopoulos keyed up again.

"Sierra 2-8-4. 10-23 at the 10-50. Looks like the calls are connected. The 10-50 and the "Shots Fired" are connected. And start me some additional units."

Before Comm could respond, I keyed up, "1-1-4-2. 10-76."

Other deputies responded as well. But it would get worse.

"Sierra 2-8-4."

"Sierra 2-8-4, go ahead."

"Code 900 times two. The car is riddled with bullet holes. Standby

DEPUTY WHILE IMMIGRANT

for 10-28." (Two dead people inside the car and a bunch of bullet holes.)

I flipped on lights and sirens to expedite my response. The sergeant updated the location and said he was at Swan and Calle Del Pantera, which was south of Sunrise. He wanted us to block the four-lane roadway in all directions. I saw his car up ahead of me in the opposite lanes. Pulling my car diagonally across the roadway, I tried to create a block as well as I could and got out. As I walked up to the scene where a silver BMW X5 stood angled toward the shoulder with all doors open. From a distance, I could make out the bodies inside. Two other deputies were already there and seemed to relay information to Sergeant Stefanopoulos. One of the deputies started running back to his car. When the Sergeant saw me, he yelled in my direction. "We may have a survivor still around here somewhere. 10-0, he's likely 10-32! Get back to your car and start roaming the neighborhood streets." I turned around and ran back to my patrol car, got on the radio and said, "1-1-4-2. I'll be a roaming unit." Another deputy had arrived and took over the roadblock.

The sergeant requested additional units from neighboring districts to assist with patrol duties or directly at the crime scene. He also asked for homicide detectives to be called out, for forensic technicians to respond to the scene, for the mobile command post to be deployed, and for the department's air unit "Survey One" to assist. The command post was a big RV-type of vehicle equipped with everything command staff would need to handle a larger operation on the scene. I started to slowly drive through neighborhood streets with my windows rolled down and overhead lights activated. We wanted our presence known, and I wanted to be able to hear noises outside of my vehicle. Additional updates from the scene with the SUV began to paint a picture. Apparently, there had been at least three people inside the SUV, possibly more. At some point, a shootout had occurred inside the vehicle. All bullet holes were from the inside out. One or more survivors were on the loose, possibly injured, and most certainly armed with a firearm. Now it was important to lock the whole area down as best we could and potentially find the survivor.

A few minutes later, Survey One keyed up and advised they were now overhead. Survey One was a neat piece of equipment. First and foremost, it was not a helicopter. When people hear a law enforcement air unit, they immediately assume that it has to be a helicopter. But ours wasn't. It was an airplane. Or in cop speak, a fixed-wing aircraft. It was an old Vietnam-era military reconnaissance plane, equipped with forward looking infrared (FLIR) camera. That was extremely helpful at night. While we were all walking around in pitch black, Survey One would look for heat signatures in the desert. A human being, for example, would show up as a bright-white figure on the screen the Tactical Flight Deputy (TFD) aboard the aircraft was looking at. Because the plane would circle at a high altitude, making very little noise, the suspect was typically not even aware that we were being led right to them. The TFD would guide our every step or route us with our vehicles directly to the location of the suspect. More than once, I looked into the utterly surprised face of someone who had been running or hiding, and who could simply not understand how we had managed to find them. A helicopter was loud and only had a searchlight to use. That was appropriate within city limits where the distances were much shorter and where there were more light sources on the ground to work with. Our distances were significantly larger, and on a moonless night, the desert could turn into a pitch-black maze.

Circling overhead, Survey One would identify areas for us to check out. Either because someone was outside or walking the streets near the incident location, or because it looked like someone was potentially hiding in a spot where one of us deputies on the ground had to go and check in person. The neighborhood streets out in that particular area were mostly narrow, winding, single-lane roadways. There were no sidewalks. The houses were mostly set back from the roadway, accessible only via long dirt driveways. The homes typically sat on lots that were at least one acre or larger. At night, coyotes roamed the area hunting for rabbits and other small rodents. As you may imagine, there were not a lot of people walking on those streets. People drove everywhere out here. It was more convenient due to the distances, and it was safer. For about an hour or hour and a half, we roamed the neighborhoods, drove to suspicious spots pointed out by Survey One's crew, followed up on concerned calls from residents of the search area, or stopped out with neighbors who stood in their driveways, lured out by all the police activity. We did not find anyone possibly connected to the crime that had just occurred.

I drove back to the crime scene, which had turned into a place buzzing with activity. The entire scene was brightly lit by mobile light posts. There were detectives, forensic technicians, deputies, and command staff. The BMW still sat where I had first seen it, well over an hour and a half ago. Sergeant Stefanopoulos was using the hood of his patrol car as a whiteboard. Using erasable markers, he had drawn a rough map of the surrounding neighborhood streets. Radio designators pointed to areas of assignment where we had been roaming. In a different color, the location of incoming 911 calls about suspicious activities had been noted and provided a nice overview of the entire area. I checked in with the Sergeant and he wiped my designator off the list on the hood of his car. He told me to standby at the scene and use the time to get my report done. Once deputies with the midnight shift arrived, I could clear and go home. Walking back to my car that I had parked just north of the command center, the OME vehicle passed me. They were there to pick up the bodies that were still inside of the X5 just down the street from me. It was one of those days where I was especially grateful to be able to use our automated dictation system to file my report, rather than having to type it. We would call an internal phone number and, using a specific access code as well as the case number, we could dictate our report to a computer server. From there, transcribers at the department would pick it up and transcribe it into a written report within 24 hours if it was a high priority call like this one.

A short while later, deputies with the midnight shift arrived. It was just after 10:00 p.m. and they would take over from there. Tired and frustrated that we had been unable to locate the survivor(s), I made my way toward Houghton Road to go home and get some rest.

When I came back to work the next day, the district commander had put out a memo saying that the department was looking for volunteers to sign up for temporary duty (TDY) at the Ajo District. Ajo was a small community on the far western edge of Pima County. How far, you wonder? From my house to the district office there, it would take roughly three hours by car. And yes, that was still within our county. Ajo used to be a mining town with its own copper mine. The mine went out of business more than 20 years ago and with that, the community out there downsized significantly. It was still home to some 3,000 people, mostly retired folks, USBP agents, and Rangers who worked at the Organ Pipe National Monument, just south of Ajo. It was a very small district, but still needed a law enforcement presence. A tiny spot on the map, bordered by the National Monument to the south and the Tohono O'Odham Nation, a large Native American reservation, to the east. A small contingent of deputies, sergeants, and a lieutenant lived out there. When you filled out your application for Deputy Sheriff, there was a question asking if you would be willing to work in Ajo. Should someone check that box, they were sure to go there, and it was a three-year tour. The voluntary TDY was for one week at a time to help alleviate a personnel shortage the department was experiencing out there. Without these deployments, nobody from the permanent Ajo District staff would ever be able to have weekend or other days off. Ajo deputies worked four ten-hour shifts per week. If you worked in Ajo, you were also allowed to participate in "Stonegarden" deployments. As I mentioned earlier, those were special deployments that targeted the flow of drugs, money, and weapons to and from Mexico. Deputies would work during their time off and receive overtime pay financed by federal grant money. It was a very lucrative opportunity for the otherwise fairly meager deputy pay. Going down to Ajo for four days and then working Stonegarden deployments for another three days would create a welcome influx of extra money. So, I signed up.

Standing in our bedroom a few days later, I went over everything I had packed for the week. It was mainly uniforms and a few civilian clothes. I also took two books, as I figured I'd have plenty of time to read. A few simple groceries in a cooler and everything went into my patrol car. Annie and I kissed goodbye in the driveway. "Be careful," she said. One of the many things I loved about her was that she never gave me the sense of overwhelming concern. Sure, at times it would have been nice to hear your wife tell you that she worries about you. But that was not who she was. She didn't worry, but rather said that she trusted in my abilities. There were times where I pitied other deputies whose husbands or wives would call several times during their shifts to check in on them. If there was a shooting or some other call that had generated a lot of media interest, deputy spouses would begin to call their loved ones to check in on them. My phone always stayed silent. And I appreciated it. It helped me keep my head free and maintain focus on the task at hand. It was on a few occasions where I heard people ask Annie, "So, do you worry a lot about your husband? I mean, it's a scary job. I don't know how you do it." She would always answer nonchalantly, "No, I'm not worried. He knows what he's doing." I loved that.

It was a long three-hour drive. After leaving Tucson and passing the far western reaches of the San Xavier district, I came upon a sign indicating the boundary of the Tohono O'odham Reservation. An area of more than 4,300 square miles under the jurisdiction of the indigenous people of the Sonoran Desert, who have lived there for thousands of years. The longest stretch of my trip led me through this barely inhabited wilderness. The beauty of the unsettled desert was striking. It was still early in the year and flowers were blooming. The blooming carpet was cut in two by the road's black pavement. Large rocks rose in the distance. Places that were known to be used as lookouts by cartel scouts. Once or twice, a USBP patrol vehicle passed me in the oncoming lane. On my whole one-hour-and-45-minute drive through the reservation and except for the area of Sells, I saw only one other civilian car. It was almost as if time stood still in this part of the world. It was easy to imagine the native people freely roaming their lands. Someone had told me that the stretch through the reservation, or "rez" as it was often called, was simply a part of the journey you'd have to get through. To me, it was the most beautiful part of the drive. Then I reentered Pima County and came upon a small settlement south of Ajo called Why. The only thing I can tell you about Why, AZ is that it has a gas station, a souvenir shop, and a campground. Right next to it, inside of the reservation's boundary, sits a small casino. It is the last settlement on the U.S. side before you get to the international US-Mexico border point of entry, Lukeville. On the other side was Sonoyta, Sonora. Tourists would come through this area on their way to Puerto Peñasco (Americans also refer to it as Rocky Point) on the Gulf of California. I made a northbound turn toward Ajo and a few minutes later rolled up to the district office. As this was the only such facility for miles and miles around, the Ajo district had a part of its office complex set aside for a few jail cells. They had a small number of Corrections Officers who would look after the few inmates. They had to be self-sufficient, with the next administrative and supply hub being in Tucson, a three-hour drive away.

One of the deputies stationed there told me where to find my trailer around back: my home for the next seven days. Behind the small Sheriff's Department compound stood a few trailers, among them one that looked similar to the FEMA trailers I had seen on TV. When I unlocked it and stepped inside, I noticed dog hair everywhere and learned that the deputy who had stayed here the previous week had brought his golden retriever with him. It seemed that about 10 percent of the animal had stayed behind. No wonder, in this heat. My shift would begin in roughly two hours, and I used the time to unpack and set up camp. It was cozy, and I was excited to get to know this area.

In a briefing by two other local deputies at the beginning of my shift, they told me how I had to be cognizant of the lack of backup out here. For the first few hours there would be three of us, but later at night there would be only two. The shift supervising sergeant would be available by phone if needed. *Okay, that was different.* Then they set up my radio as the Ajo district used a different frequency and repeater, which was located on a nearby mountain. We were not able to speak to Tucson districts directly. The sole dispatcher was housed in the office building near the front desk.

Once outside and ready to roll, one of the deputies said for me to follow his car, as he wanted to show me the nearby USBP compound. After a few minutes of driving southbound on the only road going in that direction, we reached a fortified building just off the roadway to the east. It was a large concrete building surrounded by barbed wire fences. Inside the compound was a large helipad with a Blackhawk helicopter. Two Wackenhut buses sat in the parking lot. This was the first detention facility on this side of the border. The deputy told me how agents here were extremely helpful and how they had a very tight relationship with them. No surprise there. It was good to know these guys were out here. They weren't real cops, but in a bind, it would be good to have someone nearby who you knew would be on your side.

All in all, my seven days out in Ajo were rather uneventful, though not without lessons to be learned. Here are a few of the calls we went out to:

A report was made of human remains found in the desert. One of the local deputies went out and reported back that they would conduct an on-scene investigation and return back later. It turned out to be skeletal remains. Given the Mexican voter identification card found in a bag close to the bones, it was most likely an illegal border crosser who had succumbed to the harsh environment a long time ago.

Then there was a request for assistance from USBP regarding a fleeing suspect. During that call, I had the pleasure to observe specialized USBP agents who could read "sign." Traces left by a fleeing person such as footprints, broken branches, scattered leaves, anything and everything. It was fascinating to see how they would notice the most minute detail and use it to get a sense of the direction in which the suspect had fled. After tracking the individual for about a half hour, we found him hunkered down in a bush right next to the roadway. We almost stumbled over him, as he had cleverly remained very still and calm. It taught me the valuable lesson that if you knew where and how to be still in the desert, people could stand only a few feet away from you and not notice your presence.

Deputies responded a few times to the Lukeville port of entry to pick up individuals who had arrest warrants and were identified during their attempted border crossing. They were locked up in our tiny jail and then brought to Tucson with the next transport.

And then there were the Austrian motorcyclists I stopped on their way into town. They had rented their bikes and were on a long road trip through the southwestern U.S. They got a crack out of me speaking German once they had given me their Austrian driver licenses. We talked for about five minutes, and I let them get to their hotel with just a warning. They asked me what was there to do out here at night. "Sleep," I said.

When it was all said and done, I was glad to be able to return home. Though it was slow, it had not been boring, as I had still learned something new in this unique environment for law enforcement to work in. It was the only time I worked out in Ajo.

As you know by now, all deputies use a radio designator when they communicate over the air. It is a federal requirement and part of the radio etiquette. Your designator becomes your name and sometimes, when you meet a deputy from another district who you always hear on the radio, but don't typically work or otherwise interact with, you'll remember his radio designator faster than his real name. These designators are assigned in the order people join the force. Deputies start with the number 300 or, as it would be called, on the radio 3-0-0. Hence, everybody knew that 3-0-0 was the most senior deputy out there. As you have heard before, my designator was 1-1-4-2. Some of the senior guys would make fun of us asking, "What was your designator again? One million what?" Very funny. But over the years there is obvious attrition. Deputies promote, retire, leave, and new deputies sign on. The list of designators gets longer and longer, with more and more designators remaining unused due to said attrition. Therefore, every now and then, Comm will announce that there will be a collapse of designators. Meaning that on a specific date, everybody will receive a new designator according to their seniority within the then existing sworn staff. If there are 500 deputies, the designator will then go from 300 to 800, with all designators being in use. I don't remember exactly when this happened, but at one point such a collapse was announced and beginning with a new shift one Sunday, I had morphed from being 1-1-4-2 to being 6-2-4. No big deal, you may think. But hang on a second. Remember how we would use this numerous times each and every day? It was my "name" on the radio. It took a while to get used to the new "name" and, occasionally, I messed up using my old designator. Other deputies would chime in on the radio and make fun of the mess up. When I would say, "1-1-4-2, 10-23," to advise I had arrived at the location of an incident, someone else would key up. They'd simply say, "What he was trying to say was: 6-2-4, 10-23. Can you make sure the log will reflect that?" You could hear the dispatcher smile and confirm, "10-4. Showing 6-2-4 10-23." There you go. All of this should have occurred somewhere around this time, and you'll notice the new designator moving forward.

Some deputies purposely avoided being anywhere near their home to stay away from possible conflicts of interests. Having to arrest your neighbor could be an uncomfortable affair. Personally, I thought that to be a rather remote possibility and enjoyed my time out in Beat 1. There were times where I wouldn't see my home beat for two weeks or so, and then again, I'd find myself working Vail, Corona de Tucson, and the area all the way over to Cochise County for an entire work week. I considered it a privilege.

After a domestic violence call early in the afternoon, I went out to a call of a "Cow in the Roadway." Rincon Beat 1 is a very rural area with a lot of the desert used by ranchers for their cattle. Roadway signs along one of the main roads there, Houghton Road, would read "Open Range." What most drivers were not aware of was that it meant they had to be aware of cattle on or near the road and that traffic safety was their responsibility. It was not the rancher's fault when a cow strayed close to the highway, despite the fences they had erected. The burden of traffic safety (and therefore liability) lies with the motorist.

The call text on my computer screen indicated that there was a large bull outside the fenced-in area and right next to the roadway, near the intersection of Houghton and Sahuarita Road. It said the animal had caused chaos each time it had stepped into the roadway, as cars had trouble maneuvering around it.

When I got into the vicinity of the intersection, I slowed down to look for the animal. Shortly after turning westbound on Sahuarita Road, I saw him. He was massive. Nobody had mentioned that this was a prize-worthy specimen of a cattle. Probably one of the largest bulls I have seen alive. He stood on the northern shoulder of the road, right under a mesquite tree. It was a huge bull and given the sheer size of this beast, I was not going to attempt anything on my own. I was a Deputy Sheriff, not a wrangler. In my little notebook scribbled full of names, addresses, and phone numbers, I was looking for the number of Mr. Hernandez. From previous incidents like this one, I knew he owned or leased most of the land in this area, and typically it was one of his cows. He answered right away. I described the situation and said that I thought I had noticed his brand on the bull. He knew right away which animal I was talking about, saying, "Oh, that's Gladiator (or some other equally fitting name). I'll have my guys come out to you. Give them a few minutes." It would probably take them 15 to 20 minutes to get to my location, I figured, and updated the dispatcher over the radio.

I pulled my patrol car closer to the bull, but maintained a respectful, non-threatening distance. Imagine that guy becoming defensive and ramming his giant, horned skull into the side of my car. He might be able to push my car off the road, I thought. It was still daylight, and I figured it wouldn't bother him too much if I turned on my overhead red and blues to warn other motorists of the hazard. It worked out well, even though the bull decided two or three times to step into the roadway, practically bringing traffic to a full stop. Mind you, this is not the busiest of roadways and folks here are used to dealing with livestock; however, all of the cars and pickup trucks that came upon us that afternoon also maintained their respectful distance.

Finally, after some 30 minutes, a large F350 with a horse trailer pulled up on the dirt shoulder. It was two of Hernandez's cowboys. I got out to meet them and hear what the plan would be. Both of them were very friendly, seasoned cattle wranglers with a weathered look from their lifelong exposure to the hot desert sun. They said that they would not be able to simply "hush" the bull back onto the enclosed pasture. They would need to use their horses, two horses, to successfully secure the animal. I was asked to block the roadway entirely; in case the bull made a run for it and to minimize any possible agitation. "You don't want this guy to get angry, Deputy," they said. No, I certainly did not want Gladiator to get angry. Think of the paperwork!

They unloaded their horses from the trailer, swung into the saddle, and gave me the signal to stop traffic. Another deputy had arrived to assist and blocked the roadway from the other end, practically creating a corridor of 30 yards between our two patrol cars, giving the bull room to make a run for the opposite side of the road if he wanted to. The cowboys slowly moved their horses a little closer. One of them stayed in the bull's view, the other was offset to the hind of him. The cowboy on the hind side got his lasso out, swung it over his head and successfully looped it around the bull's head. The other cowboy quickly followed suit. To my surprise, the bull only reacted after the second lasso went on and moved his massive head from side to side. Now it was clear why they approached him from both sides. Both cowboys pulled their horses back in an attempt to fixate the bull in place. Each time the bull pulled in one direction, the horse on the other end of the rope had bent its rear knees and stemmed against the bull's pull. Slowly and with a lot of soothing talk, they were able to lead him back onto the pasture, away from the roadway, where he was released again. We opened the roadway and many of the drivers, some of whom had stepped out of their vehicles to watch the spectacle, gave us a friendly wave and the cowboys a thumbs-up. I thanked both cowboys and told the dispatcher over the radio that the traffic hazard had been removed.

After typing up my report about the incident, the other deputy and I decided to meet up for dinner in a church parking lot north of I-10. The sun was setting, and we had a few good laughs about the "bull call." Suddenly, my designator was called over the radio.

"6-2-4? Copy call."

"Go ahead," I answered.

"Check welfare at Pima County Fairgrounds, 15900 East Houghton Road. Caller said she's concerned about her friend not answering her phone or her door. Caller is standing by at the campground. I'll show you 10-76."

So much for dinner.

Both of us drove toward the fairgrounds, where the other deputy was going to stay nearby in case I needed help quickly, but otherwise remain available for other priority calls. We were the only two deputies out there that night. I drove up onto the fairgrounds and made my way across the large, empty parking lot of this huge property. On the east side, there was a campground with several long-term campers in their RV or trailer. Some were retirees, often snowbirds, others were recluses who preferred to live away from the city in a place where they'd be left alone.

In the cone of my headlights, I saw a woman coming toward me, waving her arm. I stopped my patrol car and got out. I immediately noticed that she looked like a man wearing women's clothes—an odd ensemble at that, comprising an oversized blouse with a dark, floral, wide-pleated skirt and white leather platform heels, plus a brown purse. While talking to me, she wildly gestured with her hands and spoke rapidly. She got out a Kleenex and wiped away some tears, explaining how she had tried to contact her friend and ultimately decided to come out here and check. When she had opened the door to the trailer, she found her friend slumped over at the desk and believed she was dead. I asked if she had touched her friend or anything else inside; she said that she had only called her friend's name, but then got scared and called us.

I got on the radio, advised of the situation and that I would go inside the trailer to check on the occupant. My colleague, who had stayed back on Houghton Road, came up on the air and asked if I needed backup. I declined and said I'd let him know if things changed. Then I pulled my patrol car up to the trailer in question and asked the woman to remain outside by the back of my car. The lights were on inside the trailer and after putting on gloves, I slowly opened the door, knocked and announced myself as a deputy with the Sheriff's Department. No response. I slowly stepped up the two little steps and entered the trailer. It was somewhat clean, with a few things strewn about, but not too bad. Boy, had I seen worse! There was what looked like a woman seated on a chair at a desk. She was bent at the waist, her hands and head on the desk. She had shoulder length hair, and I could not see any details without stepping in closer. I looked around to see if I noticed anything suspicious, but everything seemed normal. When I came up to the desk, I maintained a safe distance, in case the person would wake up and be startled by my presence or, worse, be armed with a weapon I could not see from my viewpoint. My hand reached out and as I said again, "Ma'am?" I touched the body in an attempt to lightly shake her. My touch met a well-known stiffness, and I changed into a pair of nitrile gloves. Stepping in close now, I touched the body again, this time with my full hand, and could feel it was cold. Going through the motions, I looked for a pulse on the neck. Nothing. Then, on the side farthest from me, I noticed a small puddle of blood on the desk. Scanning the body and its immediate surroundings, I looked down at the floor and noticed her two large feet with toenails adorned in neon-colored green and orange nail polish. As I leaned in, I could see that the blood seemed to come from the mouth, as if her head had dropped onto the desk, causing some kind of bleeding injury. The hands and forearms showed a purple discoloration on the bottom half.

"Is she dead?" The woman outside could no longer bear the wait and popped her head in through the front door of the trailer. She startled me and, rather cold-hearted, I harshly responded, "Yes, she's dead." I heard her cry on the outside and told her that I'd be right be back outside.

"6-2-4"

Dispatch responded promptly, "6-2-4, go ahead."

"Code 900, start a forensic unit and OME, please."

"10-4. Copy Code 900 at 19-48 hours."

I went back outside to get my camera. The concerned friend of the dead woman stood outside freezing. Nighttime temperatures had dropped significantly over the past few days. I offered for her to sit in the back of my car with the heater going, which she gladly accepted. "If you close the doors, I'll have to come open them from the outside. They cannot be unlocked from the inside," I told her. She acknowledged, and as I walked back to the trailer, I heard the backdoor of the patrol car slam shut. From the trunk I had pulled my camera out of a plastic bin in which I kept smaller pieces of equipment, so they wouldn't fly around in the trunk should my driving become a little more "animated." Per our standard procedure, I notified the Detective Sergeant of the homicide unit about the death and my findings. He listened to my description, then said he would not send anyone out and told me what closure code to use for my report.

I went back inside the trailer and took lots of pictures. The exterior of the trailer, an overview of the interior taken from the door of the trailer, the desk, items on the desk, including close-ups of several bottles of medication (mostly hormone treatments and anti-depressants), the body, and close-ups of the body. In a wallet on the desk, I found a driver's license issued to a man. There were several notes on the desk, and in the active browser window was a web-based message board for transgender people.

Back with her friend who had tried to stay warm in the cage of my patrol car, I learned that the deceased was an activist of sorts and had been the administrator of the well-known message board. She had last heard from her friend the day prior, but often spoke several times a day, which is why it seemed suspicious that her friend had not answered the phone. I asked her when they had last seen each other and about the nature of their relationship. She said they had last seen each other the previous morning, and that they had been in a romantic relationship before but had broken up a while back. They had remained friends. Did she have any witnesses for her whereabouts over the past 24 hours? She gave me several names and places where she had been and also explained that she had spent most of her last few dollars on taking a cab out here. She also told me about a son of the victim and gave me his name and a possible address in Los Angeles. She did not know of any relatives locally and explained that it was unlikely I would find anyone around here, as the victim was a California native. After noting her information from her driver's license, I asked my colleague to come over and give her a ride to the nearest bus stop, which was near a shopping center in Rita Ranch. That's as far as we could go without abandoning our assigned beat and stay available for calls. I was concerned for her safety, because this place was way too far out of town and in the desert to simply leave her to her own devices.

While I waited for the folks with OME to arrive, I called dispatch on my phone to be connected with LAPD. The Sergeant on the other end confirmed that he had a record of a man with the driver's license addressed to the place I gave him. He also had a phone number available. I asked if he could send out an officer to make the death notification. He said, "I'll give it my best shot, Deputy. It's a busy night, so let me see what I can do for you." Just as I hung up, headlights came up behind my patrol car.

OME had sent two guys, which was helpful, so it would be easier to bag the body. We went inside, and they conducted their own separate investigation. The heavier set of the two explained a lot of things to the other one. It seemed to be a training situation. I had not seen the trainee before either. After about 15 minutes, they were done with their part and asked if I'd take the medication as evidence. I confirmed, and they said they'd make a note accordingly. The trainee brought in one of the white, sturdy plastic body bags and a white linen sheet. We laid the body bag in between the sofa and a cabinet and lined it with the linen sheet. Then the senior OME investigator carefully lifted the head of the deceased off the desk. The body was then turned sideways and in tilting it, the long t-shirt revealed the person had not been wearing any underwear. With a tone of surprise, the trainee blurted out, "Aww, dude! She's got a package!" And you only notice *now* what we're dealing with here, I thought. He certainly needed more training. Senior OME guy grabbed the body under the shoulders and junior OME guy and I each grabbed a leg under the knee to place him in the body bag. Lying in the open body bag, the body remained in the position it last had on the desk chair due to rigor mortis. Slowly and carefully using his own body weight, the senior OME guy pushed down on each knee, slowly stretching the legs out into the body bag. We were able to kind of cross the bent arms in front of the victim's chest and then zipped up the bag. They had left the stretcher outside, the three of us huffed and puffed the body out the narrow trailer door and onto the stretcher.

OME drove off, and I called LAPD again to see if, over the course of the last hour or so, they had a chance to make the notification. The call ended in the disappointing realization that my request had not even made it onto their call screen yet. So, I had to do something we usually try to avoid. Make a telephonic notification. Dialing the number the deceased's friend had given me, I heard a ring tone go out. After three or four rings, a male voice answered.

"Hello?"

"Yes, Good Evening, sir. This is Deputy Peine with the Pima County Sheriff's Department. Who am I speaking to?"

"This is Michael Ashford."

"Yes, Mr. Ashford, do you have a minute to talk to me? Where are you right now?"

"I am at home. Why?"

"Is anyone with you?"

"No, I am by myself. What is going on?"

"Sir, are you the son of Mr. Robert Ashford?"

"Oh my god, yes. Is he dead?"

"Yes, sir. I'm afraid your father has passed away."

The son was very collected and explained that he had always expected he'd get a call like this. He knew of his father's sexual identity issues and explained that his dad had come out to him on a phone call about a year ago. He said that at the time, he could hardly believe what he had heard. The son then told me a little bit about his father's life. His father was a decorated U.S. Marine with years of honorable service in the Marine Corps. After he had finished his military service, he had signed up to become a police officer with the LAPD and after twenty years had retired as a Sergeant from their service. He portrayed his father as a man's man, dedicated to serving his community. Obviously, I had expected a lot of things, but not this. It was very touching to hear the son talk proudly of his father and how he loved him, no matter what. He said his father had

DEPUTY WHILE IMMIGRANT

chosen to live in Tucson and asked me where his body would be taken. I explained that he would be contacted by OME, once they'd release his father's remains. Further arrangements could then be made through a funeral home of his choice. I offered my condolences and gave him the case number, my name, badge, and phone number, just in case he might have any questions further down the road.

The groundskeeper at the RV park secured the trailer temporarily, and I told him that the son might be in touch with him. Then I drove off, back to the church parking lot where we had taken our lunch break earlier to write my report and eat the rest of my sandwich. What a call, I thought and couldn't help but be awed by this veteran's dedication to service and community, despite his deep inner conflicts, and wondered how tough it must have been for him all throughout his life.

✯

I have mentioned all the different ways we encountered and dealt with weapons. Most of the time they were—of course—used intentionally and—more or less—properly. But then there were occurrences where they were *not* handled properly. The following is one of those cases.

It was already dark, and I had been assigned to Beat 2. Nighttime in Beat 2 could be especially challenging, as it is not as densely populated as the metro beat. There were only a few businesses, mostly along Tanque Verde Road. The majority of traffic occurred during rush hour. I was near a golf course and in the community surrounding it when a call of an accidental discharge came in. The incident location was a home for troubled youth near the intersection of Houghton Road and Tanque Verde Road. Though I took the call, it was within only a few seconds that two deputies with our Search and Rescue squad were in the vicinity. They had probably been nearby on their way to or from Mount Lemmon, their typical work environment, when it was dispatched. Racing west on Tanque Verde, I heard them advise dispatch over the radio that they had arrived at the scene. Two minutes later, I drove up the dirt driveway and saw the two Ford Expedition patrol cars in front of one of the houses on the property. We were told an ambulance was en route. Stepping into the small house, I noticed a deputy and a sergeant attending to a man who was sitting in an office chair behind a desk. Underneath the desk and flowing out toward the front was a large pool of fresh blood. The middle-aged, heavy-set man in the chair was very calm and looked on as the sergeant wrapped a compression bandage around his thigh. We carried a limited amount of first-aid equipment in our vehicle, especially to treat gun shot or other heavily bleeding wounds. A revolver laid on the desktop. "Why don't you take that and package it for evidence?" the deputy said, as he pointed at the gun on the table. I had already gloved up on the way in and took the gun to bring it back outside to my patrol car, where I had the proper packaging materials for evidence. On my way out, the medics with Rural Metro Fire Department walked in. I turned around and said toward the search & rescue deputy, "I'll grab my camera as well." He gave me a thumbs-up.

Back at my car, I opened the trunk and rummaged through the different plastic bins. From the evidence packaging materials, I took a gun box, an unfolded sheet of cardboard which would come together as a box and could then hold a handgun inside, held by plastic zip ties. Next, the camera came out, and I took a few pictures of the weapon. It was a classic 6-shot. When I opened the drum, I could see the expended cartridge with the hammer indentation. Then five more rounds. After taking a picture of it, I put the gun in the box I had assembled, the remaining rounds into one evidence bag, and the expended shell casing in a separate bag. Everything went back into the plastic bin in the trunk, and I went back inside the home. Paramedics were just coming out with the victim on a stretcher, telling me they'd go to UMC with him. I nodded and said I'd meet them there later. Back inside and while I took pictures of the interior, the deputy and Sergeant gave me a description of what the injured man had told them.

DEPUTY WHILE IMMIGRANT

The man was a supervisor at this youth home. It consisted of a group of small residential buildings, each housing several youths and one or more social workers who stayed with them. The property was set back from the main road and was surrounded by desert brush. The facility had received some threatening messages in the past few weeks and there had also been several unauthorized visitors who had to be escorted off the property. As a result, the supervisor had decided to arm himself during hours of darkness for protection. His weapon of choice was a single-action revolver, which he had tucked into his front waistband. As I had mentioned earlier, this guy was heavy-set with a sizeable belly hanging over his beltline. At the time of the accident, he was sitting at his desk working on the computer, when he heard a noise coming from the outside and decided to go check it out. As he lifted himself up from the chair, his large belly got caught by the edge of the desk. That, in return, partially cocked the hammer on the revolver and pinched him. The painful pinch made him quickly push back the chair to get his belly out from under the desk, which then caused the revolver's hammer to be released and fire the chambered round. The bullet penetrated his upper thigh, traveled diagonally through his thigh muscles and exited on the other side. It was a perfect through and through shot.

We secured his office and my colleagues left. I made my way to UMC's emergency room. UMC was the area's only level one trauma center, and it could get busy at times. I found the victim in one of the many trauma bays sitting on a bed, his legs dangling. Only seconds after I arrived, the attending physician came in and said he'd have to cleanse the wound before stitching it. "You'll just have to wait a few more minutes, deputy," he said in my direction. The doctor was joined by a nurse and the victim was asked to take his pants off. With his legs exposed now, I could clearly see the hole in his thigh. The man was still in a lot of pain but refused any additional medication. The doctor said the cleansing would be painful, but my victim just looked at him and said, "Let's just get it over with." The nurse handed the doctor a brown plastic bottle which held an equally brown liquid. The patient had laid back onto the hospital bed with his injured leg off to the side. The nurse had placed a plastic receptacle at the foot of his injured leg and then the doctor began to pour the brown fluid directly over and into the gunshot wound in the patient's upper thigh. The man immediately turned pale and arched his back in pain. He let out a grunt and clinched his jaw, but otherwise made no noise. The doctor looked at me, smiled and said, "This is usually where they pass out." The brown disinfectant was foaming out of the top wound and then came dripping out at the bottom opening, further down his thigh. It was as if I could feel the man's pain. A whole two bottles of that stuff went into the man's leg. The doctor said they would let it rest for a while and then he'd come back to stitch it all back together. The x-rays had shown the man's thigh bone fully intact. He was lucky. Before leaving to attend to his next patient the doctor stopped next to me and quietly said, "That is one tough guy. I have had a lot of grown men weep, cry, or pass out in this room. This guy has an incredibly high pain tolerance." I walked over to the man's bedside, explained how he could get his gun back and handed him a receipt for his property. Still very pale and with sweat beads on his forehead, he looked at me and said, "Thank you for everything, deputy." I smiled at him and said, "Don't thank me. I haven't really done anything. Just don't do something like that again. Get a decent holster. You were lucky tonight. I hope you get well soon." And with that, I walked back out to my patrol car.

It was not just the calls I went to that provided variety, but the seasons could also be drastically different in the Sonoran Desert: the natural area surrounding the city of Tucson. One of the starker differences was experienced when working in the Rincon District, which included Mt. Lemmon—or as we would simply call it: Beat 4. During the winter months, snow would fall at the higher elevations of Mt. Lemmon. It was a fascinating experience to start out at the foot of the mountain where temperatures were in the high sixties and would drop precipitously as you climbed uphill. Then suddenly you would notice a snow dusting in the woods alongside the roadway, which ultimately increased to a solid cover. There was a small ski lift operation at the very top of the mountain and

DEPUTY WHILE IMMIGRANT

combined with some gastronomic offerings made for a full experience of alpine fun in the snow just north of the Mexican border. At night, I could drive home from work and have a drink poolside again. This unique setting regularly caused a stampede when the first reports of snow would go out via TV, radio, newspaper, and social media in the later years. Folks from Mexico would drive significant distances to experience snow and would turn Mt. Lemmon into a mad house. Frequently, the mountain would have to be shut down entirely, meaning we'd set up a roadblock at the bottom to prevent overcrowding.

One year, I was asked to assist and spend a few hours in support of the two deputies who lived up on the mountain. The department maintained two trailer homes near the village on top of the mountain. Deputies also stored scores of specialized equipment up there (tracks for their ATVs, all sorts of mountain climbing and rescue equipment, extra shovels, chainsaws, axes, you name it) to provide law enforcement services in a mountainous environment. But with thousands upon thousands of tourists descending, or rather ascending, on this comparatively small area, additional help was needed. Typically, there would be an extra deputy with the Search & Rescue squad and one of us regular patrol deputies up there on the weekends. Did I say mad house? I mean, people parking two and three rows deep on the side of the road, leaving no space to turn around. I saw it get bad enough that an ambulance or fire engine could not have passed through. People saw the white stuff and simply quit thinking. Hundreds, possibly thousands of people, kids and adults, would launch themselves onto their snowboards, sleds, inner tubes, or whatever they could find to slide down a slope that would end in the middle of the roadway. It was complete people overload. When we anticipated that level of overcrowding being near, we'd notify our volunteer organization, who often set up at the foot of the mountain, and told them to shut down traffic going up. People, of course, didn't understand and were upset at the volunteers.

On one of the crowded weekends, I was up on the mountain, a mother called 911 to report her 10-year-old son had struck a tree stump. She reported he was bleeding and had possibly broken his leg. I responded, as did the Mount Lemmon Fire Department. It was not too far from the village, which is where I was located with my Ford Expedition. With all the parked cars, congested traffic, and people walking around everywhere, it took me forever to get anywhere. When I came up on the intersection where the fire department's access road came out, I let the engine and ambulance pull in front of me. With lights and siren, albeit slowly, we made our way to the reported incident location. Once we came near, I noticed a man waving his arms in between two rows of parked cars. All three emergency vehicles stopped, effectively blocking the only path left to go either up or down the mountain. It was as far as we could get. I got out and the man said he was the boy's father and wondered if we couldn't get any closer. We couldn't and had to run the last portion of the way uphill through cars and crowds of people. Finally, completely out of breath and wheezing like a broken hose on an air pump, we made it to the boy. I was not used to running at well over 9,000 feet elevation and quickly felt the additional strain. The kid was screaming in pain and had bled quite a bit, coloring the snow red. Medics went to work while I spoke to the father and people nearby who had witnessed the incident. It was a true accident, and unfortunately, the boy who had been sledding downhill had to pay for his lack of steering skills and his parents' lack of foresight. A few minutes later, two firefighters joined us with a gurney, and the boy was brought back to the firehouse. The medics had called for a rescue helicopter to pick up the boy from the helipad near the fire station. That became necessary as it would have taken too long for the ambulance to make it through all the traffic down the mountain, a half hour or longer, plus the time from the foot of the mountain to the nearest trauma center. The boy suffered a compound fracture and time was of the essence. A short while later, I blocked the access road so the helicopter could land safely. The boy was taken aboard together with his mom and off to UMC they went.

    Another oddity was that people would pack snow on top of the roofs of their cars or into the bed of their pickup trucks. They did so utterly oblivious of the fact that a lot of the snow would either slide off or melt on the way down. The resulting residue of snow and ice would cover the opposite lane, especially near steeper curves. The dropped snow would later turn into ice and create extremely hazardous conditions. In order to combat the urge of taking home a snow "souvenir" to the 70-degree warm valley, we set up a checkpoint of sorts and flagged down all vehicles with a snow load. The driver was asked to step out and dump/unload any excess snow they had on their vehicle. I certainly did not make any new friends that day, but it was better than someone getting killed because they didn't see the black ice that had formed at the end of a curve going up the mountain.

There were frequent rescue calls on the mountain that required our assistance. Either we were asked to assist in the search area, set up a landing zone for a helicopter, or help with identifying information helpful in the search effort. People would start in the valley wearing nothing but summer clothes or light weather gear and then get caught in a snowstorm on the mountain. During summer months, tourists and locals alike would go for a hike planned for several hours with all but one or two small bottles of water. A few hours into their hike, the effects of dehydration would set in and the search and rescue teams had to spring into gear. Deputies would risk their own lives during daring rescue efforts or spend the night with lost hikers in steep, rugged terrain to ensure their safety. There were hundreds of people entering the wilderness every day, who were ill-equipped, had no experience, and misguided expectations. Some of them ended up in dire straits, some of them suffered grave injuries, and some of them died in the mountains. The Catalina Mountains, with their proximity to the city of Tucson, lured people into the false perception of it not being such a "big deal" to go for a "quick hike." Lucky for them, we had a stellar and very prestigious Search & Rescue unit with a group of highly dedicated, specialized deputies, who took great pride in their professional skills. But regular patrol duties had to be taken care of as well. And so, it was time to get back on patrol in the metro beat. It was roughly 8:00 p.m. and night had fallen. Alex and I had just finished eating at a sandwich joint and walked back to our patrol cars. We were discussing what we'd do for the rest of the shift when priority tones blared over our radios. "Rincon Beat 3, 10-16 Physical. Units responding advise." It was a domestic violence call where the situation had turned physical. These are some of the most dangerous calls for us and for the victim. Alex keyed up and said that both of us would respond. We closed the distance to our cars running through the parking lot of the shopping center and jumped in. Start engine, lights, siren, and out of the parking lot we went. It wasn't too far from our location, but then the dispatcher got back on the air and said that the automatic location information that came through with the phone call does not match anything on our map. We might have to search a little in that neighborhood.

The house was in a neighborhood that consisted of several small side streets and dead ends near Sabino Canyon. It was a small maze to get into and with our lights and sirens turned off once we came into the vicinity of the call location we slowly cruised through the residential streets. Then Alex came on the radio and said, "I found it. Come one street up north, turn east. You'll see my car right there. I'll make contact." I sped up and was right behind Alex's patrol car within 20 seconds.

Alex stood next to the front door and was waiting for someone to answer. As I got out of my car, the front door opened, and I rushed to join Alex. "Evening, ma'am. You called 911?" "Yes, sir," she responded. Her makeup was smeared, and her eyes were bloodshot. "Anyone else inside?" I asked. She shook her head. "No, no. He's gone." She showed us inside, sobbing a few times.

"Alright, ma'am, tell us what happened." Alex had his notepad out and after a brief scan of the house to make sure there really was nobody else inside, I copied information from the woman's driver's license to record her identity. She appeared to be in her late 40s or early 50s and this was confirmed by her ID. She described how she and her husband had been at home when she went into his office to look something up on his computer. When she activated the screen, she was stunned to see a video screen open, showing young boys naked. She said the video showed the boys engaged in sexual activity with an older man, not her husband. Shocked by her discovery, she kept looking through the files, only to find more videos and still photos. All of explicit nature and all of them involving young, apparently underage, boys. While explaining all of this and describing her reaction of disgust and how repulsed she was by what she saw, she kept breaking into tears.

The doorbell rang, and the description of the incident was interrupted. I went and answered to find an adult woman at the front door. She said she was the victim's sister and had received a phone call to come over. The victim confirmed and asked to be allowed to see her sister. In order to provide some comfort, we allowed the sister in so she could console the victim and provide some comfort. However, we also asked her not to get involved in our questioning or comment on anything that we would discuss with the victim. She agreed, and the two women fell into each other's arms. However, to our surprise, the victim became more agitated rather than being soothed by her sister's presence. As we were standing in the middle of the bedroom, Alex attempted to solicit more information. "Ma'am, where is your husband now?" "Well, I confronted him about that horrible stuff I found on the computer. He had some lame excuse and acted very embarrassed. We argued, and I said that I would call the police. That's when he got really upset, stood up, and came up to me. I stood in front of the office door, and he pushed me aside, so I fell to the floor. We were yelling at each other." She described how they continued to argue as she picked up the phone to call 911. At that point, her husband turned around, went into the office, and took the computer out from under the desk, ripping the power cord out of the wall in the process—socket and all—and took off through the patio door.

I got on the radio and advised over the air that our suspect had fled the scene. The house was one of several in this small neighborhood street, with all of their backyards abutting the grounds of a local elementary school. As she provided a description of her husband, I requested air support to get some help from our eyes in the sky. The victim became more agitated and not only cried continuously but also started yelling at her sister. The sister asked, "Have you been drinking?" The question was met with a brief, "You bet I have." That statement was followed by her stepping closer to her sister, yelling profanities, and how the sister was of no help in this situation. I was still taking notes and copying the sister's driver's license when Alex decided to address the victim. "Ma'am! You need to calm down!" I stopped writing. One of the last things you want to tell someone who is highly agitated is that they need to calm down. The victim turned away from her sister and stood right in front of Alex, maybe two feet away from him. Poking Alex's badge with her finger and in a hysteric voice she said, "I haven't been fucked in 15 years. My husband likes little boys, and you want me to calm down!?" I looked down on my notepad and tried not to burst into a laughing fit. Very calmly, Alex said, "Ma'am, don't poke my badge." The sister, sensing that her sibling was about to get into trouble, pulled the victim back and said, "Let's sit down on the sofa, honey."

Survey One, the department's airplane, had been circling overhead this entire time. They set off a radio call and let us know that right now they saw someone standing outside the perimeter wall looking into the backyard straight at us. Alex immediately disengaged and ran over to the sliding glass door and attempted to open it, which wasn't as easy as it should have been. Finally, the door gave way, and he took off into the yard toward the perimeter wall. I stayed with the victim and her sister. Our sergeant had called out over the radio, announcing his presence, and he said he'd assist Alex. Someone had to stay with the victim, to make sure the suspect wouldn't return to the scene and open a much bigger can of worms that way. In closing the sliding glass door, I only saw Alex's feet disappear over the wall that bordered the backyard and separated it from the underbrush behind it.

On the radio, Alex was providing breathless updates on his location. Survey One was leading him from above. Using their FLIR camera, they had a detailed overview of the area and knew exactly where the suspect was in relation to Alex. The Sergeant said he'd be coming up a side street and would run toward the suspect from his location, effectively boxing him in. Then the TFD within Survey One told Alex the suspect had hunkered down and he was closing in on him. The radio traffic painted a vivid picture.

"6-3-8, Survey 1. Stop right there. Okay, walk about thirty yards to your right. Stop. Another 10 feet or so ahead of you there should be a bush or tree. That's where your suspect is hiding."

"6-3-8, 10-4. LET ME SEE YOUR HANDS!"

It was amazing. The kind of pinpoint accuracy the air crew had in calling all of this from a few thousand feet above the scene. Alex on the ground was probably just pointing his gun into the pitch-black of the night. A minute later, I heard Alex's voice on the radio again.

"6-3-8, 10-26 with one."

He had him in handcuffs. Unfortunately, the suspect did not have the computer with or near him and refused to account for the device. So, what could we do to find it?

The Sergeant keyed up, "Do we have any K-9 units nearby?"

"I'll check and advise," the dispatcher responded.

The Sergeant came to the scene to get a briefing from me. I gave him a quick rundown of what we had found and that besides the husband having pushed his wife to the floor, he may have been in possession of videos and photos depicting children being sexually abused. He asked if I had contacted victim advocates with the County Attorney's Victim Witness Program, which I confirmed and said they were on their way. He said that he would be waiting for the K-9 deputy, and once I was done at the scene, I should join him and the others to help with the search for the computer.

Inside the house, the two women were still in the living room and apparently had made their peace. In order to document any possible evidence, I brought my digital camera with me and went straight to the office. Turning on the lights in the small room that had a window out to the street, I saw where the CPU tower had been sitting under the desk from the impression on the carpet. Several cables were lying on the floor disconnected. Looking along the bottom of the wall behind the desk, I noticed a LAN cable was protruding from the wall. Some plaster was visible on the carpet, and it became clear that he had, as our victim had stated, simply ripped the computer out of the wall. In the process, the whole cable connection, complete with socket and screws, had come out of the wall and was probably still dangling from the computer. I snapped pictures of everything to document how rushed an exit the husband had made and to corroborate our victim's description of events.

I returned to the living room and saw that Alex had come back as well. He was sweaty and had scratches on his forearms from running through the underbrush. He asked me to take pictures of the victim for documentation purposes. Alex told her that should she develop bruising in the following days, she should report to the Sheriff's Department. He also let her know that her husband was under arrest and would be booked into the Pima County Jail. He recommended she come to the Department's administration building, where a forensic technician would document the injuries and by doing so make possible a comparison with how she looked on the night of the incident. It happened regularly that victims would show up a day or two later to have photographs taken of the fully developed bruises, where in the initial pictures you could only see redness or swelling.

Once the victim's statement had been obtained and the victim advocate had arrived, Alex and I connected with the K-9 handler. The sergeant stayed with the arrestee, so we could join the search. In trying to ascertain where our suspect might have dumped the computer, we began our search right behind the house, where the husband had been observed peeking over the wall. The police dog was able to search for items and began his search pattern in the underbrush behind the wall. Looking at the map, we figured that the husband may have run across the schoolyard or hidden on the nearby school grounds. We drove to the school's main gate and scaled it to enter the property. We walked the entire place without finding anything of significance. On one end of the schoolyard was a large trash dumpster, and it certainly was a possibility that our suspect had discarded his computer right there. I opened one of the large lids and, without hesitation, Alex descended into the trash inside. Stirring through the stinking debris and frequently yelling a variety of expletives from inside, he ended up smelly but empty-handed.

As deeply frustrating as it was, a significant amount of time had elapsed, and other calls were holding. We would have to leave it at that and turn the case over to detectives for follow-up. Alex returned to his car to relieve the sergeant and transport the suspect to jail. I checked in on the victim and the victim advocates at the house one last time. As they didn't need any more information from me, I left as well to find a quiet place somewhere to dictate my report.

One day, a group of us decided to meet at a local sandwich shop for lunch. It was a place where you could order one of those dripping, oozing, juicy sandwiches that could make your heart stop. I called it the cholesterol platter. They were a tasty vice, and I felt now and then I could probably have one of those. As we sat together, the guys were telling a story about a robbery they had responded to recently. There was a well-known, high-end spa in our district called "Gaddabout." They had three different locations in Beat 3 alone. Their clientele often included well-off customers, documented by their high-priced luxury vehicles parked in front of the building. You would find all sorts of ritzy cars patiently waiting for their drivers to be restyled. Maserati, Jaguar, Mercedes, BMW, Porsche, Cadillac—you name it. If something like this was "well known," then it was fair to assume that the crooks knew as well. And sure enough, it happened. The spa was entered by armed robbers who took money and valuables from everybody inside. A true heist like they are portrayed in the movies. Just that these were not gentlemen robbers, but rather hardened criminals who scared the living daylight out everybody in the store. Well, maybe not everybody.

Of course, 911 was called, and my colleagues responded. As they did not know if any of the suspects were still inside, everybody was ordered out in a hurry and sequestered in the parking lot. Once the place was presumed empty, a search party of several deputies went in, guns drawn, to clear the place. As they made their way through the establishment, a sergeant with the search party, armed with a shotgun, noticed someone still sitting under a hood hair dryer. Carefully walking up to the person, the Sergeant noticed it was a female customer. He walked up next to her and lightly tapped her on her shoulder. She was startled and then shocked to see the heavily armed law enforcement officer right next to her. "Excuse me, ma'am. Have you noticed anything unusual in the past 15 minutes or so?" he sarcastically asked the woman. It's hard to fathom, but this lady had sat through a robbery and the entire evacuation of the spa, sitting in an empty business for several minutes completely unaware of what was going on around her. She was escorted out, and the search continued without locating anybody else inside.

I'm not sure if you can picture the scene. There were people with half-finished manicures, women with paper towel pieces in between their toes, facial masks still applied, aluminum foil in their hair, or wet hair. Add to that your standard spa staff, who were now concerned for the client's well-being and the partially applied treatments or worse, hair colorations that were now staying applied to their customer's hair for way too long. My friend Will Novak was in charge of trying to obtain statements from folks who witnessed the robbery or fell victim to it. A tough task with so many people involved. As he was trying to handle this onslaught of statements and keep things organized, he became a little flustered. So it didn't help when a male employee of the spa ran around among his clients nipping at hair, burying his face in his palms, or throwing his hands in the air, all a grand show of "concern" for the beauty of his customers, which he now considered in jeopardy. He also kept inquiring with Will as to the time it would take to get everybody back inside. Will, meanwhile, was sitting in a pile of paper, was being bugged by people who were upset they weren't allowed in the parking lot to park their cars and he had just learned that the local TV stations had sent their breaking news crews to obtain video footage. Sitting in his patrol car, he turned to the male employee who was whining in his ear and said, "Jules! Listen! I need you to get back with the other people. We are doing our best to get this done as quickly as possible. But right now, you're not helping with the process!" Jules? Needless to say, the gentleman's name was not Jules. It was simply something Will had come up with at the time and just blurted it out.

Everybody at our table broke into hysterical laughter over the story. "Jules" became quite the story, together with the lady underneath the hooded hair dryer. Those were stories that would only happen in Rincon.

Not all stories had that sort of humor, but often enough things would go from seriously dangerous to bone cracking funny. So, it happened on a night where we were four deputies in the metro beat. Whoa! Four deputies! That meant we had plenty of backup available and still deputies free to answer other calls. Immediately, we switched into proactive mode and began to comb the entire beat for suspicious activity. As I was close, I decided to take a drive through an area we called Dodge City. It was a small bubble of the county which expanded into the city limits. A few city blocks of unincorporated county, surrounded by the city of Tucson. It consisted of an area surrounding Dodge Boulevard and Fort Lowell Road. There were a few businesses, but otherwise, it had mostly dilapidated trailers and apartment buildings. It was in the middle of an area known for its abundance of drug dealers and other dubious individuals. From our perspective, those were promising hunting grounds. The streets, with one exception, did not have any sidewalks and were sparsely lit.

It was after midnight already and I was slowly cruising down Chapel Avenue when I noticed a couple walking northbound with traffic. As there was no sidewalk in this area, they were required to walk against traffic and therefore had violated a statute. I pulled my patrol car up behind them and turned on my overhead lights. The couple briefly stopped, and the man turned halfway around as if to confirm it was the police stopped behind them. As soon as I opened the driver's side door, the man bolted across the street. "Stop! Police!" I yelled as I ran after him.

"6-2-4. 10-80 on foot. Chapel & Farr going north," I breathlessly blared into my lapel mic.

He was a few yards ahead of me when he made a sudden turn to the left and disappeared in a trailer park. As I got to the corner where he had turned, I slowed down to walk. The main drive into the small trailer park that consisted of only eight to ten trailers was unpaved. As I walked onto the dark property, I could still taste the stirred-up dust from his running. Then my safety instinct finally kicked in. I drew my handgun from my holster and used my index finger to switch on the tac light underneath the barrel. Small dust particles were dancing in the bright cone of light. He was definitely there somewhere, possibly pointing a gun at me. As my vision slowly adapted to the darkness, I noticed in my peripheral vision shadowy outlines of people standing next to some of the trailers or sitting in chairs in front of them. I could feel how they were looking at me. It was a show, and I was the main act. I quickly realized how exposed I was by standing in the middle of this dirt driveway, backlit by the distant streetlight. My silhouette made a perfect target. Slowly, my gun still pointed into the dark abyss of this run-down place, I backtracked toward the street. What was I thinking? Darting in there without any backup or even air support.

I keyed up on the radio, "6-2-4. I lost visual of the subject. He fled into a dark trailer park. I have retreated to the gate. Start me a 10-78 please."

"6-2-4, 10-4. Unit for 10-78 at Chapel and Farr, Farr and Chapel?"

Within seconds, two other units and the sergeant acknowledged and advised they were already in the vicinity. They must have had started this way as soon as I broadcasted the foot chase.

After what seemed to be a terribly long time, a patrol car with its emergency lights on came barreling toward me. The car turned off its headlights to not illuminate me any longer and pulled up across the dirt shoulder on the other side of the entrance to the trailer park. From behind me came another patrol car, and the scene was flooded with the soothing red and blue swirls of light. God, this felt good! My weapon was still trained through the opening in the fence. A former classmate of mine, Tyler, yelled from across the entrance, "Let's go!" Close behind me, I heard the familiar voice of my sergeant, "Go ahead. I've got your six." The direction of our guns synchronized with our line of sight, and we walked back into the trailer park. A flashlight behind me alternatively illuminated the surrounding trailers from right to left. People were shielding their eyes from the bright LED light. They had been watching us the whole time. On the first property to the left was an old school bus that had haphazardly been transferred into a trailer home. I banged my fist against the front set of doors. Tyler said he had dealt with the resident and a runner on a previous occasion. He was certain our guy was in here. The door was opened, and a tired looking, middle-aged man appeared. His face was weathered from years of substance abuse and long-term exposure to the hot, dry desert weather.

"Did anyone come in here within the past few minutes? Or did someone ask you to let them in here?" Tyler asked.

The answer was a dragged out "No," delivered in a questioning tone, as if it was something truly outrageous Tyler was suggesting. The man stood in the door with his hands resting against the frame of the school bus doors.

"You mind if we take a look?" I followed up.

"Do you have a warrant?" the reflexive question came back.

"No, we don't have a warrant. But we have reason to believe you're hiding someone in here who just ran off from a traffic stop," I replied.

"Well, he's not here," the man stubbornly said.

"Okay, then. We can stand here for the next few hours and wait while we obtain a search warrant, keep everybody up, and continue to turn this whole place upside down. The guy who fled ran into this property and is hunkered down here somewhere. If you let us take a quick look around inside, we'll be out of your hair in no time."

He thought for a few seconds and then stepped down and out of his bus. "Okay. Go ahead then. But don't make a mess of everything," he said.

Guns still drawn, we stepped inside. What a joke, I thought. *Don't make a mess.* This place was a raging mess to begin with. Stuff, a good amount of it seemingly trash, was stacked left and right, all the way up to the windowsill. The bus had been gutted of its seats and turned into a living room/kitchen combo. We looked behind closed doors and other potential hiding places, but quickly progressed toward a "bedroom" in the back of the bus. The covers were piled up in a bunch on top of the bed. Tyler looked at me, pointed at the pile, and nodded. I nodded in confirmation. Tyler leaned forward and grasped the edge of the duvet. With a strong pull he ripped the blanket away and revealed a young man who had cowered down underneath. We broke into a barrage of "Hands! Hands!" commands. "Don't be stupid," Tyler said. And for good measure, I added, "Nobody needs to get hurt tonight." Tyler quickly holstered his weapon before our guy could come to his senses and try to run again. He grabbed the young man's arm and asked him to turn over onto his belly. Handcuffs went on and that was it. We escorted him outside.

"Thank you," I said in the direction of the owner as we stepped back outside and walked the arrestee back to my car. He was still wearing the distinct reddish-brown T-shirt I had noticed and called out at the beginning of our pursuit, so I knew we'd apprehended the right person, and it turned out he had a warrant for his arrest. We exchanged Tyler's handcuffs for mine and put the guy in the back of my car. Then we gathered a few steps away from the car for a quick debrief.

The sergeant looked at me and said, "What was that, Peine?" He changed the tone of his voice to a high pitch, "6-2-4. It's dark out here. I'm scared." He and the other deputies started laughing and I couldn't resist either. It was a friendly laugh, though, not a mocking one. I attempted to explain and said, "I couldn't see shit. And then I noticed those guys on each side—" The sergeant interrupted me, "I'm just busting your chops, Peine. You did the absolute right thing. Don't lose your head during a foot chase. Be smart and remember that we all want to go home at the end of our shift." The deputies nodded in somber agreement. This could have quickly gone wrong. "Okay, on your way. Get him booked and then hurry up to get back out here. We've got work to do." As everybody walked to their cars, he looked at me one more time and said, "You did the right thing." As he walked away to his own patrol car, he sounded off the same high pitch voice one more time, "It's scary dark out here."

There is another noteworthy location unique to the Rincon District. It was called Fenster School. Fenster used to be a high-end boarding school. Located on a huge property next to Sabino Canyon, students were housed in rustic dorms surrounding a common courtyard. It was a place where rich people from all over the country sent their troubled children they could no longer control. For a "tuition" priced north of $30,000 a year, counselors and residential advisors would look after them. Unfortunately, staff members had lost control of their student body a while ago. Drug dealing among students was rampant. They had also begun to expand their trade beyond the boundaries of the school campus. With that, it had become a target of our investigations. In addition, staff began to increasingly rely on our interventions once situations got out of order. I vividly remember my first call to Fenster during field training. Two students were fighting, and there was real concern that it would escalate into an all-out student brawl. Upon arrival, my FTO walked into the courtyard and ordered the students who had gathered there into their dorms. But rather than following his orders, they just quietly stood and stared at us. My FTO quickly escalated his approach, drew his Taser and yelled at them "I said, get back in your fucking dorms!" Reluctantly and with audible moaning, they followed suit. That seemed ages ago now.

On this particular night, I responded because one of the residential advisors had confronted a student over suspicions of drug dealing. Over the course of their conversation, the student physically assaulted the advisor and then locked himself in his room. A backup deputy was still en route when I walked into the office building. A young woman looked at me through a set of French doors that led to the courtyard and, with a worried tone in her voice, she said, "Quick, over here! They're fighting." Without much thinking, I ran into the courtyard and saw a crowd of students in front of an open dorm room. "Step back," I yelled at them loudly. "Get back into your rooms!" As I walked up to the open door, I noticed one of the advisors had restrained a juvenile on the floor. I walked up to them, and he said, "This is the guy who hit my boss." As he said that, he pointed at the open bathroom door, where I saw the staff supervisor, fittingly a former state correctional officer, on his knees in front of the toilet.

I took control of the arms of the young man on the floor and put my handcuffs on him. We propped him up, seated with his back against the wall. Then I walked into the bathroom and noticed that the toilet had flooded, and murky water stood everywhere. The staff supervisor was still knelt in front of the toilet, his left arm entirely submerged in the filthy brown water of the toilet. "Little smartass," he said, looking in the direction of the youth who sat handcuffed against the wall. "Thought he could outsmart me by flushing his dope down the toilet. Not with me, my friend." Then his eyes widened, and he looked up at me. A broad smile emerged across his face. "I got it," he said. Slowly, his left arm came back out of that brown soup. After a few inches, the water drained with a loud slurp into the sewage pipe. Out of the toilet, pinched in between his fingers, the supervisor held a large Ziploc bag containing familiar looking green buds. It was a good pound to pound and a half of marijuana. With a tone of triumph, the supervisor said, "That little shit. Man, I wasn't born yesterday. And a toilet is neither a good hiding place for dope, nor is it an obstacle to me." He looked angry and said to me, "I have to clean up. I'll be back shortly to answer your questions. Just give me a minute to wash this off." I said, "Of course," and he walked off.

My backup arrived as I walked the young man out to my car. Office staff had provided me with his student file and as I ran his information through the Arizona Criminal Justice Information System, I noted that this was not his first brush with the law in Tucson. The plastic bag with the marijuana sat on top of the trunk of my car. Using a few kitchen towels, I wiped it dry and then dumped its contents into a paper evidence bag. The odor of fresh marijuana sifted through the air. Then I packaged the plastic bag separately and put red "biohazard" stickers on it because it had been submerged in raw sewage. One of the advisors came out, and we asked him to bring out everybody involved in the matter or people who may have witnessed anything. All in all, we had to talk to eight students and staff, which made for a pretty substantial report.

Luckily, I had a backup deputy who I could share the workload with. When the supervisor returned with wet hair and a fresh T-shirt, I learned that they had suspected the arrestee of dealing drugs for some time. After they had received a tip, he and another counselor hid in the brush along a wash that ran through the property and was often used by students to sneak off campus. When they saw the young man, they confronted him, but he ran off. Though they pursued him, he was able to get into this room and locked the door from the inside. With a secondary key, the supervisor quickly gained access, and a scuffle ensued. During which, the suspect punched the supervisor. He then turned to the bathroom, dropped the bag of marijuana into the toilet, and flushed. Due to the size of the bag, this resulted in the toilet flooding and another slippery scuffle began. In the end, the student was restrained, and the supervisor began to fish for the drug load by sinking his arm deep into the toilet.

As was to be expected, a few days later, I returned to the school regarding a different matter. Staff members told me that they were really fed up with the previously arrested boy's behavior and told the parents he would have to leave. The parents had been contacted by the school following the boy's initial court appearance. The father became very upset and asked what they expected him to do. After a bit of an explanation of the boy's antics, the father said to send his son back. School staff then drove the young man to Tucson International Airport and put him on a flight to meet with his dad… in Italy. The father was in Europe on an extended business trip. So, after being arrested for dealing drugs on his school's campus, he got to fly to Italy. Fenster School certainly was in a class of its own.

Not far from Fenster School was one of the top resorts Tucson had to offer. The Loew's Ventana was nestled in the foothills of the Catalina Mountains and only a very short distance from Sabino Canyon. It was a five-star luxury destination where the rich and famous frequently turned in for the night. Not only was their accommodation and golf course top notch, but their signature restaurant also attracted an affluent audience. It was rare that we ever had to respond to their business, but this particular night was an exception. A guest who had attended an event at the hotel reported his brand-new Ford Mustang stolen. Hotel staff had seen how it had been driven away from the main building's parking lot. While Gabriel and I responded, we received an update to this otherwise rather mundane call providing information that the car had entered another part of the large Ventana property to the south. There was another part of the resort called the Ventana Lodge, which was a few notches lower on the pricing scale than the main hotel. It had a guarded entrance and the security officer posted at the gate reported that he had seen the stolen vehicle enter the grounds of the lodge. Management there had been alerted and located the car in the parking lot.

Gabriel and I arrived a few minutes later and drove straight up to the Lodge. We were met in the parking lot by the manager. He showed us the car parked nearby. It was indeed the vehicle reported stolen earlier that night. We learned that the person who had parked it there was a guest of the Lodge. As we stood there taking notes, Jason Reynolds, a K9-Deputy, arrived with his dog and asked if he could be of assistance. He and his K9 partner could indeed be very helpful, and we gladly accepted his offer. The manager added that the suspect was not alone, but had a female companion with him. We asked to be shown to the room.

It was on the second floor, just across from a flight of stairs. The four of us walked up to the door. Us deputies quickly formulated a plan. We would knock at the door and announce ourselves as law enforcement. Jason would provide assistance with his K9 partner. We prepared for the possibility of an armed encounter and drew our weapons. Guns depressed, we stood to the left and right of the hotel room door. Gabriel loudly knocked on the door and announced us: "Sheriff's Department! Open the door!" Jason's dog became very excited by the commotion and commands familiar to him, signaling some kind of action he might get involved in. The dog leaned on the leash, which Jason held tightly. He barked once but was hushed by Jason. Gabriel repeated his knock-and-announce. No response. We gestured to the manager, who stepped up to unlock the door. Standing off to the side, he turned the key, cracked the door open, pulled the key back out, and then quickly stepped off to the side.

DEPUTY WHILE IMMIGRANT

Gabriel and I nodded at each other and with a quick turn, we pointed our guns straight down the hallway into the room. Still partially covered by the door frame, I saw a man's shoe, a white shirt, a pair of high heels, a thong, and other clothing items strewn about on the floor and leading toward the rear bedroom. Once again, we loudly announced our presence. Again, there was no response from inside. My adrenaline spiked. The silence was striking, as we had announced several times and probably woke half of the guests on this floor. Yet, nobody answered from within this room. Were they waiting around the corner, guns drawn? Had they stepped out onto the balcony? Were they in the bathroom? Were they hurt? Maybe the room was empty? Though the last option didn't really make sense. But, hey, you never know. Slowly and methodically, we made our way into the room, coming down the hallway. Using a technique called "slice the pie," I cleared the corner toward the bedroom and immediately noticed two sets of legs in the bed.

Clearing the corner further, we could see the two suspects lying in bed. They looked perfectly fine from a distance and seemed sound asleep. Jason was right behind us with his dog, who was panting heavily with excitement. Jason was leaning backward to control the dog's forceful pull on the short leash. We could not see enough of the suspects' bodies, especially their hands, to be sure there were no weapons hidden in the bed. We quickly decided to separate the female from the man first. Pointing his gun at the seemingly passed out man, Gabriel provided cover. I walked up to the left side of the bed and pulled the young, naked woman by her arm. She did not react. I shook her a bit, while trying to maintain a safe distance in case she would be startled and attack me. Slowly, very slowly, she partially opened her eyes, which is when I gave her a good yank, turned her around, and pulled her toward me. Holding a strong grip on her wrist and keeping her arm behind her back, I said in a low voice, "It's all okay. This is the police. Be quiet. We'll explain everything in a minute." My handcuffs went around her wrists, and I brought her to her legs. On a chair behind us was a bathrobe, and I wrapped it around her, showing her to sit down in the chair. Jason kept an eye on her.

Now we had to take care of our main suspect. Gabriel said to step in closer and provide cover with my Taser. The man was lying on his belly with his right arm to his side and his left arm angled in an L-shape toward his head. He would get onto the bed and use the suspect's position to gain control of his arms and quickly cuff him. Should that fail, he would try to disengage, and I would deploy my Taser. With Jason and the young woman looking on, Gabriel held out his hand and with his fingers counted down from three. Then he knelt on the bed and then quickly grabbed onto the suspect's arm. That finally woke the man up. He began to resist. Gabriel told him, "Police! Stop resisting!" The guy looked at me and saw me point my Taser at him, which seemed to convince him it was better to let things happen. As soon as he was in handcuffs, he asked, "Where's my girl?" We pointed her out to him, as she was still sitting in the chair. "You fucking pigs! Don't touch my girl. What the fuck do you want from me!?" He learned that he was suspected of car theft, and he was asked how he got to the hotel. "I drove here in my car," was his response. This was not going to be easy. The manager had told us in the parking lot that they had video evidence from several cameras on the property and the gates, which would clearly show the suspect driving the stolen car. It was agreed to let the woman go into the bathroom to put on some clothes. However, our demand for her to leave the door cracked open so she couldn't lock herself in or gain access to a weapon was met with a furious outrage by the detainee. He cussed at us and accused us of simply being interested in watching his naked girlfriend get dressed. "You better show my girl some respect," was his demand. We explained that there were no ill-intentions on our part, but that we also couldn't let her entirely out of our sights as that would create a possible safety risk for us. The man was highly agitated, most likely fueled by whatever substance he and his girlfriend had consumed prior to going to bed. Jason let his dog bark, which scared the bejeebers out of me, but failed to impress the detainee. "You think your damn dog scares me, motherfucker?" Well, it scared me as I had seen what they could do to a non-compliant human being, and I was thankful for Jason maintaining thorough control of his dog. The woman got dressed in the bathroom and came back. She was mostly quiet, but certainly not cooperative. We also put some pants and a T-shirt on the young man. He was not in agreement with anything that was going on around him and became increasingly agitated. We decided to bring him to my patrol car first. With me to his left and Gabriel to his right, we held him by his arms with his hands still cuffed behind his back. As we came up to the staircase, he moved from side to side as if he was trying to shake us off. We were not going to risk falling down the stairs. So, while this guy was cussing up a storm, waking up the entire hotel, we stopped next to the stairway and pulled out our batons. That briefly rendered our detainee quiet. We then stuck the expanded batons through his arms and crossed them over his shoulders, effectively creating an "X" across his upper back. That enabled us to lift him up and carry him down the stairs without him having the ability to trip us on our way down. The entire time, he continued to yell and scream, cuss obscenities at us, and loudly proclaim his innocence.

Once we arrived at my car, we took the batons off the man's back. When I attempted to put him in the cage of my car, he refused to enter. He put his feet against the bottom door jamb and stiffened his body, while yelling out loud through the parking lot. It took a while and Gabriel's assistance to stuff, push, and pull him into the back of my car. The man's attitude was very aggressive. He continued to yell insults at us and threatened he would one day encounter us alone or off duty and then "your badge ain't gonna help you, asshole." Finally, after a few minutes of intense struggle, he was inside, and I closed the door on him. Our sergeant arrived at the scene and requested a briefing. He told me to get the arrestee to jail and not delay the transport, as he was obviously highly agitated. The sergeant then went to talk to the hotel's manager and the other two deputies. As I took a seat behind the steering wheel of my patrol car, the arrestee seemed to have momentarily taken time to catch his breath. "Alright, man. Here's the situation," I told him. "You are under arrest for car theft. Are there any warrants out for your arrest that you know of?" Hearing about the arrest, he went into a renewed frenzy. "I didn't steal a damn thing! That's some total bullshit," he said and kicked the back of my seat. I turned my car around to drive toward the exit. As I headed through the parking lot, my arrestee had slid sideways on the plastic back bench, despite the seatbelt providing some restraint, and he started to kick against the opposite back window. Fortunately, I had a cage with metal bars against the windows from the inside, preventing him from kicking out the window entirely. I brought the car to an abrupt stop and turned myself around. "Listen! You behaving like a dickhead back there is not going to stop you from going to jail. The only thing that might happen is that we tack on additional charges if you damage anything inside this car. Your call!" His response consisted of him starting to bang his head against the Plexiglas separating him from me. I got out and opened the back door. "Stop banging your head," I yelled at him. Gabriel and the Sergeant came running toward my car. Before he reached us, the sergeant yelled out, "Get him out and hog-tie him!"

The term "hog-tie" referred to a way of completely immobilizing a prisoner, who was in danger of hurting himself or others. We dragged him out onto the pavement, where he continued to struggle with us. Using some special straps and ties, we tied his feet together at his ankles and bent his legs at the knees. The tie around his ankles was then attached to his handcuffs, rendering him mostly unable to move or at least not able to move without hurting himself in the process. We lifted him off the ground and laid him on his belly across the back bench of my car. It was decided to have Gabriel follow me to the jail. He ended up turning around when we came up on 22nd Street as the guy in the back remained calm, aside from a few mumbled curses.

While en route to the Pima County Adult Detention Complex, which was the official term for the jail, I notified Comm that I had a combative arrestee and would need assistance upon arrival at the jail. I hurried up to limit the time the prisoner had to lie the way he was in the back of my car. Upon arrival at the jail, I was met by a group of four Corrections Officers (CO) and a Corrections Sergeant. They had brought out a restraint chair, which we sometimes referred to as the "Hannibal Lecter." One of the

DEPUTY WHILE IMMIGRANT

COs was filming the entire incident with a video camera for evidentiary purposes. The sergeant opened the back door of my patrol car and introduced himself. Then he said, "So listen. Here's the deal. We can get you out of the car, take the restraints off, and walk you inside, like any other reasonable person coming in here. Or we can force you into that chair and strap you down for the safety of all of us and the other inmates. The choice is yours. What's it going to be?" While still on his belly in the back of my car, the mumble response was "That's okay. I'll be cool." Suddenly, he was not so "badass" anymore.

The COs looked at me, shrugged, and lifted him out of my car. They laid him onto the pavement and unbuckled the foot restraint from his handcuffs, enabling the man to stand on his feet. He was brought up, and the restraint was removed from his ankles. The prisoner had become fully compliant and walked inside with them, where he was immediately brought into the search area, away from the room where all the other arrestees were waiting to be booked. I turned in all my paperwork for him and went back outside. From the trunk of my car, I retrieved the spray bottle of Lysol to disinfect the cuffs and spray down the backseat of my car. Gabriel and I met later in a quiet side street to debrief and then file our reports. Other calls would need to be covered soon, and we wanted to use the lull for our administrative work.

It was not only the adrenaline-laden calls that would surprise me or add to the growing library of "now-I-have-seen-it-all" moments. Much more somber scenarios were routinely part of my shift work. While assisting a young junior deputy, I responded as backup to a Code 900 call. A woman had called 911 and reported she had found her husband deceased. Nothing too much out of the ordinary, I thought, but decided to go with the rookie to make sure he would not miss anything.

I arrived at a nice home in an upscale neighborhood of the Catalina Foothills. The primary deputy had arrived already, and together we made contact with the caller at the front door. It turned out to be the wife of the deceased. Paramedics were still at the scene but wrapping up. She explained how she had found her husband deceased in the bedroom after returning from a shopping trip. A friend was present for support as well. We asked one of the firefighters to be shown to the bedroom.

The naked body of an adult man laid on the bed the way paramedics had left him there, electrodes still attached. I took photos of the bedroom and the body for evidence. The primary deputy came in and said that the medics had not found anything unusual other than the fact that the deceased seemed rather young for a natural death and theorized about some unknown, underlying condition. We also learned that he was a medical doctor. As we proceeded with our investigation, we included the walk-in closet accessible from the bedroom. On a shelf at about eye-level, there was a type of device I had not encountered before. It looked as if it came straight from a laboratory and two large, clear plastic bags with a fitting at the bottom were right next to it. The device turned out to be a vaporizer used to enhance the effects of marijuana consumption. The widow explained that her husband had used it to conceal his habit of using marijuana. The vaporizer reportedly prevented him from smelling like marijuana after using and also did not leave the telltale green layer on his tongue. Besides the vaporizer, which we took into evidence, we found marijuana and a fair number of narcotic prescription drugs the deceased had purchased and illegally imported from Mexico. A case of "high end" drug use. Again, this went into the category of "when you think you've seen it all." A medical doctor who had mastered the concealment of his illegal drug habit.

In 2008, Annie and I were finally able to afford a vacation after going without any for the past three years. We used a special offer from a Westin Hotels to spend five days in Hawaii. Our trip to Maui was heavenly. We enjoyed the tropical environment, the beaches, the relaxed atmosphere, and the lack of daily chores. Then, on June 2nd or 3rd, I received a message from back home from coworkers. Two deputies had been injured and a TPD officer had been killed during a mad rampage of an individual. It all had started in the Foothills district, where the first deputy was injured by the suspect's gunfire. A chase across town ensued and coming through the Rincon district, the suspect had killed Tucson Police Officer Erik Hite, and fired at one of the deputies stationed on Mount Lemmon, with the bullet scraping his head. The place where Officer Hite died was only a few hundred yards from our district office. A location I had passed regularly while on shift. It was crushing to hear. Though I was not there or involved, it happened at my place of work and a fellow law enforcement officer had died—in the "quiet" district.

TPD Officer Erik Hite succumbed to a gunshot wound sustained the previous day by a suspect who had wounded one of our deputies. Following a pursuit through the streets of Tucson involving both TPD and the Sheriff's Department, the suspect turned into a small residential street east of the Rincon District Office and set up an ambush. As Officer Hite turned the corner onto the street, the suspect opened fire from a distance of approximately 80 yards, striking him in the head. The suspect continued to flee and wounded another deputy before finally surrendering. He left behind his wife, adult son, and his then one-year-old daughter. Nohemy Hite, Erik's wife, would later establish the Erik Hite Foundation that supports Southern Arizona's first responders and their families.

Fellow deputies kept me in the loop regarding funeral preparations for Erik, as we would be involved as a sign of solidarity and to help out TPD on a day that would stretch their department's resources due to their participation in the funeral. I let folks back home know that I would volunteer as needed.

When we returned from our trip, and I contacted my district, I learned that we would be heavily involved in the funeral procession. Deputies would assist with coverage of emergency calls in TPD's jurisdiction, so officers who wanted to attend the funeral could do so. We also volunteered to line the streets and block intersections during the funeral procession from the church all the way to the cemetery.

It was June 10, 2008, and as was typical for this time of year, it was seasonably hot outside with 106 degrees Fahrenheit. The searing temperature made the air above the roadway flicker. We stood on both sides of the street, dressed in our Class A uniforms and joined by thousands of civilians, who stood alongside us. I stood at the intersection of a small residential street with Speedway Boulevard on Tucson's Eastside. I had parked my car on the shoulder of the side street and walked up to my assigned post on the shoulder of Speedway Boulevard. As we stood at ease, waiting for the procession to arrive, more and more civilians arrived. Older people, families with children, people holding American flags, veterans in uniform, scouts in uniform, a broad representation of the citizens of Tucson. Over the radio, we heard that the procession had started from the church. (Videos of the procession can be found on YouTube.) The lead vehicle was a Sheriff's Department patrol car, so we knew where the tip of the procession was as they would regularly broadcast updates of their position. People kept asking me how far out they were and as they came closer, the assembly of citizens turned quiet. Then I saw the emergency lights in the distance. When the lead vehicle approached our position, we stood at attention. What followed was a motorcycle escort of epic proportions. One hundred and sixty motorcycle officers on their bikes passed our position as the hearse inched closer and closer. The lump in my throat became bigger as I thought about Erik Hite, who I may or may not have met during one of my shifts. He was born roughly a month ahead of me, so we were of the same age. He had started his service with TPD a year and a half before I had started with the Sheriff's Department. And he had worked on the Eastside, close to and intertwined with our area of operation. Finally, he had died incredibly close to the place where I reported for duty every day. It all filled me with an incredible sadness. How incredibly sad for his wife and their children! Most likely, he went to work that morning just like I did every day. Saying goodbye to his wife and children, fully expecting to be back home a few hours later. As the hearse came up on our location, we all saluted. Though I tried not to, I could not keep a few tears from running down my cheeks as his body, followed by a set of limousines with his family inside, was driven past our position.

DEPUTY WHILE IMMIGRANT

Suddenly, I felt a welcome relief from the heat as I lowered my arm from the salute once the hearse and family vehicles had passed. A procession of hundreds of police cars, some 11 miles long, followed the hearse and the family. Now I noticed that someone was holding an umbrella over my head. Without turning around as I was still standing at attention, I said from the corner of my mouth to the person I pictured standing somewhere behind me, "Thank you so much, but that's really not necessary. I'm okay. Thank you." The umbrella remained over my head and an older male voice quietly said, "No, no. It's okay. This is about the least I can do for you guys. Thank you for your service." That almost made me cry again. The feeling of being rooted in and being respected by the community we served, was incredibly powerful, reassuring, and yet reminded me of the bond that was ours to honor and preserve by the way we performed our duties every day.

A small memorial was erected at the place where Erik Hite lost his life while serving his community. From that point on, each time I had a rookie training with me or a civilian ride-along in my car, I would stop by and tell them about Erik and what happened that day. He will not be forgotten.

9

RIDE-ALONGS

Like I said, the relationship with the community we served was incredibly important. Just as they told us in the academy, "The badge you wear is not just a sign of power. It is also a sign of trust the community has in you." And there were a lot of things we could and would do during our everyday encounters with the citizens of Pima County. Kids were often especially fond of us. They wanted to look at our cars or motorcycles, check out our uniforms or the items on our duty belt. Parents would teach them to be respectful of law enforcement officers, and there were few things more enjoyable than that little girl who gave me a big hug once I had come to her level outside a Subway restaurant. The mother apologized but explained that her daughter just adored cops. I told them no apology was needed and that her daughter had most certainly just made my day.

Beside these coincidental encounters, there were also more structured ways to interact with us as law enforcement officers. There was, of course, the volunteer organization that supported us with countless hours of service during a great variety of scenarios. But there was also something I had not heard of prior to joining the force and certainly had never heard of it in Germany. It was the civilian ride-along.

At the beginning of this book, I invited you to join me for a virtual ride-along. Well, there was actually such a thing—non-virtual. As a civilian, you had the opportunity to apply for a ride-along with a Deputy Sheriff for a regular shift as long as you received approval and signed a liability waiver. And people did sign up. On occasion, I would be assigned a citizen ride-along or even brought someone along myself. During my time of service, I had family members, friends, German police officers, and a reporter from G-Town come along for one of my work shifts.

Having a civilian ride-along could be a lot of fun, but it could also be a drag. I remember a high school student who had requested it as part of a career exploration assignment from his school. If he asked me even five questions during that eight-hour shift, I'd be surprised. I constantly tried to trigger his curiosity, asked him questions, made jokes, told him about my then teenage son. But nothing came back. It was like driving around and working with a lead ball attached to my leg.

It was also a tremendous responsibility. Having a ride-along meant that I did not only have to worry about my own safety, the safety of my coworkers, the safety of those I was dealing with, but now also the safety of the person I had in tow, which was typically someone without any experience of how to handle volatile, potentially life-threatening situations. In order to create some sensitivity for the types of situations and scenarios we might encounter, I conducted a safety briefing before going out onto the streets with my ride-along. Prior to the safety briefing and getting into my car, I would invite the person back into our briefing room, and while I would gather a few items, I tried to learn a little bit about the individual themselves. Why had they asked to go on a ride-along? Once we were in my car, I would explain all the equipment and lay down some safety rules:

1) During traffic stops, you remain inside the patrol car unless I tell you otherwise.
2) When dealing with citizens, you will stay behind me or near me so I can direct you as needed should a situation get out of hand.
3) Should you be uncomfortable or fearful in any situation, leave and return to the patrol car.
4) If you leave, make sure I am aware of where you went.
5) Should we end up in a situation where a fight or even a gun fight ensues, take cover.

a. If possible, stay near the patrol car.
   b. If I tell you to, it is okay to get on the radio and let the dispatcher know what's happening in plain English.
   c. Once other deputies or police officers arrive, identify yourself as a civilian ride-along.
6) Do not engage with anyone other than me while we are on a call.
7) If you have a question, you may ask. Be prepared that I may tell you to wait until after the call.
8) Do not take any photos during the ride-along (unless explicitly permitted) or record audio or video.
9) You cannot have any guns, knives, or other weapons on you. If you do, leave them in your vehicle or we can lock them up at the station.

There may have been other things I have told them, but these are the topics I readily recall. Finally, if I felt it was appropriate to do so (it was not with the high school student), I would ask the person if they had ever handled a rifle or shotgun. If they answered positively, I would follow up with the question if they had been comfortable handling such a weapon. If the answer was positive again, I explained the unlocking mechanism for the patrol rifle located in between our seats. I said that this was only to be used if I am in immediate danger of being killed (i.e., I was overwhelmed by an aggressor and he was trying to gain access to my firearm or has gained such control already and is likely to use it against me or someone else) and only then could they come to my aid if they were comfortable doing so.

The last part was when reality would set in. That is when the mood was set to a more realistic expectation and behavior, rather than looking at the experience as some sort of joyful adventure. It was real life, real danger, real people, and often enough, real suffering.

One day, I had an interested member of the community as a ride-along. We received a report of a possible fire at the Ventana Country Club near Sabino Canyon. As the excitement was clearly visible in my ride-along's face, I tried to tone down the expectations a little. "You know, people will often call in any kind of smoke they see in the area and suspect it's a fire. That's perfectly okay, especially as we live in such a tinder dry climate out here. But many times, we arrive only to find out that it was, in fact, someone having a good time with their BBQ grill." I received a somewhat disappointed looking smile in response. As we drove eastbound on Sunrise Drive and turned left onto Kolb Road, which is where the main gate into the country club is located, we could see thick smoke billowing and flames reaching into the dark night sky. I got on the radio.

"6-2-4, I have a visual on the fire and it looks pretty substantial. If fire is not on scene already, tell them to expedite. 10-70 is confirmed!"

So much for me trying to tone things down. My ride-along gave me a dismissive look as we drove through the open gate of the country club and past the guard, who looked at the fire engine turning in right behind me. As we came up to the small cul-de-sac, we could see that it was a two-storied mansion that was on fire. And it was burning. From the scene around the building, it looked as if renovation work had been going on. I drove through the cul-de-sac and waited for the fire engine to pull in. Then I pulled my patrol car across the access street to block anyone else from driving in. Neighbors stood in their driveways, painting an odd picture with their worried faces illuminated by the orange glow of the house fire across from their properties. The fire crew went about their business and raised a second alarm, as they needed more manpower to handle the blaze. In the end, it turned out that some oil rags left by construction workers on the second floor had most likely self-ignited, causing the devastating fire.

On a different occasion, my ride-along and I were having a lively discussion about proactive policing. We drove into Dodge City and I explained its significance as a crime hot spot within Beat 3. Going at almost walking speed with rolled down windows, we cruised through the neighborhood. People were looking out the window, likely headed for their phones next to warn their buddies of our presence in the "hood." As we came up to a Circle K convenience store, there were two cars sitting in the parking lot, one of them occupied by a passenger. As I drove past,

DEPUTY WHILE IMMIGRANT

I immediately noticed the passenger's stare glued to my car, seemingly curious as to where I was going. That look was never a good sign. Looking through the shop window, everything seemed peaceful inside. There were several customers inside, and it looked as if everybody was simply going about their business. However, the passenger's look at me had spiked my "cop senses." I drove into the next side street, made a U-turn and drove back onto the main street, passing the store one more time. This time, I ran the license plate of the vehicle. Pulling into the side street next to the store, the passenger's eyes were once again stuck to my car. He looked at the storefront and then the driver came out. We were just about to go past the side of the building when I saw him grab the door handle. The second we reached the back of the building and continued on the neighborhood street, the return of my license plate inquiry popped up on the screen. The car was stolen! I immediately got on the radio. "6-2-4, confirm Code 18-0-3." The dispatcher ran the plate again and as I turned around, he confirmed that the car was indeed stolen. We came back up on the Circle K and as we cleared the side wall to look into the parking lot, we saw the suspect car exit the lot and merge into flowing traffic going westbound on Ft. Lowell. Before I could pull out onto the main street, another deputy passed me and got directly behind the suspect. It was one of the rookies. I got on the radio and told him to hold off any further action until we came to a better position. It was not a good idea to pull off a high-risk stop on a busy roadway, with two lanes going in each direction and plenty of apartment buildings left and right. He confirmed. My ride-along became excited as well and asked a lot of questions as to what was about to happen, and if this was going to be dangerous. It was one of the few times where I told a ride-along to hold their questions until later and yes, this had the potential to become dangerous. There were no more questions from his side.

Then the suspect car, whose driver had undoubtedly noticed the two police cars following him, switched into the left turn lane to turn south onto Country Club. I got on the radio again and told the deputy in front of me that Country Club was not as busy as Ft. Lowell, and we might try the high-risk stop there or even better in a side street if the driver decided to make another turn. The deputy once again confirmed. The traffic light showed red, and we all sat there waiting. Waiting and thinking. The light turned green, and I could hardly believe what I saw next. As we all pulled forward, with the suspect car pulling into the intersection to wait for a gap in oncoming traffic, the rookie deputy turned on his red and blues. *Why would he do that?* We couldn't go anywhere and had agreed to wait for a good spot for our high-risk stop. Now we were sitting at the light, giving the suspect plenty of time to come up with a plan, as we had announced our intention. Damn! I was furious and started cussing up a storm, which seemed to intimidate my ride-along. I apologized briefly and said, "Don't worry about me right now. I'm just venting."

The number of scenarios for how this could go wrong had just risen exponentially. And then there was the gap in oncoming traffic. The suspect calmly made his turn, followed by the rookie deputy and then me. He pulled up into a nearby parking lot right away, and the rookie pulled up fairly close behind him. *What was he doing?* There was almost no room for me to fan out to one of the sides as we would during a high-risk stop. We now had to stack our cars. But it got even better yet. With utter bewilderment, I saw the deputy step out of his car as if he wanted to conduct just a regular traffic stop. Good god! As I pulled into the parking lot, the suspect suddenly lifted his foot off the brakes and pulled back out into the street and then gunned it. I turned on my siren and blasted past the other deputy, who rushed to get back into his vehicle.

Yelling updates into the mic of my radio, I tried to catch up with the suspect. Approximately 50 yards ahead of us, he pulled into a smaller street going eastbound. We continued our pursuit. Despite us now driving on narrower neighborhood streets, the suspect accelerated further and bottomed out on some of the potholes. My ride-along was white-knuckling his door handle and had a truly terrified look on his face. That was actually kind of funny. I was busy and kept my eyes trained on the car in front of me—and whatever else was going on in the streets that could interfere with our pursuit. We were traveling way too fast for this environment, I thought. The rookie deputy was directly behind me, also going with lights and siren. The suspect came up on the next larger cross street marked by a stop sign, and without ever slowing down or the brake lights coming on, he crossed the two-lane roadway. That was insane, and I worried that if I didn't stop it right there, someone was going to die. I shut down my lights and siren, hit my brakes, and got on the radio.

"6-2-4, terminating 10-80. Suspect continues at a high rate of speed through neighborhood streets, exceeding 55 mph."

The response came promptly, "6-2-4. Copy 10-80 has been terminated."

We had to wait for traffic to pass until we were able to cross and proceed in the direction the suspect car had gone. I could only imagine how they might have hit one of those cars. Once we reached the other side, the suspect was long gone. We asked for assistance and roamed the neighborhood. As this was within city limits, we notified TPD as well and within a few minutes, we had a multitude of Sheriff's Department and TPD vehicles crowding the area. We received assistance from a K-9 unit and searched the place high and low for another hour or so. The suspect remained unfound. After the debriefing with our Sergeant, I finally got to catch up with my ride-along. "Any questions? Sorry for earlier," I apologized one more time. "No, you're good," he said. "I don't have any more questions. I'm just glad it's over."

It just so happened that the rookie deputy who caused the mess described above months later had a ride-along himself. (You could no longer be on probation if you wanted to take someone along for a shift.) At the beginning of his shift, he advised over the radio that he had a civilian ride-along on board. I am pretty sure the rest of our squad were all thinking the same: God help us today.

It was a swing shift and around 6:00 p.m. I decided to give, let's call him Jeff, a call to see if he wanted to meet at a local Jimmy John's to have a sandwich. He agreed, and I thought it was a good opportunity to check in with him, "feel his pulse" and get a firsthand impression of his ride-along. We sat down in the fast-food place and made small talk. I learned that the ride-along was Jeff's cousin. He seemed very excited about the opportunity and Jeff complained about how it had been a very slow call volume that day. Trying to keep things realistic, I explained how these days were important for us as well, as they enabled us to be out in the community more, be the observers, and approach people or check in with local businesses. Jeff asked if I would be okay hanging around Dodge City for a while as a possible backup. He wanted to see if he could "stir something up." That's what I was afraid of. I told Jeff to call the sergeant and if he was okay with it, I'd stick around. Jeff was hungry. He ordered a "Gargantuan" sandwich and devoured it in no time. The sergeant gave his approval, so we went to Dodge City once again.

Jeff called out traffic stops every few minutes. He was definitely trying hard. Then he called a traffic stop with a mini motorcycle. I drove past his location and saw Jeff, his cousin, and the motorcyclist engaged. Nothing seemed out of the ordinary and Jeff held up four fingers of his left hand, indicating that he was "Code 4" (all okay). I drove around the block and a short time later heard Jeff's voice shouting into the radio that he was "10-80 on foot." He was in a foot pursuit. I turned on lights and siren and returned to the location of the stop. I could not see anybody. And… Jeff's patrol car was gone. *How was that possible?* He said he was in a foot pursuit. Then he came on the air again, giving an approximate location, but he added he was not sure. The dispatcher followed up, trying to clarify, but there was no response. She called him again and again. There was no response. She called for other units to assist Jeff and I advised that I was already in the vicinity looking for him. Both windows were rolled down so I could listen for any noises. I rolled through the streets where he could possibly be. Then I saw Jeff's patrol car turning the corner coming toward me. We pulled up next to each other, and I recognized the driver. It was Jeff's cousin.

I yelled at him. "What the fuck are you doing?

"I'm sorry! I got scared and didn't know what to do. I'm looking for Jeff."

"Pull over and get the fuck out of that patrol car!"

"Okay, okay," he said, clearly intimidated.

"Stay near the car. Don't touch anything. Stay put. You understand?"

"Yes, I understand."

Holy shit! That guy just drove around in a marked police vehicle looking for his cousin. Another unit pulled up to the scene, and we decided to split the streets between us and continue our search. Jeff was either in a fight or down and, as a result, couldn't answer the radio calls. When I pulled back toward the street where Jeff's patrol car was now parked, I suddenly saw him on the side of the street, rolling in the dust with someone. I sped up my car and came to a stop right in front of them, then jumped out to help. Just as I rushed up to them, Jeff managed to slap handcuffs on the man.

"Are you okay?"

"Yes, I'm fine. Can you take over?"

"Of course."

Jeff disengaged from the suspect, who was still on his stomach, and stepped to the side. As I wanted to help the suspect back to his feet, I noticed that the handcuffs, put on in the confusion of the fight, had been badly twisted. So, I put my handcuffs on top of Jeff's and then took Jeff's cuffs off. When I turned my head to hand Jeff his set of handcuffs back, I saw him standing next to a fence throwing up his entire "Gargantuan" onto the dusty dirt shoulder.

Every few minutes, another cop car arrived and soon the whole neighborhood was teeming with police. Of course, the sergeant came out as well, and this all resulted in a lot of paperwork, possibly some discipline that I am not aware of, and a trial where the suspect was found not guilty of assaulting a peace officer. The defense attorney managed to convince the jury that the suspect was so scared and confused by Jeff—and his ride-along's appearance—that he was justified in physically resisting the arrest. He could not have been sure that Jeff was, in fact, a law enforcement officer in pursuit of his duties.

10

THE "9-9-X" CALLS

In previous chapters, I alluded to a specific set of calls which would make everybody's adrenaline level peak. It was the Code 9-9-8 and Code 9-9-9. They were our version of 911. The first indicated an officer involved shooting, the second stands for "officer needs help urgently." Each of these stands for dire scenarios where one or more of us were in immediate grave danger. They were announced by Comm with an all-stations broadcast, meaning every radio that was powered on would receive it. The announcement was preceded by a set of warble tones that would make my heart skip a beat and pay full attention to the announcement that was about to follow. The following is about two of those calls.

It was another slow night in Rincon, and I was assigned to the slowest beat: Beat 2. It was one of those nights where I kept reminding myself of the saying, "Rincon is slow, but when shit happens and especially when big shit happens, it happens in Rincon." There was no scientific or otherwise factual reason for this expression. That was just the way it was. As usual, we had two units working the rural areas of Beat 1, me working Beat 2, and two deputies assigned to Beat 3. A sixth deputy was assigned to roam between the metro area of Beat 3 and the residential and somewhat rural areas of Beat 2, in case I needed a backup. Of course, there were also the two deputies on Mt. Lemmon; however, they had already signed off and gone home, with one of them remaining available in a call-out status should the need arise.

TOM PEINE

Because it was slow, and I had not responded to any calls in the past hour or so, I called the roaming deputy on his phone and asked if he could hang out near my beat so I could run some traffic. He agreed and said he'd have to do some paperwork at the district office anyway, and that was right on the western perimeter of my assigned patrol area. Traffic enforcement was something we'd mainly do for two reasons. One was to enforce the traffic laws in hotspots where there was a cluster of crashes in the past, or where folks who lived in the neighborhood had requested for us to keep an eye on things. The second reason was that a driver who broke a traffic law could be stopped and give us an opportunity to interact with people and see if any other crimes were potentially afoot. Mt. Hood was always popular with the teenage and young adult crowd. They'd hang out at one of the vista parking lots with fabulous nighttime views of the city. Periodically, we would go to those places and enjoy the vistas ourselves. Tucson would lie at your feet like a sparkling diamond. A pulsating microcosm that lit up the dark nighttime desert, its yellow light radiating out and reflecting off the mountainside. It was a spectacular, marvelous sight. On the side away from the city, you could clearly observe the Milky Way and its myriads of stars, humbling the observer with their beauty and the imaginable vastness of the universe.

Young folks would come up here to gaze at the beauty in the valley or the person next to them. They would go there to make out, have sex, smoke pot, drink, or pursue a variety of other— sometimes illegal—activities. To keep a handle on things, the county had declared the parking lots alongside the main road up Mt. Lemmon as county parks. Posted signs would indicate that the park was closed after 10:00 p.m. and only those with a valid camping permit could remain. Needless to say, that in all my years of working patrol in the Rincon District, I have never encountered anyone in one of those parking lots at night with a valid camping permit. We would simply tell them to gather their things and move along. We'd check identification of people to see if anyone violated age restrictions, curfew ordinances, or consumed illegal substances. Every now and then further law enforcement action became necessary because someone was a little too young to be drinking that beer, should not have lit that joint right before we rolled up on them or simply should not have been out at that time of night.

Given the lack of personnel strength that night, I was not able to go up the mountain. But I decided to set up at the first four-way stop sign coming down from the mountain. I blacked out on the western side of the intersection and pulled all the way onto the dirt shoulder. From there, it was a waiting game. Cars would come racing down that mountain and blow through that stop sign without ever slowing down. There I was, in the pitch black, the interior of my car only illuminated by my computer screen and the LEDs on my radio that would occasionally light up when someone was talking on the air. Nothing was moving. The only vehicle coming down was an older Ford F150 pickup. The car rolled up to the intersection, came to a perfect stop, and then continued southbound. I was in for a true Rincon night.

Then came two signal tones indicating a priority call over the radio.

"Attention Rincon Beat 1! Shots heard at 12345 Desert Road. Units responding advise."

Both units assigned to Beat 1 came up to respond to the call. The following description was more unsettling.

"Caller states that at a residence south of his location, they heard a female screaming, then a shot was fired. Now all the lights inside the house are out."

Both deputies responded that they would expedite their response using lights and siren. When asked for further updates or a better location description, it became clear that this would not be an easy one. The area in question had houses on one or more acre lots, many of them being so-called "horse properties." It was out in a sparsely populated desert area, and it was a night of low moonlight. As the responding deputies made their way from their current position several miles away toward the incident location, they requested assistance from the air unit Survey 1. It was a single engine Vietnam-era airplane equipped with sophisticated a forward looking infrared or FLIR camera. The plane was likely to get to the scene prior to the deputies arriving on the ground. Using their infrared sensors, they could get a much better overview of the situation at night than anyone on the ground ever could. The air crew confirmed and said they were en route and expected to be overhead within a few minutes.

Our shift supervisor, Sergeant Mitchell, came up on the radio. While he informed the dispatcher that he was responding as well, you could hear his engine screaming in the background. They had a vast area to cover and really no clear picture of what was going on. They potentially needed help, and it was a long way from where I was, yet I was the nearest Rincon deputy available. I decided to respond as well. The deputy doing paperwork at the station could cover my beat.

"1-1-4-2. I'm 10-76 to the Shots Heard call. Code 3."
The dispatcher confirmed, "10-4."

No intervention or negative comment by the sergeant over the radio and my phone stayed silent as well. It was okay for me to go and help. I raced southbound on Houghton Road, lights and siren cutting through the dark of night. Radio transmissions from the Beat 1 deputies indicated that it would not be easy to identify the house in question. There were several properties that would fit the location description and the dispatcher was asked to get the original caller back on the line to see if we could identify additional pointers. Ultimately, it was narrowed down to a set of two or three properties.

When I came into the vicinity of the incident location, I took one of the side streets to see if I could find an access point to the location described by our air crew. They had arrived a while ago and surveyed the area, which helped tremendously with identifying the possible residence. All residential roads in this area were dirt roads, some of them with potholes deep enough to park my patrol car in. I imagined what this must be like during the heavy monsoon rains, when roads like this turned into raging rivers of mud. The sergeant advised over the radio to prepare ourselves to deploy with long guns once we arrived at the scene, as we did not know what type of weapons our possible adversaries could be armed with. A deputy from the Green Valley District had responded as well for support. The crew on Survey 1 had identified a ranch house with several vehicles upfront, just south of the caller's residence. One of the vehicles on the property showed a strong heat signature on their infrared screen, indicating that it had recently been running. That was most likely the place we were looking for. Upon arrival near the house in question, Sergeant Mitchell, the Green Valley deputy, and I stopped and got out for a brief strategy talk. We decided that I would leave my patrol car at the corner of the driveway with my rear deck lights activated. That way, other units who may need to respond in case the situation deteriorated would know where to go and not end up in the type of search scenario we were in right now. The sergeant would spearhead, followed by the Green Valley deputy in his vehicle, while I would walk behind the sergeant's car and provide cover with my patrol rifle as we approached the house.

Our plan was relayed over the air by the sergeant, so everyone was aware of our actions. I parked my patrol car on the shoulder, near the edge of the driveway, and turned on the rear portion of my red and blue emergency lights. Then I unlocked the gun rack and took out my Remington patrol rifle. A pump action .223 cal. rifle that should later be replaced by the more common AR-15. I locked my car and fell in behind the sergeant's patrol car. Racking my rifle, I chambered a round and with that, we began our approach toward the main residence. The way down the dirt driveway was dusty as the Sergeant's car stirred up the dry desert dirt and I ended up inhaling a lot of it. As we arrived in front of the house, we saw the vehicles parked as described by the air crew. Our cars were stacked alongside the front of the house. With full emergency lights on and all available light sources directed at the front of the house, Sergeant Mitchell used the public announcement system of his patrol car, "Police! Come out of the house with your hands up! Anyone inside the house, come out now!" We had the two initially responding Beat 1 deputies to the rear of the house. They came on the radio and said they had a female who had stepped onto the patio. She was ordered on her knees and then detained by the deputies.

Just as that last radio transmission from the deputies on the backside of the house ended, it happened. A huge bang slammed through the night, and for a split second I thought, *What was that?* Sergeant Mitchell got on the radio. "Shots fired! Shots fired!" All three of us in the front of the house instinctively ducked and turned our heads toward a shed on our left. That's where the shot had come from. Then everything happened very quickly.

The warble tones came on the radio and the dispatcher announced, "Code 998, Code 998. Rincon Beat 1 at 12345 Desert Road. All units 10-3."

Sergeant Mitchell looked at me and said, "You go that way and I'll come from here. You call out." With his hands, he indicated that we would approach the shed at a 90-degree-angle to cover the front door of the shed from both sides without creating a cross-fire scenario. Once the sergeant had made it to the south side of the shed covering the front door, he gave me a signal. With all my might, I yelled out toward the front of the shed, "Police! Come out now!" After a short delay, the door slowly opened and a middle-aged white man in shorts and T-shirt appeared from inside.

He stepped out and said, "What's going on?"

I yelled at him, "Get on the ground! Keep your hands up!"

"What the hell is going on out here?" he said with an annoyed tone.

I was furious about his non-responsiveness to my commands and worried about the man's intentions. "Get on the fucking ground!" I yelled.

I walked up from behind the cover of a vehicle and approached the man, while pointing my rifle at him. He dropped to his knees, and I kept his head in my front sight as I approached him. The safety was off and all it took was a squeeze of the trigger to put a hole in his head. The Sergeant still provided cover from the side of the building and coming up to the man kneeling on the ground, I saw from the corner of my eye the Sergeant's gun pointing in our direction. With a quick snap, I engaged the safety, swung the rifle over my right shoulder and grabbed the guy's wrist. Without having been told to do so, he had crossed his fingers behind his head. I took a fallout step forward and with that, slammed the guy forward into the dusty soil. I put my knee behind his shoulder and cuffed him behind his back, then brought him back to his feet. "Any guns or weapons on you? Anything that could poke or sting me?" He didn't answer. As I patted him down, I could smell the boozy odor coming from his mouth. Each breath he took put us into a renewed cloud of whatever he had poured down his throat before all of this unraveled.

Just as I went to put him in the back of the sergeant's patrol car and take cover behind the vehicle again, a small Toyota four-door drove down the driveway, past our police cars and emergency lights. It stopped at the side of the house. We all yelled at the occupants, guns pointed at them. "Get out! Get on the ground now!" It was a group of teenage girls, presumably the homeowner's daughters and maybe some friends. Oblivious to the police presence and activity, they had simply passed us to park their car and go inside? Apparently so. The Green Valley deputy yelled at them about how they almost got themselves shot. They were cuffed and led away, back behind the cover of our vehicles. At this point, we still had no idea what had happened earlier, who all these people were, and if anybody else was still in the house. Meanwhile, we requested a K-9 unit to assist with clearing the house and called several more times on the house for any potential folks inside to step outside. No response. The woman who was detained by deputies on the backside of the house said that nobody else was inside, but we could not simply rely on that statement.

Meanwhile, more and more deputies who had heard the distress call began to arrive and joined us at our vehicles. Eventually, 35 patrol vehicles were parked alongside the dirt road leading up to the house, making it look like a presidential motorcade (or two) had stopped by. We stood by and held our weapons on the house until a K-9 handler arrived with his dog. We were told over the radio that the only one remaining inside the residence was a scared little Pomeranian. The K-9 handler and two other deputies approached the house and let the dog loose to search the interior after giving the proper K-9 warnings. It took a few minutes until the dog emerged from inside, then the deputies went in to clear it again. Nobody else was found.

So, what had happened that brought us all out there? Turns out boozy guy and his wife got into a heated argument, during which boozy guy decided to gear up and retrieve his shotgun from the shed. As his wife sees him coming across the driveway armed with his shotgun yelling, "I'll kill you, bitch," she screams out in shock. That is what the neighbor heard. The wife ran back into the house and slammed the front door shut. Boozy guy decided to give his wife a warning and fired a round from his shotgun into the air (we didn't find any shotgun rounds lodged into the side of the house). The neighbor heard that as well and called 911. Next, the wife ran toward the kitchen and on her way hit the main circuit breaker so her husband couldn't see her from the outside. She hid in the kitchen until she heard us calling on the house and saw the red and blue lights flashing, but decided to walk out the back, where she was detained by deputies. He said he was in the shed when we arrived and intended to unload his shotgun before coming out. In doing so, he claimed the shotgun went off accidentally. We found a slug lodged into the doorframe.

Boozy guy was arrested and later charged by detectives, but as far as I remember, the matter never went to trial.

☆

I had been working the late swing shift from 6:00 p.m. to 2:00 a.m. for several weeks and truly enjoyed it. It was the busier, more eventful, call load of the late swing shift with the addition of the busier, first part of the midnight shift. The workday felt as if it was over in a heartbeat, and every day there was new stuff to be learned. Especially in a slower district like Rincon. This was the shift to be on.

We had been hopping calls for the past two hours and I had joined Andrew Thompson on a call for a DTP (disturbance of the peace). Someone from within an apartment complex had called about some juveniles who were partying in the pool area of the complex and were being very loud. Given the fact that it was well after 10:00 p.m., a valid concern. Most likely we'd encounter some drunk—excuse me, "intoxicated" juveniles.

DEPUTY WHILE IMMIGRANT

Upon arrival, we walked up to the pool area, which we easily found as we were led by loud chatter, laughter, and other noises. Once at the pool, we found two boys and a girl. They all had obviously consumed their fair share of alcoholic beverages, judging by the empty beer cans on the table and the smell coming from the three young mouths each time one of them spoke. They all admitted to drinking alcoholic beverages, and we began to issue juvenile arrest paperwork and call parents.

The younger of the two boys and the girl were dealt with pretty quickly. Andrew had called their parents and summoned them to our location. They lived nearby and promised to show up promptly. Once they showed up, the parents took custody of their children. A citation listing the committed offenses was issued and signed by the parents, here "Disorderly Conduct" for the noisiness after hours, and "Minor in Possession of Alcohol" (most teenagers would call it simply MIP). With their signature, the parents promised to appear with their children in front of a juvenile judge once summoned by the court. We got the kid out of the back of the patrol car, took off their handcuffs, and reunited them with their stern-looking parents. Personally, I believe the punishment at home was probably worse in most cases than what the judge would impose, which was perfectly fine in my book. Most of them we would not see or deal with again. Of course, there were our regulars, or "frequent fliers" as we liked to call them; even at this juvenile age.

That left us with the remaining young man, who turned out to be a few months into his 18th year on this earth, which means he was "blessed" with the ability to take responsibility for his misdeeds himself. He received an added charge of "Contributing to the Delinquency of a Minor" because he, as an adult, was present while the other kids got wasted. The difference a few weeks can make. While Andrew filled out the citation for the older boy, I assisted in order to move this whole thing along and ran the young man over the radio.

To our surprise, the dispatcher returned with the transmission of "6-2-4. Code 10?" Now that meant she wanted to know if the person I had inquired about was within earshot of my radio, a request typically made prior to the dispatcher alerting us about outstanding warrants.

"Negative. Go ahead," I responded.

"Subject is 10-88 Mike out of our agency."

He had a misdemeanor warrant for his arrest, issued for a charge made by our agency. Now we had to take him to jail, no cite and release.

Andrew walked over to him. The young man, though clearly somewhat intoxicated, had been very cooperative with us, as had the other two. He sat handcuffed on a chair by the pool. Andrew said, "Dude. Are you aware you have a warrant out for your arrest?"

"Yeah, I figured as much. I had court and couldn't go that day."

Andrew followed up with, "Okay, buddy. You'll have to take care of this tonight because we will take you in. Okay? You're going to be cool about this?"

Not really having any other choice, the young man was smart to acknowledge his error and continued his compliant behavior. When Andrew was about to put him in the back of his patrol car, the young man said that he seriously needed to use the bathroom. He explained how they had been drinking a lot of beer and his request made sense. The last thing any of us wanted was a urine-soaked backseat. Andrew looked at me and asked if I'd follow him to the nearby Circle K to give his young arrestee some relief. There were no other calls holding on the screen and I agreed. It was only a quarter of a mile down the street, anyway.

We rolled up on the Circle K, where the night clerk gave us a friendly wave. They were always happy to see us around at night. It kept the thugs at bay. With the arrestee, we entered the store and told the clerk we just needed to use his bathroom really quick. "All three of you together?" the clerk joked. We joked back, saying, "Sure thing. You know we're scared of going anywhere alone." He laughed and nodded in our direction. Once inside the bathroom, the arrestee's handcuffs were brought to his front and reapplied. That way, he could take care of business himself. Andrew cautioned him, "Don't do anything stupid! It's not going to work out and you will most likely get hurt. So be nice, take a piss, wash your hands, and off to jail we go." The young man nodded and made some comment in an attempt to be funny, which didn't work. Andrew advised dispatch of our location and what we were doing.

As we are standing there, waiting for drunk boy to finish peeing, the radio silence was broken by a series of warble tones.

"Code 9-9-9, Code 9-9-9. 6-5-8 requesting assistance urgently at Deer Circle."

Shit! That was Alex, and he was just about a mile from our location. He had some minor radio traffic earlier, but only something about another DTP, nothing serious. And now he set off an emergency call?

"6-2-4, 10-76."

I looked at Andrew and he said, "I'm okay. Go!"

Drunk boy was still peeing and trying to make conversation with us, when I took off through the bathroom door. I ran out of the store and didn't hear what the clerk was saying behind me. In my head, I scanned the map of our beat and tried to picture where this small side street was. I thought it was just down the road off of Kolb Road, near the Rural Metro Fire station.

I unlocked the driver's side door, jumped in, and looked at the computer screen. There it was in big, bold, red letters: Code 999, and I was assigned to it. The only other unit in the vicinity was Carlos Ramirez, but he came from Beat 2 and was probably a good 15 minutes out. The engine started. I turned myself in the driver's seat to look out the rear window and flipped the car around. Headlights on, emergency lights on, sirens blaring, I went past the gas pumps and onto Sabino Canyon Road. Racing down the road, I knew Alex would hear the sirens from afar and know I was coming. Help is on the way, buddy!

Coming up on the intersection, I made a right turn onto Kolb Road and drove toward the fire station. Fortunately, there was very little traffic, and I could go as fast as possible. Just beyond the fire station, Deer Circle came up on the left-hand side. I turned into the cul-de-sac and saw Alex's red and blues ahead of me. I parked my car on the opposite dirt shoulder and got out of my car. Alex was standing in the driveway and had his Taser in his hands. In the twitching red and blue emergency lights, I could see the sparkling reflection coming from the copper wires that lead my eyes to a man who was on the ground. Alex was yelling at the man, telling him to "Stay on the fucking ground! I told you before! If you try to get up again, you'll get tased again." With that being said, I heard the man on the ground yelling out loud in pain, and then I saw him fall back. Alex had just sent him on another ride of 50,000 volts—best regards from Taser, Inc. Instinctively, I had drawn my weapon from its holster and pointed it in the direction of the man on the ground.

Yelling in Alex's direction, I said, "What the fuck is going on, man?" His response didn't instill any confidence that we could quickly come up with a solution for this scenario.

"I don't fucking know!" Alex screeched back at me.

I saw that the man on the ground was lying in an area with some liquid on the ground. When I pointed my gun at him, the tac light of my weapon illuminated the scene and revealed that this guy was rolling in what seemed to be blood.

I repeated, "Dude, what the fuck?"

Alex said, "I know! There's another guy inside. He ran back in through that door. I was dealing with this dude here when he showed up in the doorframe and said he would cap me."

Okay, this did seem pretty serious.

"Where is he now?" I asked.

"No idea. He ran back in and shut the door behind him."

"Anybody else in the house?"

"Your guess is as good as mine."

I looked at the guy on the ground who moaned and once again attempted to get up. Alex hissed another "Stay down!" at him. As the man did not comply, he went on yet another Taser ride.

I said, "You need to cuff him up. This is not going to stop otherwise."

By now, I had trained my gun at the interior door at the back wall of the open garage, where Alex had described the second guy had disappeared. Alex said, "The guy is full of blood!"

"Go for it, man," I tried to encourage him.

DEPUTY WHILE IMMIGRANT

Alex rushed up to him, turned the man over on his belly, and cuffed him. As he led him back to his patrol car, Carlos came screaming around the corner with his patrol car. He parked his car and joined us, taking cover behind Alex's car.

He pointed his gun at the house and asked, "What's going on?"

I yelled a quick, "Cluster fuck!" back at him and then relayed what little I had understood.

Alex requested the response of an ambulance to the scene, so "bleeding man" could be properly attended to. All we could do at this point was wait for more units to arrive. With just the three of us standing out here, it was way too dangerous to take further action. We each stood behind some sort of cover and each of us had a different part of the house in our front sight.

Alex explained he had responded to a DTP call in this vicinity. As he slowly drove through the neighborhood with his windows rolled down to listen for any noises, he had turned around at the end of the cul-de-sac. All was quiet, and he was about to leave when he passed the house we were now pointing our guns at. Looking down the driveway, he noticed the garage door was open. Illuminated by the porch light and the interior garage light, he saw a man standing in the driveway. Alex made the decision to get out and ask if the man had heard anything suspicious, when he noticed the man was bleeding heavily from one of his hands. He asked if he needed help and what had happened. The man stated he didn't need Alex's help and that he had slaughtered a rabbit. Alex said the amount of blood present would have indicated a rabbit slaughter fest, and the man's response did not make any sense to him. Then a second man appeared in the doorframe in the back of the garage. "Get out of here! Leave us alone. If you come any closer, I'll cap you." Alex obviously felt threatened and "bleeding man" started walking toward him. Alex drew his Taser and warned the bleeder to stop and not come any closer. The other man disappeared inside the house and slammed the door to the garage shut. Bleeding man was still advancing on Alex, which is when he deployed his Taser, sending the bleeder to the ground. That's when he called out the Code 999.

After what seemed like an eternity, several other patrol vehicles arrived and Sergeant Cross. He had come up from Green Valley some 20 miles away as the closest on-duty sergeant. On this night, we were without a sergeant and Carlos was our acting supervisor. After he received a briefing, Sergeant Cross advised Comm of the situation and instructed us to build a search group of three deputies. The rest of the deputies, who began to arrive in short order, would cover the front and back of the house. Deputy O'Connor and I joined the search team.

After loudly announcing our increased presence over the public announcement system, the search party approached the interior door at the back wall of the open garage. Let me paint the picture of Deputy O'Connor. He is a true character. He's heavy set and slightly shorter than me, maybe 6'1". And he had a funny, duck-like gait. In front of his body, he held, in a depressed position, an AR15 rifle that had so many accessories on it, it looked straight out of Star Wars. With this motley crew, we knocked and announced at the back door, and then entered the interior of the house.

Slowly and methodically, we made our way through the house, room by room. Clear, clear, clear. We had made no contact by the time we came to the living room. There was blood on the floor everywhere, and it certainly seemed more eventful than a rabbit slaughter. Off the living room went a hallway. There were three doors. Two on the left, one toward the end on the right. O'Connor tried the first door on the left and turned the knob. It was locked from inside. "Open the door! Police!" he yelled. Nothing. He tried to kick the door in with a forceful kick. The door held. He kicked again several times, so hard it made the walls shake and the pictures in the hallway swing from side to side. After the third kick, the door gave way and opened with the cracking noise of bursting wood. While the third deputy covered the hallway with his handgun, O'Connor and I went inside. The room was dark inside, lit up only by the flickering light coming from a TV screen. Two Latino men, one standing by the window, the other sitting on the bed, were inside. A small TV on a

DEPUTY WHILE IMMIGRANT

dresser had porn running on it. Some nasty movie, showing an older guy having sex with two girls, who looked way too young to be in a movie like that. The two men, neither of whom seemed to speak English, were handcuffed. When we brought them out into the light of the living room, we noticed white powder around their nostrils. "They were doing coke in there. Probably snorted all the evidence," O'Connor said.

Two other deputies came in behind us and led the handcuffed men outside. We continued down the hall to the second door on the left. The door opened without problems. Inside was a young girl, who later turned out to be the 15-year-old daughter of the homeowner AKA bleeding guy. She sat on her bed with her face in her palms, crying. When asked if she was okay, she didn't answer. She was led outside by other deputies for further evaluation. That left us with the door at the end of the hall and on the right. Entering into that room revealed the last person. A tall man in his thirties with a dark complexion. He was taken into custody without a fight as well. On the wall in that room was a dart board and a bunch of beer cans on a table, some posters, not much else.

Having cleared the entire house with a secondary sweep, we came back outside to learn what our fellow deputies had pieced together from those we had encountered. The homeowner, in his booze-filled head, apparently had decided to perform a daring stunt with a knife. He had put the dartboard on the table and placed his hand on top, spread his fingers and then rammed the blade of the knife in the space between his fingers, going from left to right and then back. As he had increased his speed of doing so, he—no surprise there—missed on one occasion and instead of ramming the blade into the dartboard, sliced his hand open. The two Latino men, both of whom turned out to be in the country illegally, had consumed copious amounts of cocaine and apparently were readying themselves to have sex with the homeowner's juvenile daughter. It was disgusting and extremely disturbing.

The father was arrested on a variety of charges. Tall guy had a warrant for his arrest and the two Latino men were turned over to Border Patrol, who responded to the scene to pick them up.

Finally, and after all the dust had settled, Carlos, Alex and I were summoned by Sergeant Cross. He had a heart-to-heart with us and made it very clear that our radio communication was terrible. Since Carlos had arrived on scene, there were no further updates, leading the responding units to believe that something so bad was afoot that we didn't even have time to get on the radio. In return, this led to a massive response to the scene, which could have been prevented, had we provided decent updates. Six more deputies and the sergeant would have sufficed. It was made abundantly clear to us that we had unnecessarily tied up a lot of department resources, which now had not been available elsewhere. A mistake that I would remember for the rest of my law enforcement career and going forward turned me into an updater-in-chief of sorts.

When I started this chapter, I was driven by those most memorable stories. Stuff that sounds cool and would be entertaining to read. But as I am going through this process, I increasingly wonder what makes an experience "memorable?" Is it the amount of adrenaline felt during the action? Is it the unfolding tragedy? Or is it something different altogether? Suddenly, my choices of what stories to share seem random. There were so many stories. The more I write, the more I remember. And the more I remember, the more I begin to realize that I could fill volumes with all of them. So, what do I leave out? What do I include? Haven't other deputies or officers experienced much worse? Does something have to be considered "bad" to be noteworthy? I also feel conflicted about laying all of this out there, sharing these moments that have a special kind of intimacy to them, at least for those who experienced them.

Some of these "stories" are so much more. They are points in time that brought together a variety of different people in one place, sometimes facing seemingly impossible choices. People dial 911 because whatever they are experiencing has gone out of control and you respond to bring back that sense of control, of order, of safety. Yet, there are also moments that leave a mark on everybody who was there. When I write about having had my finger on the trigger or pointing my gun at someone, I leave out the fact that in my head and at that time, I was already a step further along in the potential sequence of events. Here is one: Standing behind a tree for cover and pointing my rifle at the head of a former coworker who made suicidal comments online and was now standing in her doorway, gun in hand, waiting for our next move. In my head, I had already pulled the trigger and saw the back of her head splattered all over the doorframe. In my head, I had already written the first three paragraphs of my report, explaining the rationale behind my decision to end this woman's life. Fortunately, it never came to that in reality. But I had already been there. That picture is still in my head. The decision was made, and my finger had, in fact, slowly taken the slack out of the trigger. The difference between the reality in my head and the reality outside that apartment door was a split second. Experiences like that don't just go away or fade with time. The challenge is that there are a lot of those experiences. The unrealized realities of the speed of thought, of trained scenario imagination to prepare for a variety of outcomes and not be caught off guard. These so-called immediate action drills—think of five different ways the call could develop—leave their own scars. Scars not so different from the tangible experiences in the there and then.

You know what is memorable to me? The camaraderie—the knowledge that you can blindly rely on your fellow deputy or whichever cop may be standing next to you. Like them or not, they'll be there for you. Memorable are the reactions of those involved in criminal or emergency situations. Victims, perpetrators, witnesses, bystanders. Their reactions range from ignorance to open grief, from angry outbreaks to utter disbelief. The embrace of a lost child by their father and mother upon reunification. Oh yes, and before I forget, elation. Those who were lucky to escape unharmed. Those who were found to be innocent, despite accusations to the contrary. Tears of elation are a thing.

Fact is that some stories should not be retold as their occurrence in real life was traumatic enough for all involved. A repetition of those events is most likely not going to do them justice.

11

FROM DEPUTY TO DETECTIVE TO PIO

While life as a Deputy Sheriff in a patrol assignment certainly offered all the variety one could possibly ask for in a professional assignment, it left me feeling unfulfilled after the first few years. Looking back at the end of the day, it increasingly felt as if I simply provided a Band-Aid. Following a 911 call, I'd show up, establish facts and circumstances to the best of my abilities—good abilities. That in turn would lead to the determination if a crime was committed or not and if I could identify a suspect. If there was a suspect, the next question was if there was probable cause, or facts and circumstances that presented a reasonable indication that this or this particular person(s) had committed the alleged crime. With all those conditions met, I would arrest and—if it was a felony crime—transport the individual to jail for booking. Finally, I would file my report to hand things over to detectives for further processing. While this description is wildly reductive because it omits the myriad of non-criminal calls and other combinations of circumstances which would lead to a similarly large variety of actions and possible follow-ups, it captures my mindset at the time. Arrive on scene, fix what's broken or stop a crime in progress, cite or arrest suspect, write it all down in a report, rinse, next call, repeat. Only the actors and circumstances changed. And the "interesting" cases? Well, they were handed off to the Criminal Investigations Division, or CID. You know, detectives and such. It was the other side of the coin I felt I was missing out on.

So, after some four and a half years on the job, I used the next process to fill openings within CID to throw my hat in the ring. Interestingly, becoming a detective within the Pima County Sheriff's Department was not considered a promotion but a reassignment. Still, one had to submit an application and go through a selection process involving a panel interview. With help from my coworkers and a bit of preparation for the panel, I was successful and was reassigned to a detective position. My initial assignment was to the Fraud/Financial Crimes section, presumably based on my background in banking and finance, but who knows?

Work as a detective was vastly different. Cases, their victims, perpetrators, and scenarios became not only more intense due to the increased severity of crimes investigated (detectives handle felonies only), but now I would take them home with me. Not literally, but mentally take them with me. Contemplating my next investigative move, preparing for a grand jury or court testimony. Plotting my next step in the investigation to finally nail the suspect.

My first cases mostly dealt with run-of-the-mill fraud offenses. Nigerian lottery scams, where the victim responded to emails and/or phone calls informing them of their large win in the Nigerian lottery amounting to millions of dollars. All that stood in between riches and the victim's current financial status was the payment of an administrative fee related to Nigerian regulations. Transfer the money to an account or go to a Western Union branch and deposit cash. Shortly after that deposit, you will enjoy your newly attained affluence. Right? Of course not! Amounts lost by victims to this sort of scam ranged from a few hundred dollars to well over $10,000. Most victims were embarrassed about falling for the scam, with no chance of ever recovering their money or catching the perpetrator. Close second were the romance scams with a similar story line. All you have to do is replace the lottery win with finding true love and the Nigerian administrative fees with help to cover travel expenses for prince charming, now stuck at a foreign airport on their way to you, but with no remote access to their own money. Please help!

But there were more interesting cases. A particular case that comes to mind involved a scheme to lure regular income folks to invest in a complex enterprise to open a theme park on Native American land near the entrance to Grand Canyon National Park. The fraudster was a representative and fundraiser for the project who had traveled to China and brought potential Chinese investors back to Arizona. Surreptitious recordings showed his prowess in presenting a fantastical picture of this lucrative theme park. Without going into too much detail, after three months of work on the case, I had amassed six volumes of file folders containing records and evidence. The story was gripping, and the crime committed well disguised, yet it broke federal as well as state laws. After briefing my Sergeant about it, I had to explain that I had no idea how deep this rabbit hole would go and that I was not sure if I might need more time and more resources to investigate. She told me that we were not equipped to handle cases of this magnitude and to present it to the State District Attorney for evaluation. If they thought it worth pursuing, they would have the means to properly and fully investigate it further.

That said, I took my case synopsis to an appointment with the local Assistant State District Attorney. He was intrigued when I called him over the phone to set up our meeting. That intrigue morphed into all out excitement once I laid out a reader's digest version in his office over a cup of bland office coffee. Once I turned over my six-volume investigative file, he all but turned into a blood hound. In an interview with the suspect and his attorney a few weeks later, we decided to use the fraudsters' outsized ego against him. We questioned his background and his ability to win over investors, purposely misrepresented numbers of the project, diminishing its portrayed dollar volume, and so on. It worked like a charm. Not only did he correct us, but he outright explained and described those of his actions that were elements necessary to turn his conduct into criminal activity. His lawyer became increasingly irritated, trying to contain his client.

He kept saying, "I strongly advise you to not respond. Just don't make any more statements! Gentlemen, we have nothing further to add."

Only to be shushed by his client with a swipe of his arm and a statement like, "No, no, no. I can explain this. What they're saying is just not accurate."

It was beautiful. After the two left the office, we both smiled at each other and shared our feelings of glory. The suspect ultimately agreed to a plea deal and did time at the Arizona Department of Corrections.

Right around this time came my first exposure to the local news media. A particularly noteworthy scam made the rounds in Pima County targeting gas stations and convenience stores. Making the public as well as business owners and their employees aware of it, seemed a perfect way to not only prevent the crime from reoccurring but it was also a way to possibly generate additional leads and nab the suspect(s). My sergeant called the public information officer or PIO and told him about the case. A short time later, the PIO showed up at my desk to get a more in-depth briefing. After hearing me out, he said this would be perfect for a media pitch and said he would get back to me.

Later in the day, I learned that we were expected at the TV station of Fox 11, the local Fox News affiliate, for the recording of a segment of their "Fox11 Fraud Unit." I explained how the fraudster would call a local convenience store, pretending to be a member of the chain's upper management. He or she would come across very assertive to the clerk answering the phone, often leaving them intimated by this "call from above." The "manager" would then explain how earlier in the day a customer of the store had fallen or eaten something that made them sick. The customer then supposedly threatened to sue the chain for damages. Thanks to the persuasive skills of the "manager" however, the customer could be convinced to settle the case outside the justice system. This is where the clerk came in to help. He was instructed to put together items the customer had agreed to accept as compensation for their grievance. The items included cash, but then regular store items such as toothpaste, packaged food, or cigarettes. The "manager" then told the clerk how they were on their way from out of town. They would send a courier in the meantime, typically a cab driver, to collect the items and for the clerk to hand them over to the cabby. I explained that convenience store chains are covered by liability insurance and how there was no need to resort to rag tag tactics like those described. A few days later, the city police ended up arresting the suspects based on a tip that came in after the TV segment had aired.

In the summer of 2010, my wife and I decided to host an exchange student for one year. Annie had been approached by a coworker, who had hosted herself and told Annie what an enriching experience it was. After some discussion at home and including our son Tobias in the process, we decided to go for it and with the beginning of the 2009/10 school year, we hosted our first exchange student, Dennis, from Germany. After Dennis' departure in the summer of 2010, we decided to take a little break and host again the following year, this time for only one semester. And in January, Vickie from Austria stepped into our lives. On January 8, 2011, all four of us got in the car to drive out to the mall and give Vickie a first impression of the American shopping experience. As we got off the Interstate and drove into the city proper, the radio program I had been listening to in the car was interrupted for breaking news. The report stated that our local member of Congress, U.S. House Representative Gabrielle Giffords had been shot together with additional victims outside a Safeway store at the intersection of Ina and Oracle Road in what was our Foothills District. Of course, I knew very well where that location was. Initial information was scarce, and my head raced. That had to be an all-hands-on-deck call. This weekend, I was one of two detectives on call. So, if my sergeant needed me, I trusted he would give me a call. In my futile attempt to picture what a crime scene like that might look like, a rather chaotic visual came to mind. Lots of cops, from multiple jurisdictions, rescue personnel, and probably all the detectives they could get ahold of. I told myself, "Don't jump to conclusions! If additional personnel are needed, commanders will coordinate with their sergeants. That is what on-call detectives are there for. If there is a need, I will be the first to receive a call."

All of that meant I had to bring the family back home and be ready to go right back out. For a second, I considered calling the sergeant. Should my presence be required, I could have Annie drop me off near the crime scene and then take the kids home. Yet, that was not a very good option given the fact that I would be without a vehicle. Also, if I called the sergeant in the midst of the anticipated chaos of such a busy scene, I could perfectly picture a response along the lines of "This place is a fucking mess! I'm busy with phone calls and coordination up to my eyeballs. Don't you think I would have called you if I needed additional people here at the scene? And who would cover any other regular calls coming in that may require a response?" Yeah, not helpful. While Annie kept trying to explain to Vickie what had just transpired and how this is likely to receive international news coverage, I drove us back home to Vail. After waiting for a few more hours, I couldn't stand it any longer and called my sergeant. He answered promptly.

"Oh hey, Tom. I totally forgot about you."

"Sarge, are you at the scene in the Foothills?"

"Yes, of course! Everybody is here!"

"Oh, I thought you'd call if you need any help, as I am on call this weekend."

"You're on call? I actually called in someone else from the unit."

"Oh, no! I am so sorry! I had no idea. If you—"

"Listen, Tom. We have more than enough folks out here. The FBI is here and took the lead.

Stay where you are and come into the office tomorrow morning. I am sure we are going to need some fresh eyes on all this in the morning. Keep your phone handy."

"Of course, sir. Will do."

"Alright, thanks. Bye."

Rats! Here we have a major crime with multiple victims, and "everybody" was there to help, except for Tom. I was mad and disappointed at the same time. I was too hesitant, too concerned about my boss's reaction, about getting in the way. It would have been better to do what others had done. They got into their car and simply showed up at the scene to offer their help. "Everybody" was there.

The next morning, feeling utterly useless after what now seemed like a total rookie move, I went straight into the sergeant's office.

"Morning! Good you're here. We're still putting today's assignments together. Be ready to head out to the scene of yesterday's shooting. We need fresh people out there. Yesterday was a bitch. It's massive and processing will take days. The FBI has the lead and will continue to send additional people. I'll let you know when it's time to go and who to report to once you get there."

"Got it. Thank you, sir."

It turned out I was not the only one who had not dropped everything they were doing and went to the scene. Now they put together a secondary detective response team, pretty much everyone who had not responded the previous day or had done so later in the day.

Later that morning, when I got to the scene, the extent of what happened quickly became obvious. Nearly the entire parking lot was taped off with crime scene tape. The areas not taped off were covered by reporters and cameras. Compared to other scenes, the area appeared massive. I reported to the incident commander for assignment. We had taken the role of further processing the crime scene as needed and conducting follow-up interviews. Detectives had begun to notify owners of the vehicles that had were left behind the previous day, as they were part of the crime scene. After everything had been documented, photographed, and otherwise processed as needed, the owners who had shown up were escorted to their vehicle and then shown which path they could use to exit the scene. Now there was room to give the parking lot a closer look.

One of the FBI agents called us all together and announced we would be conducting a line search. Should we note anything of possible evidentiary significance, we would raise our hand and call out loud to stop the line from proceeding. An FBI agent would then come to our location to examine what we had found and determine the next steps.

As soon as we began to line up, the media on the other side of the crime scene tape came alive. Reporters came up to the front, cameras were repositioned to film every one of our moves. And that is how I ended up on national news as a tiny dot in a line of other dots moving across a parking lot. Later on, the cameras would receive additional fodder. The FBI issued us metal detectors, directing us to comb all the planters and areas around trees throughout the parking lot. Same drill, call out if you find anything. Anything!

The afternoon was filled with additional follow-up work. People had called in all kinds of information. Together with an FBI agent, I went to one of Tucson's employment centers where the perpetrator had shown up in the weeks leading up to the assassination exhibiting unusual behavior. We spent about an hour questioning personnel who had contact with him and then returned to the scene. Next, I was tasked with taking reports from some of the hundreds of people who had called in to offer what they considered helpful information.

The report I filed for one of these phone calls described the following: "The female on the other end of the line (…) explained that she had previously dreamt of scenarios that she felt implicated the shooting of January 8, 2011 as documented under this case number. She went on to explain that she had dreams on August 8, 2010, and on January 7, 2011, in which she saw her mother in front of a Walmart store. In connection with this picture, she saw the number 1801 and felt it could stand for the date of January 8 or potentially a telephone area code or a Walmart store number.

The woman added that she also saw bees or potentially ants in her dream and now understood that this were indicators for bullets, hence the reference to Saturday's shooting.

In summary, this was the information (she) provided and then offered to provide notes she had made, if needed. At the beginning of our conversation, she also mentioned that she had already contacted the White House and spoke to the Secret Service; however, nobody there felt that her premonition was of any value, so she called the Sheriff's Department. I noted (her) contact information, and we disconnected."

Needless to say, not all information was helpful.

When I went to grab some food at the "Beyond Bread" located in the parking lot and still open for business, I had to stand in a long line of a mix of cops and reporters. Two people ahead of me, I recognized Brian Williams, the anchor of NBC Nightly News. This really was a big deal for not only our national news media, but outlets from all over the world who had descended on Tucson with their hordes of reporters and transmission trucks.

Miraculously, Congresswoman Giffords survived the attack despite being shot in the head. The shooter took six lives that day, including that of 9-year-old Christina-Taylor Green. She was born on September 11, 2001.

Within a few days, we all returned to our regular duties while the attack lingered in the news for some time. Detective work was more in-depth and therefore interesting, but it was also much more singular in its scope. Pleading with victims not to send money to Nigeria or some other exotic place to release a win from a lottery they never played felt like a Sisyphean task. One of my fellow detectives, who had joined the CID ranks during the selection process preceding mine, told me about an opening in the Sex Crimes unit he was currently working in. He felt I would be a good fit for the team. It was considered one of the top assignments, following Homicide as a close second, albeit unpopular. Dealing with victims of rape, incest, abuse, child sex abuse, prostitution, and other unspeakable offenses was not necessarily considered a hot ticket. Yet, besides working for the Homicide unit, it was the only unit detectives were not simply assigned to or rotated through. They were handpicked by the supervising sergeants and with agreement from the section commander. After several conversations with the detective who had initially approached me, I spoke to the Detective Sergeant for the Sex Crimes unit and received her approval. A few weeks later, I packed my things and moved onto the second floor of the Southern Arizona Child Advocacy Center, where we were collocated with detectives from the Tucson Police Department and employees of the state's Child Protective Services. Over the course of the coming months, I went to many classes and began to hone my skills as a detective investigating crimes against children.

I thought back of a class in the academy where the instructor, the department's ombudsman at the time, gave us the following instruction: "I want you to turn to your classmate seated to your right and tell them about the most recent sexual encounter you had. Be specific, be detailed, be professional about it. I'll give you a minute to think about it and prepare. On my signal, the person seated on the left will start. Your classmate will take notes. Then you switch. One minute starts now." After about a minute, she said, "Okay, are you ready? This is uncomfortable, isn't it? You can relax. I don't actually want you to tell your fellow recruits about your last sexual encounter. What I want you to do is remember this moment, and how you felt when you interview a victim of a sex crime to tell you about what happened. This is difficult stuff!"

Working in the Sex Crimes/Crimes Against Children unit is different from other assignments due to the sensitive subject matter and the requirement to treat victims equally sensitive so as to preserve their best memory of the incident without worsening the trauma they already experienced and while allowing them to maintain their dignity. My cases all involved abuse or sexual abuse of children ranging in age from infant to teenager. It is one thing to interview an adult about a violent sexual encounter and have them recall the incident in detail. It was a whole different ballgame to do the same with children. It was impossible for me to understand how any person was able to commit acts of physical or sexual violence against a child, let alone be sexually aroused by it. *How on earth?* Now add the fact that a lot of them were abused as children themselves. It was a lot to take in and deal with. Yet, I had to maintain a professional demeanor and secure as many statements and evidence to provide for a successful prosecution of the suspect, if such a person could be identified.

The cases I became exposed to and had to investigate were horrific by any measure. Yet, I had never felt as determined and like I was in the right spot at the right time as I did then. I was in a position to make it stop and to help bring justice to the victim. But how do you bring justice to a sexually abused eight-year-old? While sparing you the details, it is hard to put into words my excitement when receiving a phone call from our contracted DNA lab concerning an item of evidence I had submitted a few weeks earlier. On the night of the incident report and following a forensic interview of the victim and her brother at the Children's Advocacy Center, I spoke to the parents and confronted them with the fact that their daughter had indeed been sexually abused by a relative. After containing the perfectly understandable outrage and anger of the victim's father, I asked them if their child might still have any unwashed items of clothing from her time spent at the relative's place. After a few seconds, the mother's eyes widened and she said, "Her backpack! She had a backpack with her. I hung it on the back of her door, and I think her underwear may still be in there."

I called for a patrol unit to escort the parents' home, check the backpack for any clothing items, and secure them if found. Within the hour, a deputy called me on my cellphone and said they had found a pair of the girl's underwear in her backpack, and he would turn it into evidence. Jackpot!

That is what I submitted to the DNA lab for analysis. Fast forward three months and the analyst was on the phone with me. She would not have called unless it was good news. The analyst explained how she was able to extract DNA from the girl's underwear. It contained DNA foreign to the girl. Further analysis showed the extracted cells to be saliva cells containing DNA that pointed to the identified suspect. I am not sure I ever felt as conflicted ever again. Disgust for the now confirmed act of abuse, sorrow over what the victim had to endure, anguish over the need to confirm to the victim's parents that their relative was indeed the perpetrator, and then pure joy and deep satisfaction that this had most likely been the last time ever the suspect committed abuse like this.

But even in this particular unit we had lighthearted moments. Such as the time where we investigated a case involving the seizure of a large amount of pornography. Suspicious that the seized footage contained depictions of child sex abuse, we had to view the material. Now add the fact that this specific type of offender often hides the illegal footage within legal adult pornography, we had to watch the entire stash. And we are not talking about a few tapes or DVDs. No, this was a sizeable collection. Oh, did I mention that this was not as straight forward as a whole section of illegal footage being hidden amidst the legal kind? Often the illegal footage was cut into tiny snippets and hidden either throughout one single, legal film or potentially several different films to avoid easy detection. Forget about fast forwarding through the footage because that way you were likely to miss illegal snippets. It all had to be watched in real time. This led to several days of all detectives within the unit, two women and five men, watching porn on VCRs, DVD players, and TVs placed throughout the office and in pretty much every cubicle all day, while trying to continue our regular work as well. Each of us had a batch of movies assigned. On one of those days, porn running throughout the office in virtually every corner, the Bureau Chief and the CID Commander unexpectedly walked in. Unable to quickly turn off all the sexually explicit scenes flickering on various screens and at our desks, it all just kept running. We waved from within our porn-saturated cubicles and extended a friendly welcome to the Chief and the Captain. Stunned momentarily and unsure of what they had just walked into, the Chief was the first to speak up, saying they were there to speak to the sergeant. It was then that she happened to emerge from her office and quickly chaperoned the two commanders inside, away from the graphic content, offering an explanation as to what they had just observed.

 I spent some two years in Fraud/Financial Crimes and in Sex Crimes/Crimes Against Children, seeing the other side of the coin, the work following the initial investigation conducted by patrol. Being the ones who see it all through to the end or the courtroom. Conviction of a crime or determination of innocence. During those years, I spent countless hours in interview rooms filled with stale air and lies. Listening to victims and their stories about the crimes committed against them often left me shattered. There is no next call to go to and leave this behind. These interactions were up close and personal. The buck stopped here with me, or at least that is what it felt like.

 Coming home at night, I often went to bed seemingly sleeping like a rock. Sometimes I came home and immediately went to take a shower as if I could wash off the filth or to just clear my mind after interviewing a suspect. Maybe I had held their hand (touching sometimes worked wonders) or told them how I could "see that the victim was cute" and how they probably "didn't mean to hurt" them, all in order to illicit incriminating statements. Waking up in the morning, however, was akin to rising from the dead. It took a comment from my wife, who told me one morning that I must have had a bad dream. She described waking up in the middle of the night to my making all sorts of noises. Grunting, weeping, and then jerking around in bed as if fighting with someone. When I went to see my dentist for my semiannual cleaning and checkup, he asked if was grinding my teeth. I told him that I was not aware of it but shared my wife's descriptions. Consequently, he recommended I use a mouth guard to prevent permanent damage to my teeth. A mouth guard? Wait a minute! Was this job of mine, the job I loved, I obsessed over, I felt called to do, where I could truly help people, was that job turning against me? Or was I simply too weak? Maybe I just couldn't stomach it. Was I that little boy again, who was bullied by the bad boys in elementary school, just when it mattered most?

Fast forward a few months. While on an off-duty job at a church on Sundays, I spoke with our then current public information officer. Through several conversations, I learned that she was in the process of studying for the sergeant's exam and how department leadership was looking for a potential successor. Would I possibly be interested? I took the idea home to talk to Annie about it and eventually agreed and stepped into the assignment that would bring it all full circle.

After 40 years spent as an outsider to policing, a career in the finance industry, and fulfilling sales career, I had gone through patrol assignments, been a detective, and felt better equipped than ever to go out and tell the story of this department and my coworkers. After an interview with senior command staff, my application was accepted, and I became the official on-the-record spokesperson for the department. An assignment that brought its own new challenges. It was me who would now put the department on the record with statements that had potentially wide-reaching consequences in court proceedings, civil litigation, the outcome of investigations, or in general the public's perception of who we as members of this department were and what we stood for. It included the demanding work of maintaining and improving the relationship with local print, radio, and TV media outlets. Last but not least, I inherited a budding Facebook followership of some 900 users. Command staff at the time had considered social media "kiddie stuff" and neither saw any real value in it nor did they pay particular attention to it. This was in 2012. Oh, and then there is the added fun factor of being on call 24/7. Should I desire to have a drink at night or travel anywhere outside of Pima County, I needed to inform my supervisor in advance so that a substitute, typically the supervisor herself, could be scheduled for the duration of my anticipated inability to respond.

From the day I started, I loved it. It felt as if everything I had learned and experienced throughout my previous careers and with the Sheriff's Department simply fell into place and nicely jelled into this job profile of public information officer. Once the transition period ended and my predecessor left for her new position, I immediately began to change things. One example was the press releases from the other large law enforcement agency in town, the Tucson Police Department. Every day—for the past I don't know how long—they were printed out from their electronic version. Trees and paper waste be damned. They were then neatly two-hole punched and hung up on a clipboard in our unit's cubicle bay. As nobody ever seemed to look at it and it being 2012, I took the whole thing down and threw it in the trash. We never printed them out again and nobody ever asked for them or missed them.

Arizona, and Pima County in particular, continued to be in the news for some time because of a newly adopted 2010 Arizona legislative act titled "Support Our Law Enforcement and Safe Neighborhoods" that became nationally known by its bill number SB1070. It was a new law forcing local enforcement to contact Border Patrol or other federal immigration officials if we had reason to believe a person we were in

DEPUTY WHILE IMMIGRANT

contact with was in the country illegally. Never mind that we had done so all along. Anybody who believed law enforcement was not following through on this obligation could now sue the agency. Working for a Sheriff who was a Democrat in a county considered to be a politically blue island in the otherwise red sea of the state of Arizona, often brought us special attention. Controversy sells. Also, our Sheriff Clarence Dupnik, with more than 30 years in elected office, was not a man known to mince his words. He made clear that he was opposed to the law, as he called it unnecessary nonsense. Actually, he coined a new term and said he considered this new law "political fornicaboobery." Not surprisingly, we were informed by the Sheriff's executive staff that he had agreed to an interview with NBC News national correspondent Mike Taibbi. On the day scheduled for the interview, the team rolled up with a producer, production assistant, videographer, sound engineer, lighting specialist, and of course Mike Taibbi himself. It took them almost an hour to set up the room where they were going to film the interview.

Once the team declared they were ready, we informed the Sheriff, and he came down to meet the NBC News team and Taibbi. Turned out the two knew each other and after sitting down immediately fell into rather jovial banter with Taibbi telling the Sheriff that he would still "kick your ass on the golf course." There were a few more minutes of what was considered warm up talk and then they started for good. Quiet on the set! Lights? Sound?

"Sheriff Dupnik, what is fornicaboobery?"

"Oh, it can be whatever you want it to be." Big smile from the Sheriff.

"We are looking at this new law, SB1070, which has ignited a tremendous amount of discussion, not just here in Arizona, but nationwide. It has brought up allegations of racial profiling. Sheriff, do your deputies profile?"

Pause. Sheriff smiles broadly. "Absolutely they do. Profiling is an essential part of our job. Deputies look for suspicious behavior, demeanor that indicates somebody is trying to hide something, a car with stolen license plates. They profile because that is what they do. It is what people want us to do. But it doesn't matter what skin color the person has. It has nothing to do with the individual's racial profile."

For a moment, I thought my sergeant, who stood next to me listening to the interview, was about to faint; until the Sheriff added his clarification. I thought it was brilliant. To me, it was a wonderful example for carefully weighing the question you were asked, paired with wit and the grit of a lifelong career as a cop.

Back to my regular duties, I became best buddies with the staff of our Communications Center. The supervisor would call me regularly on duty and just as regularly off duty to inform me of media inquiries they had received or about a sergeant or other supervisor in the field who had requested my response to a scene. I would drive out to the crime scene and receive a briefing. In coordination with scene commander, on-scene detectives and often times their supervisor, we would determine what information could be released to the public without jeopardizing the ongoing investigation or subsequent prosecution of the case. There was also the calculus of asking the public for help quickly where that was deemed appropriate and useful. Then I stepped out in front of the cameras or got on the phone with the radio station and gave a statement. This would happen at all hours of the day. Sometimes the news desk of a local TV station would call me about something they had heard over the scanner before anyone from Comm or otherwise had a chance to brief or even advise me that something noteworthy had happened. This was especially challenging when we had a Code 998 or Code 999 and the warble tones went out. And all the news desks had an array of scanners running 24/7, listening to every bit of radio chatter they could pick up on. Every station in town knew what those tones meant. They would call me and say, "One of your guys is in trouble. Can you call us when you have a chance to check and get some information? We hope they're okay." While it was the obvious thirst for sensational or breaking news, they seemed mostly reasonable about these types of calls.

All those callouts seem to blend together in hindsight. Especially on that day where it all started with a callout to a traffic fatality in the afternoon. After scene response, briefing, and subsequent stand-up interviews, I managed to head home to try to grab dinner, but as soon as I walked into the house, my phone went off about a rescue operation underway. Media had shown up at the base of the mountain where deputies had set up their command post. Nobody had time to deal with the media, because they obviously were focused on the rescue operation. So off I went, did my thing, and came back home around 9:30 p.m. going straight to bed. Within 15 minutes, my work phone rang. It was our homicide supervisor telling me they had a murder on the southside and needed help with media that was present. I was there until well after midnight, when I got called to another traffic fatality. At roughly 3:00 a.m., I sat down with a few other deputies at an IHOP to get some toast, eggs, and, most importantly, coffee. While we sat and reminisced about our lives on the thin blue line, my phone rang and I was called out to a scene where they had found a young man shot in the head next to the highway. And so I went to the scene, got a briefing, well you know… When I showed up in the office to start my workday at 8:00 a.m., I went into the sergeant's office because she had a question about one of yesterday's media reports and to brief her on all the callouts. I stood in the doorway, looked at her, and she asked me something. I had to ask for her to repeat her question and she said, "How long have you been up?" I had to think for a few moments and said, "I'm not sure—27 or 28 hours maybe? Why?" Not allowing this conversation to go any further, she said, "Go home now. Do you want someone to drive you? I got it from here. Get some sleep. Come back in tomorrow and we'll discuss then."

Things turned for the better when the department decided to assign a second PIO to the unit, so we could rotate on-call duty and get a chance to recover after a week. Tracy Suitt was an outstanding partner on the PIO front. It felt like we could tackle anything together. While it took a little getting used to the coordination part and not simply run with everything by myself as soon as I'd show up at a scene, it turned out to be a thing of beauty. It is fair to say that to this day, I have not had as much fun, joy, or feeling of belonging and partnership in my job as in those days. I will always cherish those moments with the Community Resources team.

Let me finish this chapter with an episode we could call "What are the odds?" It was late morning when I received a call from Comm telling me that we had an "Aircraft Down" call. A small turbo-prop plane had crashed near Ryan Airfield. Traffic investigators were en route, and fire was already on the scene. Of course, the local news outlets had picked up the radio traffic on their scanners and already had teams headed to the scene by the time I drove west on Ajo Way.

When I got to the scene, not much was visible from the roadside, except for a bunch of fire trucks and Sheriff's cars sitting on the shoulder. Thankfully, I got there before reporters and had a chance to receive a briefing from Traffic Unit's Sergeant Mitchell. The highly specialized deputies with the Traffic Unit conducted the initial investigation and security of the scene, but eventually they would turn it over to investigators with the National Transportation Safety Board or NTSB. I learned that the NTSB had been notified and someone was on their way to our location. As we walked into the desert brush just off the roadway, I saw the crashed fuselage of the small, single-engine plane lying on its back. The pilot had been removed from the aircraft by a Border Patrol agent, who was first on scene. The body exhibited all the telltale signs of desperate attempts by emergency personnel to save his life. Despite their efforts, they had been unable to revive him, and I had a fatality to report. It later turned out he was a lecturer at the University of Arizona College of Engineering. He was the only occupant of the plane.

It took some time for all the news outlets to arrive, get their facts, their interviews, and then some remained at the scene for live shots. As we were gathered on the side of the road, a lady with a dog approached our group and asked to speak to me. She said she wanted to make a report. I asked her to hold on for a second and led her away from the gaggle of news reporters.

"Deputy, I think there is a dead person out there in the desert."

"Where?"

"Down the road. In the desert," she said, pointing north on Postvale

Road. "I let my dog run off leash and he went off into the desert next to the road. Then he got all excited and would not listen when I called him. And when I got to where he was, on the ground, I think that's a human body out there."

"How far from here did you say this was?"

"Oh, just down there."

She once again pointed toward Postvale Road and I guessed somewhere between 500 to 700 yards from our location. I asked another deputy to take her statement and note her personal information. Then I went over to Sergeant Mitchell and asked, "Are you sure there were no other occupants on the plane?"

"Yes, we're sure it was only the pilot. Why?"

"A lady just walked up and said she found a body just off Postvale, a few hundred yards from here. Can't be a coincidence."

"Let's send a deputy over there to check it out."

One of the deputies on scene was instructed to have the woman go back and point out the location to him. Within the next hour, we had homicide detectives working down the street from us, where there was now a crime scene taped off. Following the woman's direction, deputies discovered that a human body had been wrapped in a plastic tarp and disposed of in a shallow grave. Now what are the odds that this woman's dog would come upon that smell on the day a plane crash happened nearby?

12

REFLECTION

It's been a long journey from the first social engagement all in English, which was a Christmas dinner party by Annie's Army command in Wuerzburg, Germany in 1997, to patrolling the streets of a southern Arizona city. Sitting around a large set of tables in a German guesthouse, I was the curiosity item of the night. Thankfully, I was blissfully unaware of the fact at the time. Listening to me speaking, Annie's coworkers whisperingly asked her, "So, where did you find the Brit?" She smiled and said, "He's not a Brit. He's German." My knack for foreign languages and the German school system with its focus on proper Oxford Queen's English had left their mark. During our stay in Massachusetts, people kept asking if I was from Canada. And today? Well, I'm not sure what I sound like today. When speaking German to family members and friends back in the fatherland, they say I have an American accent. Well, there you go.

And here I was, speaking publicly on behalf of a U.S. law enforcement agency. "What a ride!" keeps going through my mind. But it wasn't always all happy-go-lucky. There—obviously—were a lot of other things that happened during that time. Experiences that became part of the mix just as much as all those described in the chapters above. My life out of uniform went on as well, with all its trials and tribulations.

In 2008, Annie came home from a doctor's visit one day, opened the door that connected the laundry room with the garage, walked from there into the dining room, and threw her purse on the table. She had an alarmed, stressed look on her face. Something very significant had happened. Puzzled by her demeanor, I asked, "What's going on, honey?" She looked at me and blurted out loud, "I have cancer!" Then she burst into tears.

I only remember being completely stunned by the statement. The rest is fairly blurry. She had gone to the doctor because she had experienced a persistent swelling in her neck and thought it was time to go and get some antibiotics or other strong medication to address it. A cancer diagnosis was absolutely not on her radar. After a second opinion and additional tests, she was conclusively diagnosed with tonsillar cancer. She saw the second Ear, Nose, and Throat specialist on a Monday and was pushed into the operating room the following Thursday. Everything happened at warp speed. Doctors were concerned and chose the more aggressive approach of surgical removal first, to be followed by radiation and chemotherapy once she had recovered from the surgery.

Later that particular Thursday morning, the surgeon came to see me in the hospital waiting room to tell me they had performed a tonsillectomy and neck dissection, removing 32 lymph nodes in the process. A biopsy later determined that the cancer had spread to one of her lymph nodes, but it appeared that was as far as it went. The following months consisted of recovery from the painful aftereffects, dealing with a dislodged stomach tube, which required an ambulance trip to the emergency room, chemotherapy and its side effects, and radiation to her neck and throat area. The biggest relief during that time, besides Annie's incredible fighter spirit, was my mother-in-law. She packed a few suitcases and came from Huntsville, AL to Tucson in order to care for her daughter while I could continue to work without having to worry about Annie being home alone. The radiation had the lasting side effect of burning most of Annie's salivary glands, causing not only persistent dry mouth but also greatly affected her sense of taste. For the first few months after treatment ended, most of what she ate seemed to fall into two taste categories: tuna or cardboard. She also had to have several of her teeth removed as the radiation had greatly damaged them, in turn requiring some substantial dental restoration. Finally, and most consequentially the skin and tissue on her neck were not just burned, but also scarred, making it sensitive to heat and causing muscular tension throughout her neck. Thankfully, she came out okay on the other end and was declared free of cancer in 2013. My wife impressed me deeply during that time. Her overall attitude, her willingness to fight, and her grit are truly remarkable. She never gave up or even allowed herself to consider that there could be an outcome other than complete remission. She is a fighter, my best friend, and the love of my life.

The experience of fighting cancer affected not just my wife, but of course me as well. It left a permanent mark and changed my perspective. In the days following her transport back to the hospital because of her dislodged stomach tube, the support I received from my coworkers was indescribable. The partially dislodged tube had caused a near-fatal infection, turning the first few hours of her hospital stay into a touch-and-go scenario. My entire squad offered help should I ever need it.

When I showed up to work later that day and asked my sergeant if I could swing by the hospital to check on my wife, he only looked up from his desk and said, "What are you doing here? Why are you not with her? Which hospital are we talking about?"

"She's at St. Joseph's, sir."

"Well, that's in our district, isn't it?"

"Yes, sir."

"Don't go home. Head over there in your patrol car. While you're there, keep your radio on and stay 10-8. I'll take care of the rest. We'll call you when we need you."

"Sir?"

"Go, Tom! Get out of here! Take care of your wife. I know where to find you."

"Yes, sir. Thank you! Thank you so much!"

"Yeah, yeah. Go on now. Drive safe!"

Until my wife turned a corner for the better and her condition stabilized, I would swing by St. Joseph's periodically during my shift, checking out over the radio for a Code 902, briefly check on Annie, spend a half hour with her and then head back out into my beat. Once she was back home, I was often assigned to Beat 1, so I could head home should anything serious happen. Fortunately, that was never necessary and other than cherishing my sergeant's big heart, I never actually needed to ask for anything from anyone or take any serious time off from work. His gestures and my coworkers offer to assist if needed were more than enough to carry me through this trying time. It made all the difference in the world.

My time in the academy and my professional metamorphosis brought back a lot of memories from my time in high school. The time where I first attempted to become a police officer. After almost two years into my law enforcement career in Arizona and in preparation for an upcoming family visit in G-Town, I reached out to my old English teacher, Juergen Erdmann. He was still at my old school. I told him that we had planned a trip to visit my parents. Would he be up for a meeting and catch up on old times? He was absolutely delighted. I was glad to hear that given the fact that I had given him a lot of grief as a student, earning the occasional noogie as a "reward." But he even went a step further and asked if I would come to the school and give a presentation to his current English class. Of course, I agreed. Wow, this was truly coming full circle. After speaking to my sergeant and writing a memo to request approval to take my uniform to Germany and wear it for the presentation, we added that as the icing to the cake. On October 6, 2007, I visited my alma mater and gave presentations to all English classes for the 9th and 10th grades. It took the entire German school day from 8:00 a.m. to 1:00 p.m. and I had a blast. So did Juergen. It was so much fun. Whoever heard of German high school students seeing a U.S. deputy sheriff in full regalia in their classroom giving a brief presentation about life in the U.S. and then answering all their questions? Did I mention that we did all of this in English? Only at the very end of each presentation did I reveal that I actually still spoke German and how I used to be a student of Mr. Erdmann. You can imagine the facial expressions.

Juergen was equally excited and had notified one of the local newspapers about my visit to the school. Following the presentations, we met with a reporter and a photographer, who published an article the following day. Before we departed, the reporter, Gabi Grund, asked me if I would be up to her visiting me back home in Tucson. She told me that she was a fan of the U.S. and traveled there frequently. She would love to write a more in-depth story and maybe observe me during a day at work. I said I would have to check with my wife and the Sheriff's Department first and get back to her later. Annie was up for it right away and thought it was a great idea. Upon my return, I spoke to my superiors, and they agreed for her to come and go for an extended ride-along. In November 2007, she knocked on our front door in Vail.

The article ended up as a large feature piece in one of G-Town's local papers called "Westfalen Blatt" complete with a large lead-photo showing me seated on the hood of my patrol car—with my fly open! A memorable choice by Gabi to drive home the picture of the invincible U.S. cop. The headline was "The Sheriff is from Guetersloh," a wordplay on the title of an old, silly, and very corny German song that went wildly popular when published in 1979 called "Der letzte Cowboy kommt aus Guetersloh" or "The last cowboy is from Guetersloh." The translated German refrain says, "The last cowboy is from Guetersloh and he is searching for freedom somewhere." Readers in G-town readily picked up the reference and even during visits with my parents years later, people would still bring up that article and say they could hardly believe what they were reading when it was published.

My father passed away in October of 2017, and I went back to G-town for several months to look after my mother (who was in a nursing home following a brain aneurism years earlier) and care for her affairs. It was then that I met with Juergen again. I had been back to the school for another round of presentations a few years earlier, so we stayed in touch. When I told him how both friends and family had encouraged me to write down my memories about my time as deputy sheriff, he was intrigued and immediately offered his assistance. We met on several occasions, and he was gracious enough to be the first person who heard lines from the initial raw manuscript of this book. It was a wonderful time that often led us to reminisce about the old school days, which turned into a memorable bonding experience.

The aftereffects of Annie's radiation treatment became more of an obstacle in the years following her initial treatment. The hot and arid climate of Southern Arizona became an aggravating factor. Dealing with a chronically dry mouth in an environment that could see humidity levels drop into the single digits was difficult, to say the least. The exposure of her scarred neck to direct sunlight and the dry heat did their part to add to the misery. She tried silk scarfs, high collars, all sorts of things. In the end, we had to face the music and Annie called me on a promise I made to her when she gave in and let me pursue my dream career. Back then I told her, "Should you reach a point where you just cannot handle it anymore or become truly unhappy or it turns out to be financially unfeasible, you can tell me and I will drop it all right then and there. I promise." Given the altered circumstances of not my job, but her health, living in this climate, had become unbearable for her, and I had to make good on my promise. Annie started to put in for jobs in more temperate climates and landed employment with the U.S. Army Corps of Engineers in Portland, OR. In November 2015, after almost 10 years on the job, we packed up our belongings and moved northwest to Oregon.

It was a difficult goodbye with tears, lots of hugs, handshakes, and well wishes. Being a cop had become such a big part of my persona that it was challenging to let go. I couldn't just take it off like a coat. You're not only a cop when you're on the job or in uniform. You're a cop 24/7 x 365. You're not always on duty, but you're still a cop. To this day, I feel awkward carrying a bag in my right or strong hand and feel more comfortable switching it to the left, despite the fact that I no longer carry a sidearm.

Upon arrival in Portland, I considered joining a local police force and went on a few ride-alongs with local law enforcement. It was a real eye-

DEPUTY WHILE IMMIGRANT

opener, for now I could observe with my own eyes and ears how other departments conducted their policing. It never quite lived up to the high standard I had been trained to and how we had conducted police business in Pima County. In order to bring in some money while still searching for a permanent job, I joined a private security firm in downtown Portland. They had a contract with local retailers to keep unwanted individuals out of their stores and off the streets in front of their businesses. They also had a cooperative agreement with the Portland Police Bureau that enabled us to reach officers by radio after detaining someone if further investigation was warranted or if an arrest for violation of a criminal offense was needed. The armed officer positions were filled only by former law enforcement officers. I didn't stay very long and eventually ended up getting hired by the State of Oregon as an investigator of adult abuse. When an internal posting at the agency announced the opening for a position of Communications Officer within our program, I applied and switched back into my public information role. It is what I have done ever since. It is the profession where I found my true home, my comfort zone.

Policing has changed a lot since my days on patrol or in law enforcement. Bad apples, hyper vigilance, and an us-versus-them mentality became more prominent, fueled by political fire. It had already started during my time with the Sheriff's Department in Tucson. At some point, a discussion broke out about our self-image as law enforcement officers. Were we more the "warrior" type or more the "guardians?" Personally, I never quite understood the need for such martial terminology. Why couldn't we just be peace officers? People working for their fellow citizens in enforcing the rules the community had given themselves. Caring for them in the process, earning their respect, and protecting them decisively when necessary. Why did it need some silly stereotype? That discussion became a real thing, and today I see it as the beginning manifestation of a broader change that was already afoot.

I was very fortunate in that I had a good support system. The age at which I entered this profession definitely played a role, giving me the ability to create some space between me and my every-day work experiences, helping me put it all into perspective. In 2011, I happened upon one of my most valuable teachers, the abbot of the Theravadin temple "Wat Buddhametta" in Tucson. As his student, I learned about the power of stillness, about the power of awareness and mindfulness. Through meditation and contemplation of a variety of teachings, clarity arose within me around the fact that the universe of our experience constantly strives to maintain an equilibrium. We are the ones who create and divide it into definitions of good and bad, pleasant, unpleasant, or neutral. Yet, in fact, there is no such thing. It is our perception, our thought process around these experiences that tries to categorize them. It is our way of making sense of things. It was a true revelation. I arrived at a point where I was able to "see" and begin to develop a deep appreciation for the interconnectedness of everything. It was a new, a very different perspective—a paradigm shift. And it made perfect sense given the backdrop of the daily deluge of human experiences, often times on the extreme end of what a person may have to endure in a lifetime. "Carpe diem" took on a meaning so powerful that words to describe appropriately what it means to me today escape me.

Racial and economic disparity, paired with the belief that certain political groups support law enforcement while others supposedly do not, have increased polarization. If police start to separate from the people, misunderstandings increase, as does ill will. Poor training and discussions if law enforcement should fulfill the role of guardian or warrior are beside the point. Police need acceptance from its citizens. Police need cooperation and, most importantly, trust. Where that is missing, it needs to be addressed right away, for without it, the police force is just that—a force. Following public discourse in the time after my departure from law enforcement initially seemed to increase my disconnect. What I saw and heard did not reflect my own experience or my understanding of how it all should work. Was my head in the clouds again? The switch to a communications role put me in a place where I feel I now belong. It is where I can provide the most value to others. Explaining and making accessible the work and actions of those who work in public service is very fulfilling to me. Yet, I still feel intimately connected to those who wear the badge. I walked in their shoes, and I know what it feels like. That connection will never completely fade away.

With all that said, you have to be willing to pay the price. Saying "what you will experience will include moments you cannot unsee" belies the ever-lurking darkness and constant effort required to keep from turning cynical in the worst possible way. This is the place where my plea goes out to all police leadership: Encouraging your employees to practice self-care has to go beyond the verbal declaration of how important it is. Mental health support for law enforcement is not something any officer or deputy should have to ask for. It should be part of a routine, just like departments provide gyms, workout programs, and obstacle courses; counseling and decompression exercises or assignments need to become par for the course. It will keep our peace officers in a better place mentally and strengthen their resilience. Mandatory or better "customary" debriefing after stressful or high-impact events will help alleviate the stigma. An officer or deputy should not have to fear for losing his/her job because they sought mental health support. It is time to decide what kind of law enforcement workforce we want to have: One that increasingly deals with the compound effects of trauma after trauma, which ultimately may lead to post traumatic stress disorder, or would we rather have enforcement professionals who are mentally cared for, and who feel safe and secure in their line of work without the urge to "stuff it all into a corner of their soul they otherwise rarely access." The effects are not necessarily obvious and easily noticeable. It took about a year and a half after leaving the job until my symptoms began to emerge. Fortunately, I worked in a field where I was surrounded by professionals who knew what trauma informed care is all about. When I met with my counselor for the first time and explained how my experiences over the years "weren't all that bad," how I had not been to actual combat or killed anyone, she smiled at me. Yes, I too had been drinking from that potion, which makes you feel invincible. It is a (proverbial) brew regularly passed around in first responder circles. As the cup goes around, you pronounce your invincibility and how none of what you go through has any detrimental effect on you. This ritual and cup is especially popular among men. Unfortunately, it is all too often replaced by a cup or glass filled with alcohol to dull the pain when they're alone with all their experiences.

As residents who are subject to policing, we should ask for better, actually make that "the best." What we definitely should not do is sit in our reclining chair watching the latest YouTube video of a law enforcement encounter and scream, "The guy wasn't even armed. The cop should have…" Don't! I am serious. Just do not ever do that! You have *no* idea what you would have done. The footage you are watching on your sofa is not what they experienced. You did not see it, smell it, hear it, feel it. You just got a fraction of a glimpse, possibly edited. It's not the same. I'll stop there. What we can do, however, is find an answer to the question "What do we want?" A well-balanced, regularly evaluated and cared for corps of peace officers or one that self-evaluates and self-medicates while armed to the teeth? It can be done. It needs to be done. And the ones who join the force today and their leadership are the ones who need to bring this care into existence.

Anyone who is contemplating a career in law enforcement should be aware that it will subject you to a raw, unfiltered look at life and all its facets. It is a noble profession that asks a lot of its members. You have to maintain professionalism in the face of adversity, follow the evidence, enforce the law, while using your discretion so you don't over-enforce. Protect the weak, help the victims, bring chaos back under control, mitigate among disputers, and let tourists take a picture with you. It can be beautiful, awe-inspiring, brutal, appalling, repulsive, fascinating, invigorating, glorious, and heartbreakingly mean and depressing, all at the same time. But that's life. It is yin and yang, black and white, and all the shades in between. You can't have one without the other. That is the ultimate clarity I gained from working in this unique profession. Value every day, every hour, every minute of your life, for they are invaluably precious time. Love it while it lasts. Driving home from work in my take-home vehicle on I-10 one day, I listened to a song that seemed to hit the nail

DEPUTY WHILE IMMIGRANT

on the head. I turned the volume up high and loudly sang along, moved to tears by Natasha Bedingfield's "Unwritten." It has been rewarding, at times taxing, and certainly left scars. For myself, I can wholeheartedly say, it was absolutely worth it—every minute of it. Looking back and especially now that it's written down, I am happy to say, "I am glad I didn't buy that Harley."

REFERENCES

Pima County Sheriff's Department Ten Codes

10-0	USE CAUTION
10-3	STOP TRANSMITTING
10-4	ACKNOWLEDGEMENT
10-8	IN SERVICE
10-16	DOMESTIC VIOLENCE OR DISTURBANCE
10-20	LOCATION
10-22	DISREGARD
10-23	ARRIVED AT SCENE
10-26	DETAINING SUBJECT
10-28	VEHICLE REGISTRATION INFO
10-31	CRIME IN PROGRESS
10-32	ARMED WITH (WEAPON)
10-35	LIMIT RADIO TRAFFIC, MAJOR CRIME
10-37	SUSPICIOUS VEHICLE
10-41	BEGINNING TOUR OF DUTY

REFERENCES

Pima County Sheriff's Department Ten Codes

10-42	ENDING TOUR OF DUTY
10-43	INFORMATION
10-50	TRAFFIC COLLISION, UNKNOWN INJURY
10-60	IN THE VICINITY
10-70	FIRE
10-76	EN ROUTE
10-78	BACKUP
10-80	CHASE IN PROGRESS
10-85	EQUIPMENT FAILURE
10-88	RECORDS INDICATE AN ARREST WARRANT
10-90	ALARM (SILENT/AUDIBLE)
10-95	PRISONER IN CUSTODY

REFERENCES

Pima County Sheriff's Supplemental Codes

Code 3	EXPEDITE, USING EMERGENCY EQUIPMENT
Code 4	NO FURTHER ASSISTANCE NEEDED
Code 5	STAKEOUT IN AREA
Code 10	WITHIN EARSHOT – RADIO
Code 11	HOMICIDE
Code 1803	STOLEN VEHICLE
Code 81	SUSPICIOUS PERSON
Code 103	SHERIFF'S ADMINISTRATION BUILDING
Code 115	PIMA COUNTY CORRECTIONS COMPLEX
Code 900	DEAD BODY
Code 902	HOSPITAL FOLLOW UP
Code 926	WRECKER
Code 998	OFFICER INVOLVED SHOOTING
Code 999	OFFICER NEEDS HELP URGENTLY

ACKNOWLEDGMENTS

My biggest supporter and the one who planted the initial seed for this book has been my wife, Annie. She has been most spectacular in her endurance of my doubts and self-loathing throughout the process of me writing this book. She has also been a true inspiration through her fighting spirit and her approach to life as a whole.

Thank you very much to my proofreaders, who helped bring this project across the finish line. I owe a debt of gratitude to Juergen, Nicole, and Amy for giving the manuscript its final polish.

Juergen Erdmann was my high school English teacher. After many years, we reconnected a few years ago, and he ended up being the first person besides my wife to hear some of the first lines of the manuscript for this book. We ended up spending several late nights going through ideas and giving parts of the manuscript a first critique. It really only struck me afterwards that without his efforts and dedication for teaching during my teenage years, I would have never been able to lead a life here in the United States and ultimately write this book.

A meeting with German reporter Gabi Grund turned into a long-lasting friendship. Gabi still works in my hometown of Guetersloh and was the source for some good inspiration. When I first broached my idea to write a book with her, she was immediately supportive. During her visits and several ride alongs while I worked in a patrol assignment, she took some memorable pictures. I definitely channeled my "inner Gabi" when I wrote the opening for this book.

Arne Rostek visited me in Tucson, AZ as a young German police officer. We connected through our membership in the International Police Association, which is how he found me. Arne has been the most steadfast and persistent supporter when it came to seeing this project through to publication. Thank you, Arne!

As a budding reporter on her final stretch in college, Molly Smith visited Tucson, AZ as part of the New York Times Student Journalism Institute and shadowed me for several days. The photos she took during that time are some of the most personal and intimate of my time as a law enforcement officer. Her questions in preparation for her article lead

ACKNOWLEDGMENTS

me to a different perspective of my work in law enforcement, as a public information officer, and why I loved what I did so much.

A shoutout also goes to my friend and coworker La Rosk for his creative input on several occasions, as well as the concept for the book cover.

Initially, I simply wrote down particular episodes I experienced during my days on patrol, unsure as to how they would eventually congeal into a readable manuscript. I got stuck and one day decided to call Fernanda Santos, author of "The Fire Line," for advice. We had previously met while she was Bureau Chief for the New York Times in Phoenix, AZ, while I was serving as Public Information Officer for the Pima County Sheriff's Department. She was gracious enough to give me some important pointers and tips, which ultimately broke the proverbial "creative ice" and unleashed my keyboard.

My coworkers and fellow members I had the privilege of working with at the Pima County Sheriff's Department were among the finest people I have met. Their dedication to the law enforcement profession was exemplary, and I felt safe in their presence. My fellow deputies, corrections officers, and civilians who were and always will be my family.

ABOUT THE AUTHOR

TOM PEINE is an accomplished Public Information Officer with a diverse background in public affairs and communications.

Tom was born and raised in Germany. He has a German education in the banking business and initially worked in the finance industry. In 1997, he met his second wife, who is a natural born American citizen. Following a switch to the software industry, he took on the roles of sales manager and global account manager. He emigrated to the United States at the age of 36.

Eventually, Tom naturalized, became a U.S. citizen, and chose to join the ranks of law enforcement. Just shy of his 41st birthday, he began attending a law enforcement academy and became Deputy Sheriff in Pima County, AZ. After almost ten years serving his community, he and his wife moved to Oregon and later temporarily returned to Germany where he worked as a strategic outreach specialist for the U.S. Army's 7th Army Training Command. They returned back home to the United States in 2020 and currently reside in the Northeast. To learn more visit TomPeine.com.

ABOUT THE AUTHOR